THE AGE OF THE CALIPHS

Dedicated in deep gratitude

to my revered teacher

Geheimrat Prof. Dr. Carl Brockelmann (1868-1956)

The Age of the Caliphs

by Bertold Spuler

Translated from the German by
F. R. C. BAGLEY

With a new Introduction by
JANE HATHAWAY

Markus Wiener Publishers
Princeton

Second printing, 1999

For information write to: Markus Wiener Publishers
231 Nassau Street, Princeton, NJ 08542

Library of Congress Cataloging-in-Publication Data

Spuler, Bertold, 1911-
[Geschichte der islamischen Lander. English]
History of the Muslim world/Bertold Spuler: with a new introduction by Jane Hathaway.
Vol. [2] has new introd. by Arthur Waldron.
Previously published:The Muslim World. Leiden: E.J. Brill, 1960-<1969 >
Includes bibliographical references and indexes.
ISBN 1-55876-095-4 (v.1)
ISBN 1-55876-079-2 (v. 2)
1. Islamic Empire—History. I.. Title.
DS35.63S68 1994 94-11585
909'.097671—dc20 CIP

Printed in the United States of America on acid-free paper.

CONTENTS

MAPS

TRANSLATOR'S PREFACE

Under the general editorship of Professor BERTOLD SPULER of the University of Hamburg, a group of specialists is preparing in German a series of "Manuals of Oriental Studies" (*Handbuch der Orientalistik*). The series is likely to form a most valuable compendium of modern knowledge in this vast field.

The sixth volume of the series is to be a "History of the Islamic Countries" (*Geschichte der Islamischen Länder*), surveying as a whole the development of the many lands in which the religion and civilization of Islam are, or have been, predominant. Parts I and II of this history have already been published by Messrs. E. J. BRILL of Leiden, Holland; they are *Die Chalifenzeit: Entstehung und Zerfall des Islamischen Weltreiches* (1952) and *Die Mongolenzeit* (1953), both from the pen of Prof. Spuler. They have been translated under the titles *The Muslim World: a Historical Survey*: Part I, *The Age of the Caliphs*; Part II, *The Mongol Period.* Part III, *Neuzeit,* has also now appeared (1959).

The translations have been approved by the author, who has added passages and notes which do not appear in the original.

The transliteration system used is, so far as possible, formal and consistent. It may be helpful for reference to articles in the *Encyclopaedia of Islam.* Gratitude is due to Messrs. E. J. BRILL's printers for the great trouble they have taken.

MCGILL UNIVERSITY
MONTREAL, CANADA,
AND DURHAM UNIVERSITY,
ENGLAND

F. R. C. BAGLEY

INTRODUCTION: THE AGE OF THE CALIPHS IN WORLD HISTORICAL PERSPECTIVE

An Indonesian mosque, a medieval Andalusian medical treatise, an Egyptian handbook on government, an Anatolian sufi order, a sixteenth-century Persian miniature, and an illuminated Nigerian Qur'ān are all part of Islamic civilization. Clearly, Islamic civilization is a global phenomenon, transcending both the tenets of the Muslim religion and the community of Muslim believers to encompass the cultural legacy to which members of all predominantly Muslim societies have contributed. This legacy is artistic, architectural, musical, mathematical, medical, literary, legal, political, theological, and spiritual. By the same token, Islamic history is much more than the study of the Muslim religion's development over the past fourteen centuries. Rather, it is the study of the culture generated under the aegis of Islam in all the societies to which the religion spread. In short, Islamic history is by its very nature world history. World history as a discipline seeks to integrate diverse peoples, regions, and cultures within a common framework. Islam provides just such a framework, perhaps more readily than others of the world's great religions, for in the course of centuries, Islam has integrated a large and diverse group of societies in a comparably large and diverse group of regions. At a time when the historian's lens increasingly adopts the perspective of the global village, the historian must recognize Muslims and the societies to which they belong, from Senegal to Malaysia, as agents of world history.

It is appropriate that Bertold Spuler's *The Muslim World* should be reissued in this era of global consciousness. While Spuler may never have considered himself a world historian, *The Muslim World's* three volumes have a global sweep. Moreover, they point to some of the very integrative themes critical to world historical method today: the incorporation of many disparate regions into a series of world systems, Arabo-Muslim, Mongol, and European; contact and mutual influence among alien cultures; geographical aids and impediments to integration. Spuler's first volume, *The Age of the Caliphs,* originally published in German in 1952, traces a subtle course of cultural integration as it follows the rise of Islam and the evolution of the early Muslim empires until the sack of Baghdad by the Mongols in 1258 of the Common Era. The story of these six centuries is one of cultural contact, borrowing, adaptation, and, frequently, conflict. It is played out over a geographical area that includes much of the eastern hemisphere.

Islam, it was once fashionable to say, was born in the full light of history. While it would be difficult to assert that other major religions were born in obscurity, it is nonetheless the case that Islam arose in a region at the crossroads of several major civilizations. Mecca in the early seventh century of the Common Era did not belong to an empire, but it lay uncomfortably near the spheres of influence of two of that age's largest, mightiest, and most belligerent empires: the Byzantine, or, to use Spuler's terminology, Eastern Roman, and the Sasanian, or Persian. These two sprawling polities divided much of the Mediterranean region and the Levant between themselves. In the Arabian peninsula, they vied for influence through the instrument of two northern Arabian kingdoms. Muhammad, the prophet of Islam, would certainly have dealt with merchants from these two empires who plied the caravan route through the Hijaz, transporting the fabled spices and incense of Yemen. He would also have been familiar with Greek Orthodox and Nestorian proselytes from these two empires, although their influence on him was perhaps not quite so great as Spuler would like to believe. The material culture of the early Islamic polities and the religious rites that evolved within them are replete with Byzantine and Persian influences, from the face veil for elite women, a custom adopted from the Byzantines, to the Zoroastrian-influenced emphasis on ritual ablutions. Early Muslims also adopted practices from other neighboring cultures, notably from the Jews who had fled Yemen in the wake of the Abyssinian invasion of 525 C.E., and from the Abyssinians themselves. As time went on, the Muslim empires drew influences from regions farther east into which they expanded, notably India and China. At the same time, they began to leave their own marks on the societies they touched; thus, Turkic converts incorporated many Arabic and Persian words into their languages, and sufism spread into Central Asia, India, and sub-Saharan Africa.

Indeed, the inception of the caliphate itself embodies themes of cultural contact, clash, accommodation, and integration. The Prophet's migration, or *hijra,* from Mecca to Medina in 622 C.E. brought the immigrants (*muhājirūn*), most of whom were northern, or Qaysi, Arabs, into contact with the Medinese population of predominantly southern, or Yemeni, Arabs. On the Prophet's death in 632, the Medinese and Meccans initially disagreed on a successor (*khalīfa,* whence "caliph"); the Medinese favored allowing each group to choose a caliph from within its own ranks. Ultimately, the Meccans prevailed and established the tradition that the caliph must be from the Prophet's own clan of Quraysh. Nonetheless, this fundamental division endured.

As the Muslim polity expanded, conquered non-Arab populations grew to resent their exclusion from the government and army, despite the fact that they were paying taxes to support those very institutions. Under policies set by the second caliph, ʿUmar (634-644), the settled non-Arab population resided outside the garrison towns (*amsār,* s. *misr*) inhabited by the conquering Arab armies. The easternmost territories that the Arab armies conquered, above all Khurasan in what is now eastern Iran and northwestern Afghanistan, were far removed from the capital at Medina and consequently were never garrisoned. There, the soldiers blended into the settled population and became tax-paying cultivators, deprived of the pensions that the state doled out to the garrison-town inhabitants. Dissatisfaction grew even among the garrison troops themselves when the third caliph, ʿUthman (644-656), decreed that they must remain within the towns permanently, foregoing the opportunity to launch commercial enterprises among the conquered populations. This sort of resentment contributed to ʿUthman's murder by mutinous troops from the Egyptian garrison and to the ensuing series of civil wars, each known as *fitna,* that pitted supporters of ʿUthman's family, the Umayyads, against supporters of the Prophet's son-in-law ʿAli. These *fitnas* resulted in a fundamental schism within Islam between Sunnis, or those who favored community consensus in the selection of a caliph, and those who believed that ʿAli and his descendants had an inalienable right to the caliphate. Eventually, the ʿAlids would evolve into the Shiʿite branch of Islam. But the civil wars had established the ʿAlid movement as a haven for the disenfranchised elements of the Muslim community, notably Yemeni Arabs and non-Arabs.

Tension between the enfranchised and the disenfranchised increased under the Umayyad caliphate (661-750). With the exception of the pious ʿUmar b. ʿAbd al-ʿAzīz (717-720), the Umayyad caliphs have acquired an unsavory reputation among scholars and ordinary Muslims alike. They are typically regarded as elitist and chauvinistic, a Qurayshi dynasty who created an "Arab kingdom" that reserved wealth and status for the ruling family and the Syrian Arabs who made up the bulk of their fighting forces. They are faulted both for the grief they dealt the family and adherents of ʿAli and for their negligence of the broader Muslim community's welfare. In recent years, however, historians have begun to revise, or at least to elaborate on, this view. Spuler was perhaps ahead of his time in his appreciation of the context within which the Umayyads ruled. He would no doubt have welcomed the recent strides in archaeological and numismatic research that have added to our understanding of Umayyad culture, the more so since very few written records of Umayyad rule remain. We are now able to recognize the extent of the cultural synthesis that the Umayyads achieved. Having moved the

Great Mosque of Damascus: Courtyard (ca. 715 A.D.)

Muslim capital from Medina to Damascus, deep in former Byzantine territory, they were susceptible to numerous Byzantine influences, which appear in their administration and architecture. The Great Mosque of Damascus, built by largely Greek masons on the site of an orthodox church, itself resembles a Greek basilica. It is decorated with Byzantine-style mosaics which, however, do not depict human figures but show a vista of vegetation and styl-

Great Mosque of Damascus (ca. 715 A.D.)

ized buildings. Umayyad palaces clearly draw on Roman and Byzantine models and are even decorated with sculptures of the caliph, unique examples of this form of figural representation in Islamic art. Following the reign of Muᶜāwiya (661-680), whom Spuler describes as a patriarchal Arab nobleman, the splendid isolation of the Umayyad caliphs in their lavish palaces, such a departure from the custom at Medina, resembles that of the Byzantine

Entrance to the hunting castle Kasr al-Heir al-Gharbi near Damascus (ca. 850 A.D.)

emperor. We now know, furthermore, that the Umayyads contributed substantially to imperial bureaucracy and a regal court culture.[1] These were not ᶜAbbasid innovations, as Spuler and other scholars of his generation believed; rather, the ᶜAbbasids built on Umayyad precedents. The Umayyads were even the first Muslim rulers to mint their own coins. They adopted the Byzantine gold denarius (dinar) outright, initially even engraving it with the caliph's likeness.

Under the Umayyads, the Muslim conquests continued to advance, into Central Asia and India in the east and into Spain in the west. Umayyad armies even besieged Constantinople in 717 and 718. As the conquests continued, larger and larger numbers of non-Arabs came under Muslim rule. According to what was until recently the conventional wisdom, non-Arab, and above all Iranian, dissatisfaction gave rise to the ᶜAbbasid revolution, which brought the Umayyad caliphate to an end in 750. Spuler adheres to this conventional wisdom, as one would expect an historian of his generation to do. Indeed, he takes the Iranian factor farther than many of his contemporaries, not only stressing that the core of the ᶜAbbasid armies consisted of Persians from Khurasan, but anachronistically evoking a Persian national genius waiting impatiently to break free from the fetters of Arab domination. Hence he asserts that such antiestablishment movements as Kharijism and above all Shiᶜism became "representative of Persian interests" as early as the late Umayyad period (p. 46). (Here, he seems to ignore the fact that until the rise of the Safavid empire in the sixteenth century, most Iranians belonged to the Shāfiᶜī school of Sunni Islam.) More recent historiography has pointed out that while the ᶜAbbasids won a large following among Iranians, the movement was led by Arabs and, moreover, enjoyed the support of quite a large number of Arab Muslims, including the Muslim establishment at Medina.[2]

In fact, the ᶜAbbasid movement was no more Persian than the Umayyads were Greek. It did, however, attract and patronize many Iranians, just as the Umayyads had patronized many Greeks. In fact, the contrast between Umayyad and ᶜAbbasid cultures in many respects mirrors the pre-Islamic rivalry between Greek and Persian cultures as embodied in the Byzantine and Sasanian empires. In founding a capital at Baghdad, near the old Sasanian capital of Ctesiphon, the ᶜAbbasids opened the Muslim community to profound Persian cultural influences. ᶜAbbasid painting, architecture, and court culture incorporated Persian elements. Still, it would be misleading to speak of a Persianate ᶜAbbasid culture that rejected all Greek influence, for the Sasanians had themselves been highly hellenized, and their hellenism filtered into ᶜAbbasid culture. The marks of hellenism appear in the explosion of Muslim science and philosophy under the ᶜAbbasids. In addition to composing original works, Muslim scholars translated classic Greek works into Arabic; the caliph al-Ma'mūn (813-833) even opened a school of translation in Baghdad. Through this process, works of classical Greek scholarship reached Muslims while most of Christian Europe languished in the throes of the Dark Ages.

Silver coins of the Umayyads

At its height, from 750 through the mid-tenth century of the C.E., the ᶜAbbasid empire embodies Islam as a world civilization. The ᶜAbbasid realm stretched from Spain in the west to India in the east. As a number of scholars have pointed out, it was possible for a merchant to travel from Córdoba through Cairo and Damascus to Baghdad while conversing in a single language, Arabic, and using a single currency, the ᶜAbbasid dinar. Merchants, scholars, and government officials did travel, contributing to a massive circulation of people, money, goods, and information within the empire. Commerce and diplomacy extended beyond the ᶜAbbasid domain, as well, reaching the Khazars and Bulghars to the north, China to the east, the lower Indian peninsula and sub-Saharan Africa to the south.

Spuler treats not only this golden age but the entire period from the ᶜAbbasid caliphate's inception in 750 until the Mongol conquest of Baghdad in 1258 as one coherent ᶜAbbasid era. In this, he differs from more recent historians, who take the ᶜAbbasid regime to have lasted only two centuries in actual fact, after which its authority was usurped by regional potentates. Of these, the most notable were the Persian Buyids (945-1055) and the Seljuk Turks (1055-1092), both of whom took over Baghdad. The potentates in the eastern part of the Muslim realm at least recognized the ^{c}Abbasid caliph, now little more than a figurehead, from whom they derived spiritual legitimacy.

In the west, however, a fundamental challenge to the caliphate arose in the form of the Fatimids, an Ismā^{c}īlī Shi^{c}ite counter-caliphate that established its seat in Tunisia before founding Cairo in 969. The rivalry between the two caliphates was an epic struggle, every bit as intense as the ^{c}Abbasids' struggle against the Umayyads. Like the early ^{c}Abbasids, the Fatimids employed propagandists (dā^{c}īs), who roamed ^{c}Abbasid territory, attempting to subvert the Sunni regime from within. Yet even this intense antagonism did not deter commerce between the Fatimid and (nominally) ^{c}Abbasid realms; as the documents of the Cairo Geniza make clear, trade was fairly brisk between Fatimid Egypt and Iraq and points east, as well as between Fatimid territory and the Crusader states.[3] Under the circumstances, we might perhaps speak of a commercial impetus that transcended individual political regimes.

The emergence of the Fatimid counter-caliphate abruptly divided the Muslim realm into eastern and western zones. In so doing, it separated the ^{c}Abbasid caliphate from its subjects in Spain, then under the rule of a branch of the Umayyad household that had escaped the ^{c}Abbasid conquest. In the face of this isolation, the Umayyad prince ^{c}Abd al-Rahmān III declared himself caliph in 929. Under this new Umayyad caliphate, Muslim Spain enjoyed its greatest period of cultural efflorescence. Córdoba was for a time the premier capital within the Islamic domains, and arguably in the world. From this point on, Muslim Spain's history takes a trajectory distinct from that of the Muslim east; it is now tied much more closely to the fortunes of Morocco. Spuler, indeed, devotes the final section of his book to Spain. Outside of the famous Spanish gold-

Bāb al-Futuh, Cairo (10th Century)

Great mosque in Córdoba (961-966 A.D.)

en age poetry, relatively little was known of Umayyad Spain when Spuler wrote. Recent archaeological finds, above all at the caliphal palace at Madīnat al-Zahrā' outside Córdoba, have shed new light on Spanish Umayyad court culture; meanwhile, new historical studies have uncovered the links between the Spanish Umayyad caliphate and the two more powerful caliphates.[4]

If the ᶜAbbasid golden age represents an era of political, religious, intellectual, and commercial integration, the period of decentralization and fragmentation that followed is one of diverse cultural contacts and heterogeneous influences on the Muslim polities. The potpourri of Persian and Turkic potentates who diluted the ᶜAbbasid caliph's power came from a variety of cultural traditions which they brought to bear on the culture of the courts at Baghdad and at their regional capitals. An advantage of Spuler's expertise in Turkic, and particularly Mongol, history is that he recognizes the profound influence of Turkic usages on Muslim polities even at this early date. In North Africa, meanwhile, the ᶜAbbasid-Fatimid rivalry prompted the indigenous Berber populations to assert themselves, playing off the two regimes against each other. In Spain, the beginning of the Christian reconquest in 1085 brought Christians and Muslims into unprecedented contact. This contact culminated in the twelfth-century translation movement in reconquered Toledo, where Muslim and classical Greek learning was translated from Arabic into Latin, making these works accessible to Europeans for the first time.

The most famous—or infamous—contact between Christians and Muslims during this period was of course the Crusades, to which Spuler gives ample attention. It is often tempting to treat the Crusades as a forerunner of early modern European imperialism. Spuler perceptively puts the Crusades in perspective, noting that the Muslims regarded the Crusader states in Syria and Palestine as a relatively minor nuisance. Of far greater consequence, in their estimation, was the Christian *reconquista* in Spain, which had its first major successes shortly before the First Crusade, and which Muslim observers tend to view as an integral part of the crusading mission. In assessing the First Crusade in the eastern Mediterranean, Spuler offers the piquant information that the Crusaders attacked the wrong group of Saracens. The European kingdoms were incensed by the Seljuks' prohibition of Christian pilgrimage to Jerusalem after they had conquered the city from the Fatimids in 1071; by the time the Crusaders attacked, however, the Fatimids had retaken the city. The roughly two centuries during which the Crusader states clung to the Syrian littoral provided fewer opportunities for contact than one might expect. The Crusaders conducted some trade with their Muslim neighbors and, inevitably, adopted certain regional customs. Spuler stresses

Muslim influences on the chivalric military culture of medieval Europe and notes Muslim additions to European material culture. Intellectual exchange, however, was meager, in stark contrast to the fruitful exchanges that occurred in twelfth-century Toledo. Yet we would do well to remember that the Crusader states were dealing with vigorous Muslim powers that posed a constant threat to their existence. The scholars of Toledo, on the other hand, had the luxury of sifting the intellectual legacy of the vanquished.

After the tenth century, the territory once ruled by the ᶜAbbasids never again enjoyed such a level of integration until the height of the Ottoman Empire in the sixteenth century. Between the mid-tenth century and the Mongol invasions in the thirteenth century, the Muslim lands became progressively more fragmented. By the time the Mongols invaded, the authority of the ᶜAbbasid caliph extended no farther than the immediate vicinity of Baghdad. Even the local potentates lacked unity; the Seljuks had lost authority to regents (*atabegs*) who ruled individual regions, notably the Zangids in Iraq and Syria. On the other hand, the domain of the Fatimid caliphate had returned to the Sunni fold after the caliphate gave way to the Ayyubid dynasty, founded by Salāh al-Dīn Yūsuf b. Ayyūb, known in the west as Saladin, the client of a Zangid *atabeg*. Notwithstanding, Ayyubid Egypt and Syria constituted yet another regional power paying lip service to the ᶜAbbasid caliph. Spain and Morocco, meanwhile, followed an entirely different course under the puritanical Almohads (1130-1275), self-proclaimed Berber caliphs who professed allegiance to neither the ᶜAbbasids nor the Fatimids. Generally, in assessing the distinctive cultural development of Islamic Spain, Spuler too readily ascribes such unique phenomena as golden age poetry and the Almohads' acceptance of philosophy to the influence of the individualistic spirit of neighboring western Europe. Such a position is, of course, blatantly anachronistic, given the absence of any coherent tradition of individualism in Europe at that time. To describe the Almohads as open-minded for tolerating philosophy, furthermore, downplays the rigorous puritanism of their movement.

While such observations on "the Muslim mind" may be slightly off target, they keep Spuler's work from being a dry recital of facts. Although the core of Volume I is a chronological narrative of political events (surprisingly detailed for such a short work), Spuler supplies a running commentary on the maturation of Islamic culture and never loses sight of Islam's contact with other cultures and its place in world history. He is particularly adept at recognizing continuities between practices of the various Muslim polities and the ancient empires that preceded them. The rivalry between the ᶜAbbasids and

Fatimids he perceives as yet another manifestation of the competition between the civilizations of the Tigris-Euphrates and the Nile valleys, observable since the dawn of civilization. This constant awareness of the historical continuum prevents Spuler from viewing Islam as a timeless, monolithic, self-sufficient entity, and compensates for a few early remarks that smack of Christian European chauvinism. It is also one of the qualities that make Spuler a world historian.

In fact, if Spuler were writing now, in the full light of the world history movement, he would probably broaden his interpretive framework to include a number of other world historical themes reflected in these first six hundred years of Islam. Indeed, what keeps his short introductory volume current is that it can serve as a template for comparative and integrative examinations of Islam's evolution. For many readers today, the work raises a number of world historical questions, many connected with how an evolving empire responds to the challenges posed by its own expansion. The ᶜAbbasid golden age, which is arguably the high point of Spuler's narrative, embodies a particularly striking array of world historical themes. One could easily speak of the ᶜAbbasid empire during this period as a world system as defined by Janet Abu-Lughod or Immanuel Wallerstein, with a central zone at Baghdad and multiple regional centers at Baghdad, Basra, Nishapur, Damascus, Cairo, Qayrawan, Córdoba, and other towns.[5] Bulghars, Khazars, Russians, Hindus, Berbers, Abyssinians, and even Franks and Goths populated the ᶜAbbasid empire's periphery.

This ᶜAbbasid world system participated in and linked two major ocean trading zones: those of the Mediterranean Sea and the Indian Ocean. Although the requirements of travel in these two oceans were different, and although it was extremely rare for a single merchant to trade across both oceans, Mediterranean and Indian Ocean goods circulated throughout the ᶜAbbasid domains. The ᶜAbbasid provinces bordering these two bodies of water traded avidly not only among themselves but also with Byzantines, Franks, and various Indian Hindu principalities. In short, either ocean in the Islamic Golden Age warrants a study as a coherent economic and, to some extent, cultural unit, comparable to Fernand Braudel's study of the Mediterranean in the age of Philip II or K.N. Chaudhuri's multi-century study of the Indian Ocean.[6] S.D. Goitein's extraordinary opus *A Mediterranean Society,* based on medieval documents preserved in a Cairene synagogue, offers a multi-faceted portrait of the southern and eastern coasts of the Mediterranean during the waning years of the ᶜAbbasid and Fatimid caliphates, and provides a model for what such an integrated study could achieve.[7]

More specific issues of Islamic empire-building are similarly susceptible to world historical analysis. One might mention several to which Spuler, no doubt of necessity in such a brief survey, gives little space: urban development; slavery, including the distinctive brand of military slavery practiced in many Islamic polities; the seclusion of women; and treatment of minorities.

Islam has often been described as an urban religion inasmuch as it arose in a thriving commercial town, and political power in Islamic states has typically concentrated in cities. Shortly after Spuler completed the present work, the Islamic city emerged as a major focus of inquiry. Scholars such as the late S.M. Stern questioned whether Islam itself imposed certain forms and functions on a city: the central mosque and market, the enclosed quarters and narrow, twisting streets.[8] In recent years, André Raymond has achieved something of a breakthrough in the study of Ottoman-era cities by pointing out a regional and climatic dimension to urban topography and residential design that transcends the religious dimension.[9] Thus, for example, an upper-class family house in Cairo bears more resemblance to one in Christian Spain than it does to one in Anatolia or Yemen. Richard Bulliet has demonstrated that the narrow, winding alleys so frequently associated with the "typical" Islamic city resulted from a lack of wheeled vehicles, which had been displaced by camels.[10] In short, urban layout and residential construction take their places as regional phenomena that can be studied in a particular geographical, as opposed to merely a religio-cultural, context. By the same token, urban challenges such as water management, maintenance of public order, defense against invasion and brigandage, and relations with the rural hinterland can be reassessed in such a global perspective.

The need for a reliable source of military manpower posed a problem from the early years of the first Islamic empires. The Rightly-Guided caliphs, the Umayyads, and the ᶜAbbasids had all relied initially on regional populations who supported their causes: the early caliphs on bedouin tribes, the Umayyads on Syrian Arab contingents, the ᶜAbbasids on Khurasani warriors. The danger always existed, however, that these privileged military elites would turn against the regime they had supported and draw on their regional power bases to oppose or manipulate it. The Prophet's companions had experienced this eventuality at the time of his death, when the bedouin tribes who had accepted Islam, considering their covenant with Muhammad to have lapsed with his death, rebelled against his successors. As a result of the civil wars that ensued, known as the Wars of the Ridda (apostasy), Islam spread throughout the Arabian peninsula. Months of warfare convinced the early

Samarra

Samarra ornaments

caliphs of the need for strict control of the tribes, which they achieved through the garrison towns, but did not prompt them to seek entirely new sources of manpower. This innovation developed under the ᶜAbbasid caliphs, whose Khurasani troops frequently wrought havoc in Baghdad. Toward the middle of the ninth century, the caliph al-Muᶜtasim (833-842) began to purchase Turkish slaves from the Central Asian steppe, convert them to Islam, and train them as his personal soldiers. In 836, he founded a new capital at Samarra, north of Baghdad on the Tigris. This new capital was populated solely by the caliph, his retinue, and these military slaves, who were known as *ghilmān* (s. *ghulām*) or *mamlūks*, divided into quarters based on their places of origin. Relatively recent research suggests that the use of *mamlūks* did not originate with al-Muᶜtasim; *mamlūks* of one sort or another can be observed under the Umayyads and perhaps even under the early caliphs.[11] Al-Muᶜtasim and his successors, however, were the first to employ *mamlūks* systematically and on a large scale. Their strategy was to remove young Turkish men from their families and lands of origin and train them in the caliph's capital, so that their only loyalty would be to the caliph. The *mamlūk* system was adopted by numerous other medieval powers, notably the Seljuks, Ghaznavids, and Ayyubids, and would remain a viable source of military recruitment in a number of Muslim polities well into the nineteenth century. Nonetheless, the *mamlūks* could themselves form a formidable interest group; later ᶜAbbasid caliphs came to be utterly dominated by their *mamlūks*. And in the most momentous instance, the *mamlūks* of the Ayyubids displaced their masters and established the Mamluk sultanate (1250-1517) in Egypt, Syria, southeastern Anatolia, and the Hijaz.

The systematic acquisition of large numbers of *mamlūks* contributed to the ᶜAbbasid empire's and its successor regimes' status as world empires, for it brought them into regular contact with the lands outside the borders of Islam from which *mamlūks* were traditionally procured. Yet this solution to the problem of reliable sources of manpower becomes a more intriguing world historical issue if we compare it to the solutions adopted in non-Muslim polities. Although slavery, including palace, or elite, slavery, was widely practiced in a number of non-Muslim polities, such as the Byzantine and Chinese empires, no major non-Muslim regime adopted military slavery on the order of the *mamlūk* system. The *mamlūk* system was best suited to polities in which the ruler controlled all rights to land, as was the case in Muslim territories. This allowed the ruler to assign the usufruct of specified lands to his *mamlūk* commanders so that they might support troops with the revenues. In polities in which a hereditary landowning nobility existed, such provision for a class of foreign military slaves would have been difficult, if not impossible, since the slaves' interests would have clashed with those of the nobles. This is not to suggest, however, that a feudal society with a hereditary nobility necessarily precluded the use of military slaves. It would be useful to investigate what criteria led to various forms of recruitment worldwide.

It seems clear, in any case, that the *mamlūk* system in the first instance appealed to states in an age when swift cavalry attacks were the principal form of battlefield encounter; *mamlūks* from the Central Asian steppe were

Sultan Hasan Mosque in Cairo (14th Century)

therefore valued not only because they had no extraneous allegiances but also because they were highly proficient horsemen. In most cases, the chiefs of such cavalry forces depended on the assignment of plots of land where they could graze their horses, breed new ones, and train mounted troops. When salaried, gun-wielding infantry began to overshadow cavalry under the Ottomans, the importance of landed estates correspondingly declined. A more obscure question is what part military personnel played in the political, economic, and cultural lives of various polities. A number of Seljuk *ghilmān* participated in mysticism and became noteworthy scholars. The *mamlūks* of Egypt and their offspring also patronized religious establishments and produced literary works, often of some note.[12]

If we consider slavery in general, we open a much broader field for comparative global analysis. Although Islam does not forbid slavery, the Prophet considered it meritorious to manumit slaves; furthermore, Islamic law is far less restrictive in issues of slave status than classical Greek or many medieval and early modern European codes of law. Yet Muslim polities, like their counterparts elsewhere, made extensive use of slaves, *mamlūks* and otherwise. African slaves were heavily employed in agriculture, although as is the case with many features of rural life under Islam, we know relatively little about the full extent and conditions of this form of slavery. The wretched conditions of the slaves who dredged salt from the marshes of southern Iraq under the ᶜAbbasids came to light because of their well-documented rebellion. This rebellion, known as the Zanj revolt (Zanj being the Arabic term for most categories of sub-Saharan Africans), was massive in scope and lasted from 869 through 883. Yet how many parallel instances of exploitive agricultural slavery existed is not fully known.

Far better documented is domestic slavery and what has been called elite slavery, encompassing *mamlūks* and court slaves. Elite slavery appears to have been a common feature of Mediterranean and Asian empires from antiquity through quite recent times; in fact, the early Muslim empires probably adopted it from the Byzantines and Persians. Often the *mamlūk* system itself yielded a contingent of slave courtiers who might be current or former military commanders. Slave women were also purchased from the same regions and married to male slaves or to the ruler; otherwise, they might be installed in the ruler's harem.

The harem, a private space where women resided, is almost a cliché of Islamic culture, yet it, too, had precedents and parallels in other empires. The Byzantines and Chinese, for two prominent examples, kept royal women and children secluded from public contact. In fact, it has recently been pointed out that royal seclusion, in whatever polity it occurred, served to seclude not only royal women but royal men, as well.[13] Chinese and Byzantine emperors and Muslim caliphs alike lived in splendid isolation designed to separate them from the ranks of their subjects. The need to preserve the ruler's inner sanctum explains in large part the existence of elite slaves loyal only to the ruler. The epitome of such slaves were eunuchs, employed by numerous empires, from the ancient Persian to the Byzantine to the Chinese to virtually all Muslim empires.[14]

Muslim rulers' treatment of their non-Muslim subjects is an emotional and highly contentious subject, and one that is dogged by implicit and explicit comparisons to treatment of Jews under European Christian rule. On this subject, Spuler comes closest to Christian chauvinism in narrating Muhammad's expulsion and massacre of the Jews of the Arabian peninsula, going so far as to cite Muhammad's ability "to make supernatural manifestations justify humanly reprehensible actions" (p. 9). Spuler might have produced a more balanced and historically accurate narrative had he given due weight to the complex relations between the early Muslim community and the Jews of Medina, which were not at all those of a clearly dominant power and a vanquished foe. Spuler has little to say about the later treatment of Jews,

Former synagogue in Toledo (1200-1250)

Christians, and Zoroastrians as protected "Peoples of the Book" under the regulations of the Pact of ᶜUmar. Given his sensitivity to ancient precedents for Islamic practice, it is somewhat surprising that he does not note the influence on the Pact of Byzantine directives regarding treatment of Jews.[15] Many studies of religious minorities under Islamic rule compare their circumstances to those of Jews in Europe; during the period covered by Spuler's first volume, Islamic polities seem far more tolerant. Jews and Christians participated fully in commerce and attained high positions at many Muslim courts. Their circumstances deteriorated when the surrounding society suffered economic hardship and military defeat, as occurred in isolated instances throughout the period. In polities subject to unusual stresses, such as those situated on the borders of the enemy Christian lands and those under the sway of zealous sectarian movements, minorities' circumstances were, naturally, straitened. The subject is an exhaustive one that would arguably have

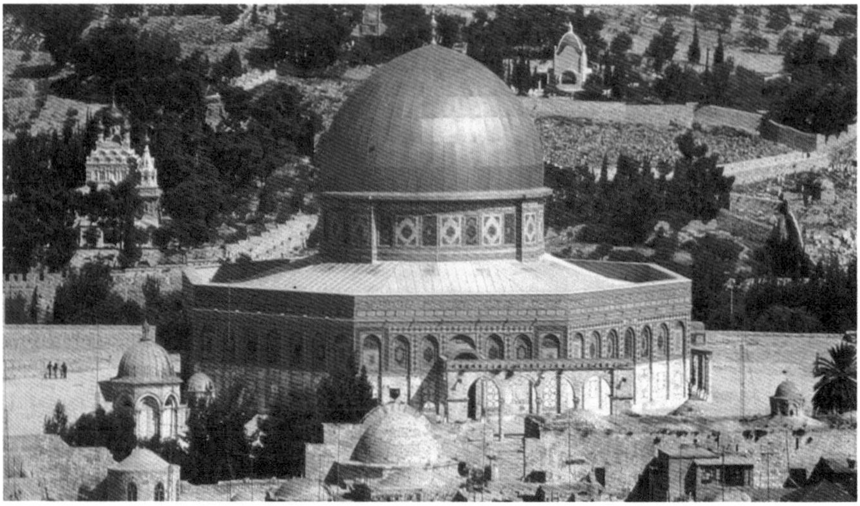

Dome of the Rock, Jerusalem (7th century A.D.)

overwhelmed Spuler's book had he given it more than passing attention.

If Spuler were writing and lecturing today, his views would no doubt be regarded as politically incorrect and even insensitive. His identity does not hide itself behind his narrative; it is clear that he adheres to Christianity and considers it in many respects superior to Islam. His analysis of many milestones in Islamic history, furthermore, rests on anachronistic conceptions of nationalism, which he attributes to Persians and Arabs alike, and of western European humanism. Even given these shortcomings, however, his understanding of Islamic history and its geographical and chronological context is remarkable. He wrote before many of the most searching, revisionist monographs on the early centuries of Islam had been published. His work presages the more recent global syntheses of Islamic history that these monographs have made possible. Despite its dated sensibilities, Spuler's first volume retains its value as an example of what Islamic history in the context of world history should be: orderly, comprehensible, concise, and conscious of the larger picture into which Islamic history fits.

Jane Hathaway
New York
August 1994

NOTES

1. See, for example, S.D. Goitein, *Studies in Islamic History and Institutions* (Leiden: E.J. Brill, 1966), pp. 168-196.
2. For a discussion of the historiography, see R. Stephen Humphreys, *Islamic History: A Framework for Inquiry,* revised ed. (Princeton: Princeton University Press, 1991), pp. 104-127.
3. S.D. Goitein, *A Mediterranean Society,* 6 vols. (Berkeley and Los Angeles: University of California Press, 1967-1993): for example, Vol. IV, *Daily Life* (1983), section ix, B, 1, *passim.*
4. Antonio Vallejo Triano, "Madīnat al-Zahrāʾ: The Triumph of the Islamic State," and Renata Holod, "Luxury Arts of the Caliphal Period," in *Al-Andalus: The Art of Islamic Spain,* ed. Jerrilynn D. Dodds (New York: Metropolitan Museum of Art, distributed by Harry N. Abrams, Inc., 1992), pp. 26-48; Olivia R. Constable, "At the Edge of the West: International Trade and Traders in Muslim Spain (1000-1250)," unpublished Ph.D. dissertation, Princeton, 1989.
5. Janet L. Abu-Lughod, *Before European Hegemony: The World System, A.D. 1250-1350* (New York: Oxford University Press, 1989); Immanuel Wallerstein, *The Modern World System,* 3 vols. (New York and San Diego: Academic Press, 1974-1989).
6. Fernand Braudel, *The Mediterranean and the Mediterranean World in the Age of Philip II,* trans. Sian Reynolds, 2 vols. (New York: Harper and Row, 1972-3); K.N. Chaudhuri, *Asia Before Europe: Economy and Civilization of the Indian Ocean from the Rise of Islam to 1750* (Cambridge and New York: Cambridge University Press, 1990).
7. Goitein, *A Mediterranean Society.* Professor Goitein planned for many years to prepare a book on the Indian Ocean trade, for which extensive notes existed. His *Letters of Medieval Jewish Traders* (Princeton: Princeton University Press, 1974) gives some indication of the insights such a work might have offered. I am grateful to the S.D. Goitein Laboratory for Geniza Research, Princeton University, for the opportunity to view his notes.
8. S.M. Stern and Alert Hourani, eds., *The Islamic City: A Colloquium* (Oxford and Philadelphia: Cassirer and University of Pennsylvania Press, 1970).
9. André Raymond, *Grandes villes arabes à l'époque ottomane* (Paris: Sindbad, 1985).

10. Richard W. Bulliet, *The Camel and the Wheel* (Cambridge, Mass.: Harvard University Press, 1975); Morningside ed. (New York: Columbia University Press, 1990).
11. David Ayalon, "Aspects of the Mamluk Phenomenon," *Der Islam* LIII, 2 (1976): 196-225.
12. Speros Vryonis, Jr., *The Decline of Medieval Hellenism in Asia Minor and the Process of Islamization from the Eleventh through the Fifteenth Century* (Berkeley: University of California Press, 1971), pp. 240-244; "Seljuk Gulams and Ottoman Devshirmes," in *Byzantium: Its Internal History and Relations with the Muslim World* (London: Variorum Reprints, 1971), originally published in *Der Islam* XLII (1965), pp. 224-252; Barbara Flemming, "Literary Activities in Mamluk Halls and Barracks," in *Studies in Memory of Gaston Wiet,* ed. Myriam Rosen-Ayalon (Jerusalem: Institute of Asian and African Studies, Hebrew University, 1977), pp. 249-260.
13. Leslie P. Peirce, *The Imperial Harem: Gender and Sovereignty in the Ottoman Empire* (New York: Oxford University Press, 1993).
14. On this subject, see Orlando Patterson, *Slavery and Social Death: A Comparative Study* (Cambridge, Mass.: Harvard University Press, 1982), pp. 314-331.
15. Stanford J. Shaw, *The Jews of the Ottoman Empire and the Turkish Republic* (New York: New York University Press, 1991), pp. 18-19.

MUḤAMMAD

ROME AND PERSIA

During the early centuries of the Christian era, the Roman empire evolved in such a way that it could not ultimately be preserved as a single entity. From it were formed two half empires, divided by a line running roughly north and south but still joined, in spite of increasingly clear-cut language differences, by bonds of common civilization and similar religion. Soon, however, growing sentiments of national and cultural independence among the oriental peoples caused the east in its turn to split into two halves. One consisted of those parts which could be considered Greek or hellenized — Greece and the adjacent Balkan territories to the north (except where romanized), Asia Minor and the lands bordering the Black Sea; the other of the area inhabited by Aramaic-speaking peoples in Syria, Palestine and Mesopotamia, and Egypt with its Coptic population. This cleavage was intensified by schisms within Christianity. Thus for the first time the eastern half of the Mediterranean region came to be divided by a line cutting it into northern and southern halves. Subsequent events were to show that this line — the spiritual frontier between Europe and the East — would become the more important and would be prolonged through the whole length of the Mediterranean Sea.

For new forces were beginning to stir — forces which had stood outside the East Roman empire and were now to intervene decisively in world history. The Persian empire, under the Achaemenids, the Parthian kings and then the Sāsānids, had always maintained itself as an independent force confronting the Greco-Roman world; and early in the 7th century it seemed as if this empire might succeed in detaching the southern half of the Byzantine domain. After passing through an internal crisis late in the 5th century, the kingdom of the Persians had been rebuilt under Khusraw I Anūshīrvān and had risen to be a great power. Under Khusraw II (590-628), in an unparalleled series of victories (613-15), they advanced into Palestine and Syria; Egypt fell into their hands in 619 and Asia Minor, too, appeared in danger. But one of the greatest of the Byzantine emperors, Heraclius, after reorganizing the East Roman state and summoning the last forces at his call, overcame the Persian empire in two mighty campaigns during the years 623-5 and 627-8 and compelled it to retrocede its newly won territories. This was a struggle of the giants. Thousands of soldiers, equipped with the most advanced technical apparatus of the time and following every precept of the art of war, were locked in battle. Who would then have heeded the news that in this same year 624, in a country quite beyond the view of the contemporary world — in a desert valley of Arabia — two bands of Arabs had fought a battle, and that the smaller (perhaps of 350 men) had defeated the larger (of about 1,000)? Yet of the war between the two mighty empires no living trace remains; whereas the victory of the 350 in Arabia determined that today, from Rabāṭ on the Atlantic Ocean to Java, in the Tatar Republic around Kazán on the Volga and at Timbuctoo on the southern edge of the Sahara, the call to prayer to the One God, Allāh, rings forth in the Arabic tongue. Within these limits lie the lands of Islām, the lands with which the following pages will be concerned. By mastering Byzantine and Persian soil, Islām welded hitherto hostile regions together; by its conquests of Egypt and Spain, it also severed long-standing regional connections. The East and West Roman empires, or their successor states, were reduced by half; their segments lying south and east of the Mediterranean Sea became Islāmic, and in one blow an end was put to the unitary political and cultural evolution of the Mediterranean basin.

THE PRE-ISLĀMIC BEDUIN

What led to this transformation, which began a new phase in world history and suddenly put into the forefront of affairs an area whose previous life had been remote from every historically significant development? Arabia, the peninsula stretching between Egypt, Abyssinia, Persia, Syria and Mesopotamia, might well have formed a centre of gravity in world politics but for the great drawback of its physical characteristics. Most of the country is desert, and only in the far south and at the north east extremity did Abyssinia and Persia succeed in acquiring bases. Only certain coastal stretches were accessible to higher civilization and had, indeed, over many centuries developed such a civilization of their own — though this was already in decline. The outside world was content to let Arab caravans bring their country's chief products to Syria and Mesopotamia and take the risk of travel through its unpopulated expanses. One of the commercial centres of the country, the city of *Makkah,* thus became one of its political hubs also. The local merchants had built up an aristocratic mercantile republic, and had known how to exploit a local sanctuary, the *Ka'bah,* for their commercial ends. In view of its importance as the emporium for a great part of Arabia, the city with its environs was regarded as inviolable; and the merchants had brought about that three consecutive months and another single month of each year were considered sacred. In them caravan traffic could proceed without danger of attacks by competitors or Beduin. The second element in the life of the peninsula consisted of the Beduin, that section of the population which was accustomed to free and unrestricted roaming in the broad, lonely spaces and lived according to its own desert-determined laws. Organized into separate tribes under *shaykhs* who in turn formed tribal alliances on the basis of real or fictitious kinship, they fell into two great groups, the Northern and the Southern Arabs (whose habitats had, however, by that time largely shifted). The main concerns of the Beduin were the preservation in all circumstances of tribal unity (though outsiders might be adopted into the tribe), the most far-reaching hospitality, and the vendetta as a guarantee of survival. Every man must know that killing a member of another tribe would bring retribution, not only on the murderer, but also on the whole of the murderer's tribe. But since, in the frequent desert skirmishes, in the fights over water-holes and flocks, cases of violent killing were bound to occur, a chain of blood feuds, each leading in turn to further retaliation, stretched through Beduin history — sometimes to be broken by larger clashes between various groups, which were long celebrated in poetry as the "*Ayyām al-'Arab*" — "(Famous) Days of the Arabs." Between the two elements of the population, the merchants and the Beduin, a passable relationship had been worked out, as each was dependent on the other.

THE RELIGIOUS POSITION

Arabia lay at a focal point where world faiths, as well as political forces, met; but here again the physical characteristics of the land had prevented the rapid spread of a definite creed and permitted the ancestral religion to survive. All was indeed not well with this religion. Neither the Beduin, nor the merchants or the citizens of the small agricultural towns, had any strong religious sentiment, and they therefore left intact the traditional religious forms, which recognized both a number of local deities of each sex and, above them, an almighty lord of the heavens known simply as "God" (in Arabic *Allāh*). Yet little interest was taken in religious questions; the reasons why the sanctuary of the Ka'bah (a black stone, probably of meteoritic origin, built into the wall of a rectangular edifice) was still carefully maintained were that it secured the inviolability of Makkah and that the yearly pilgrimage made to it by the surrounding tribes brought financial advantage to the city's inhabitants.

CHRISTIANS AND JEWS IN ARABIA

As has been the case in every age and among every nation, a life so essentially worldly, so indifferent to matters of metaphysics, could not satisfy those whose minds were open to religious questions. On these speculatively inclined souls, influences emanating from the surrounding world religions were now at work. In Arabia itself, communities of Jews were established, who had organized themselves like Arab tribes and largely adopted Arabic speech, but held fast to their Mosaic law. In North Arabia and the Yaman, these Jews had been able to win proselytes, including at times local princes. In addition there were to be found a few Manichaeans, followers of a dualistic religion which had arisen in Mesopotamia in the 3rd century and spread to Persia and also to Egypt, North Africa and other parts.

Much more important were the Christian influences. These had penetrated the country in many forms — in the Monophysite form from Syria and Mesopotamia, and from Persian territory in the Nestorian. For long past, the Arab tribes settled by the East Romans and the Persians as frontier garrisons on the margins of the fertile lands of Syria and Mesopotamia respectively had for the most part adopted the Christian faith. From here, and at the same time from the Yaman, then under Christian Abyssinian rule, it had penetrated to the interior of the peninsula. A not inconsiderable number of tribes had at least superficially turned to Christianity. At the Yamanite city of Ṣanʿāʾ and on the island of Socotra there were Nestorian bishops. Central Arabia, together with the region around Makkah, still lacked organized Christian settlements, but influences derived from the teachings of Jesus deeply stirred the emotions of the seekers after faith above mentioned. To these was added the influence of the Jewish communities, which should not be underestimated. Such men, called *Ḥanīfs,* of whom there were probably quite a number and whose names are partly known to us, made a certain impression upon their environment; and this was supplemented by an organized Christian missionary activity, carried on perhaps in part directly by Ḥanīfs, but in part also by real missionaries of that faith.

THE YOUTH OF MUḤAMMAD

The preachings of these persons had a certain basically identical pattern. After proclaiming the end of the world, when the good would be rewarded and the wicked punished, they pointed to God's creative might, revealed in nature and in the vital rain, a proof to men of His goodness, but also a summons to them for a corresponding and morally earnest change of heart. It may be inferred that once, among the hearers of such a sermon, was a man who came from a honourable but not well-to-do family of Makkah, who having been orphaned when very young and brought up among relatives had in his youth performed quite menial tasks such as tending cattle, and who only after obtaining the post of bailiff to a rich widow named ***Khadījah*** and after the latter's decision in her 40th year to marry him because of his amiability and discretion, had at the age of 25 come into settled and comfortable financial circumstances. The man who at some unknown time heard such a sermon was called ***Muḥammad*** and belonged to the family of the ***Hāshimites*** of the tribe of the ***Quraysh*** in Makkah. In his younger years his inclinations had been altogether worldly, and his attachment to the religious and moral notions of his countrymen had been strong; but from the age of about 30 onwards, he began to develop into an introspective, spiritually minded man. Quite clearly, during the preacher's sermon, the prediction of the end of the world, with its retribution of good and evil, had tremendously stirred him: had shaken him to the depths of his soul. He withdrew more and more frequently into solitude, to be able to devote himself undisturbed to his contemplations. His trains of religious thought, his fears of the eternal destruction which threatened him and his Makkan compatriots if they continued their present worldly and virtually godless life, solidified gradually into concrete form: into voices which he began to hear, into faces which he began to see.

He was perhaps about 40 when, some time in the year 610 while asleep in a cave in the mountains around Makkah, he heard a voice and then, on waking, saw a figure, whom he later identified with the archangel Gabriel and who charged him with the duty of *Prophethood*[1]. The words, which imprinted themselves indelibly on his mind, are still preserved today; the first part of a ***Sūrah***, that is a section of the holy book of the Muslims, had come into being. Whether the beginning of the 96th or that of the 74th Sūrah was first revealed is a point on which neither

[1] *Nubūwah*, from *Nabī (Prophet)*. C.f. A. GUILLAUME, *Prophecy and divination among the Hebrews and other Semites*, London 1938.

Muslims nor Westerners are fully agreed. Both contain a charge to him to warn his fellow countrymen and to reprove mankind. Later, when opposition had arisen against him, Muḥammad himself described the circumstances accompanying the revelation in Sūrah 53, Verses 1-7, and Sūrah 81, Verses 19-25 [1], which show that in this apparition he saw the conclusive sign of his calling. He won no credence for his claim; only his wife Khadījah, to whom on his return home he related his experiences and who must have long been familiar with his ideas, immediately recognized in him the Prophet of his people, and all the more readily so because a religiously-minded kinsman of hers — a Ḥanīf — acknowledged Muḥammad's vision.

In reality Muḥammad's chief concern was to warn his people, and above all, his unreflecting fellow-citizens; and he evidently found satisfaction in God's gift to the Arab nation of a Prophet who would communicate the divine will to them (as the *Qur'ān* several times stresses) in "clear Arabic speech". After the first revelation, there was rather a long intermission in the supernatural apparitions; then the whole weight of the divine inspiration descended upon Muḥammad. In one new admonition after another, forcefully expressed in the style of the old Arab soothsayers *(kāhins)*, he found pictures of unexampled grandeur wherewith to forewarn his people of the doom which threatened if they did not follow him in the way of repentance and God's will (cf. Sūrahs 81-86).

The Christian polemic of earlier times was unquestionably wrong when it saw in Muḥammad an epileptic or an impostor, a man who consciously uttered untruths in order to act against God's will. Of the sincerity of his Prophetic consciousness there can be no doubt.

ISLĀM

The religious ideas which Muḥammad represented were designated by him with the name of *Islām,* that is, entry into the state of salvation. They were acceptable, however, to only a very few of his fellow citizens, to certain members of his family, like his cousin, 'Alī, to a respected notable, Abū Bakr, who was distinguished for great prudence and probity, and to a few slaves. The great mass of the Makkans were unmoved by the new "Prophet"; when Muḥammad began to preach, they were glad to be diverted by a story-teller who related to them legends of the Persian heroes. Muḥammad himself cherished hopes of support from the Christians

[1] Quotations are from the Egyptian official edition of the Qur'ān, Būlāq (Cairo), 1918/19 (1337 A.H.).

and Jews, with whose concepts he regarded his revelation as basically identical, and he did not hesitate to converse with such of his Jewish fellow-countrymen, in particular, as came his way. Through them he learnt the main elements of the Jewish traditions, especially those bearing on popular piety, albeit in forms which were much distorted and which he probably often misunderstood. These also influenced the revelations which he uttered at this time. Soon both the Jews and his heathen opponents observed that the revelations contained manifest misunderstandings, and they did not hesitate to hold this up against him. Though occasionally embarrassed, Muḥammad nevertheless maintained unshakeably that the messages were divinely inspired and, if subjective, then rightly so, in that the religious thoughts by which he was moved merged insensibly into the trances in which the revelations were communicated to him. Such Jewish and Christian narrations, and also Arab national traditions, gave Muḥammad material for the stories of the Prophets with which he sought to warn his people and bring them to his obedience. These were constantly reiterated and expressed in an increasingly erudite style, tedious to Western tastes and markedly different from the highly poetic revelations of the earliest period.

Little by little the band of Believers grew. A few persons of high ranking origin joined, including the rich ʿUthmān and the energetic ʿUmar. Muḥammad's relatives were divided. Abū Ṭālib, his uncle and adoptive father and the father of ʿAlī, though remaining a pagan, steadfastly and most nobly fulfilled the duty which honour imposed on him of protecting his orphaned nephew against the Makkans. Another uncle, however, turned sharply against him and was consequently dubbed by Muḥammad, in one of the earliest Sūrahs, with the nickname "Father of Hell". (This Sūrah is one of those modelled on the old Arabic invective poems). But all the concealed and open hostility, and even a temporary boycott of his family which caused them bitter distress, was of no avail; the followers of the new Prophet could not be suppressed. Nor could they win over the majority of the Makkans. A severe blow befell the Prophet personally when, in the year 619, first his loyal helpmate Khadījah and then Abū Ṭālib died, one shortly after the other. Though his family did not even now deny him their protection, his position became perceptibly more difficult. A section of his followers, including his son-in-law ʿUthmān, emigrated at his bidding to Abyssinia; the Prophet counted on the sympathetic support of that Christian state against the pagans. His position nevertheless became so delicate that he decided, partly at the instance of relatives and friends, to concede to the Makkans a recognition of their three chief goddesses as at least intercessors with God. Soon, however, he was overcome by remorse for this departure from strict monotheism; and after some delay, he revoked the decision as an inspiration of Satan. This made his position no easier. On realizing that a compromise was no longer possible and on learning, moreover, that in spite of all family considerations attempts were being planned on his life, he began to seek an opening for his work away from his native city.

After one or two attempts had failed, such an opening presented itself. The town of *Madīnah* (then generally called *Yathrib*), about 250 miles north of Makkah, was so rent by disputes between two hostile tribes, the ʿAws and the Khazraj, and by clashes between these tribes and three Jewish tribes which were also settled there, that a compromise could only be brought about by an outside arbiter. Envoys from the town approached Muḥammad and invited him to transfer his residence thither. The Prophet gladly took this opportunity. After sending his followers in advance and taking precautionary measures (though in the event the Makkans did not pursue him), he himself, together with his trusted friend Abū Bakr, moved to Madīnah in September 622 and settled in that town. In so doing, he effected the final breach with his native city. The *emigration* from Makkah to Madīnah had taken place — the event, known as the *hijrah*, from which Muslims rightly date the beginning of their era. Their calendar, in accordance with a later decision by Muḥammad, is based on a year which (since intercalation is banned) is purely lunar and consequently sometimes 10 and sometimes 11 days shorter than a solar year; with the result that the individual months move through the seasons and 33 Muslim years correspond approximately to 32 solar years. (The *hijrī* year 1379 began on July 7, 1959).

MUḤAMMAD AT MADĪNAH

Henceforward, Muḥammad's role at Madīnah was well established; serious obstacles were never put in the way of his authority in the town. The economic situation and the accomodation of his followers who had migrated from Makkah did, indeed, present difficulties at the start. The Prophet sought to overcome them by creating blood ties between the new settlers, the *Muhājirūn*, and the natives, the *Anṣār* (Helpers); and above all, by issuing a municipal ordinance which obliged all the town's inhabitants, irrespective of their religion, to settle internal disputes jointly and share in protecting the Muslims. The non-Muslim Arab inhabitants and also the Jews were forbidden to enter into alliances against the interest of the Muslims. This constitution, whose wording has been preserved for us, displays a statesmanlike ability which Muḥammad developed then and in the following years and which, together with the captivating amiability of his person and his repute among his followers, was to be an essential factor in his success.

It was evident that Muḥammad could not be content to confine his activity to Madīnah, but would be obliged to seek a decision in regard to his native city of Makkah. But as the Makkans themselves did not think of taking the offensive against him, it was he who had to open hostilities. For this purpose he adopted means which went completely against the hallowed traditions of the ancient Arabs and repeatedly gave offence to his followers — for instance, when he caused a Makkan caravan to be attacked during a sacred month. Public opinion was only partially placated by divine revelations which justified his proceedings, and by the material profit. This was an indication of a tendency which in his last years became more and more conspicuous in Muḥammad — namely, to make supernatural manifestations justify humanly reprehensible actions, such as the attack on the caravan or, later, the move against one of the Jewish tribes of Madīnah on the ground of a revelation permitting the breach of a treaty if one of the partners to it was suspect. The standpoint of the observer in this matter will depend wholly on his attitude towards Islām: if he sees in the Qur'ān an assemblage of divine revelations, he will consider such humanly questionable actions to be divinely justified: if he does not attribute to the Qur'ān this supernatural character, he will be bound to disapprove of Muḥammad's endeavour to justify reprehensible actions by allegedly divine commands.

ATTITUDE TOWARDS CHRISTIANS AND JEWS

Muḥammad's attitude towards the two revealed religions, the Christian and the Mosaic, with which he came into contact in Arabia, changed considerably with the growth of his Prophetic consciousness. Initially he had believed that both denominations would forthwith recognize him as standing in the line of their heritage and therefore concur with his preaching. When nothing of this sort came to pass, and when the Jews more and more drew his attention to contradictions in his revelations on Old Testament themes, he turned against them with mounting repugnance and seized upon what was, in the circumstances, the appropriate expedient — that of describing their traditions as intentionally falsified and presenting himself as the restorer of the religion of Abraham, founder of the Kaʿbah and its cult. In so doing, he of course renounced the claim to be the first Prophet of his nation. This assertion was not open to disproof, though it was not well grounded because neither he nor his followers could read or understand the scriptures in their garb of foreign tongues. Even had they been able to do so, it would have been an easy thing to suggest that these writings had been deliberately altered by the ancestors of their then living devotees and that references in them to Muḥammad had been excised. Common people, who know nothing of textual criticism or the comparative history of religions, are quite powerless against such a reproach, and even today a convinced Muslim will, when the Scriptures and the Qur'ān are compared, hold fast to this view and so put every objection out of court. For Muḥammad it meant that his alleged oversights were not errors, but rectifications by which the "falsifications" of his adversaries were unmasked.

Muḥammad's changed attitude towards Judaism and Christianity had several practical results. He abandoned the rule of facing in prayer towards Jerusalem, which he had introduced either in the late Makkan or early Madīnan period, and substituted for it that of facing towards Makkah (the *qiblah*). Instead of the feast on the 10th of Muḥarram, corresponding to the Jewish Day of Atonement, he introduced an entire month of fasting, Ramaḍān, during which food and drink may be taken only at night. It is possible that in so doing he was swayed by Manichaean examples with which he may have become acquainted at Makkah. Similarly the classification of the earlier Prophets, including Jesus and non-Biblical Arab Prophets, into a chronological series of revelations (in which, however, his followers made occasional errors) may perhaps have been borrowed from an analogous idea of Mani [1]. Friday was now designated as the principal weekly day of prayer, likewise in imitation of other religions, but at the same time in deliberate divergence from them. (This may, however, have been an adaptation from ancient Arab institutions [2]). The bells of the Christians and trumpets of the Jews were replaced by the call to prayer (*adhān*), proclaimed by the muezzin (*mu'adhdhin*) from the minaret.

---

[1] Cf. JOSEF HOROVITZ, *Koranische Untersuchungen*, Berlin and Leipzig, 1926, p. 28, 46 (*Studien zur Geschichte und Kultur des islamischen Orients*, IV); HANS HEINRICH SCHAEDER, in *Zeitschrift der Deutschen Morgenländischen Gesellschaft*, 79, 217, passim; RUDI PARET, *Das Geschichtsbild Mohammeds*, in "*Die Welt als Geschichte*", 1951, p. 214-224. For Muslim polemics against Christianity, c.f. ERDMANN FRITSCH (Bibliography, p. 123) and the literature mentioned therein.

[2] Cf. OTTO SPIES, *Über der Ursprung des Freitags als Gottesdiensttag im Islam*, in the *Bonner Biblischen Beiträgen*, I: *Altteslamentl. Studien Friedr. Nötscher zum 60. Geburtstag*, 1951, p. 246-264.

BADR

These reforms and ordinances turned the Muslims into a tighty-knit community. Muḥammad had long shown disregard of old Arab concepts when they appeared detrimental to his interests. He could now think of asking his followers who had emigrated from Makkah to make war against the city of their fathers, if only because this offered them a hopeful prospect of rich booty. How much self-enrichment meant for the Muslims on such occasions had already been shown after the attack on the caravan during the holy month; it had assuredly helped to placate the conscience of the Believers. The Prophet therefore chose a caravan belonging to the Makkans as the target of his next attack. Its prudent leader succeeded, however, in bringing it through safely by devious routes. The covering force of Makkans, about 950 men with 700 camels and 100 horses, appeared to be in a position to return home without a struggle. But once having made ready, they preferred to seek a real fight. At *Badr*, on the caravan highway, they met Muḥammad's troop of little more than 300 men; and the Prophet, though so heavily outnumbered, did not hesitate to make the first assault. The Believers attacked with great ardour and good discipline, while the Makkans fought in the old loose formation of the Arabs. After a severe and relatively bloody struggle (during which the Prophet cast a spell over the foe, which reputedly turned the scales against them), the Makkans were beaten and the only real military victory of Muḥammad's Prophetic career was won.

BELIEVERS AND "HYPOCRITES"

The battle of Badr in 624 was described in an earlier allusion as one of the most important, in its results, of world history. It confirmed the Prophet in his conviction that God sustained his cause. It gave a new strength to the self-confidence of the Believers and singularly raised Muḥammad's reputation among the surrounding Beduin tribes. The number of Believers in Madīnah increased. The "*Hypocrites*", a group of inhabitants who only outwardly adhered to Muḥammad and had been expressing their inward aversion with increasing frankness, gradually ceased to play an important part and to exist as a self-conscious group. One of the Jewish tribes of Madīnah [1], which became objectionable to Muḥammad, was forcibly expelled from the city. There were fanatical

[1] The three Jewish tribes at Madīnah were the Banū Qaynuqāʿ, Banū Naḍīr and the Banū Qurayẓah.

followers enough who, at the bidding of the *"Apostle of God"*[1], would eliminate by murder any of his opponents whom he desired to see out of the way.

UḤUD

In the following year Muḥammad once more attacked a caravan; and the Makkans, who had hitherto limited themselves to ransoming their prisoners of the Battle of Badr for large sums, were bound to take counter-measures unless they were to abandon their cause without a struggle. At considerable expense they gathered together about 3,000 men with an equal number of camels and 200 horses, against whom Muḥammad could set only 700 men following the desertion of 300 "Hypocrites" from his army soon after it had set out. Nevertheless the Makkans, who lay close at hand, did not prevent the Prophet from taking up a favourable position on the mountain of *Uḥud* near Madīnah. So violent was the onslaught of the Muslims, and such their steadfastness, that victory would again have been theirs had not their archers, who were defending the left flank, abandoned their position to take part in plundering the enemy's camp. The leader of the Makkan cavalry, *Khālid ibn al-Walīd,* now attacked and penetrated to the rear of the Muslim army, which soon broke when a false report spread that the Prophet had fallen. In fact he was only wounded and his men rescued him. The Makkans let pass their opportunity of putting an end to the power of their adversary by an attack on Madīnah, which was undefended.

MUḤAMMAD IN OLD AGE

Muḥammad's prestige among the Believers and the neighbouring Beduin tribes had suffered a severe blow. Among the former it was restored by a revelation blaming the result of the struggle on the divine wrath over their indiscipline (Sūrah 3, Verses 153 ff.); and a measure of respect was reinstilled into the Beduin by means of several small military expeditions. A leading grudge was satisfied by besieging and banishing the second of the three Jewish tribes in Madīnah. In 626-627 a new threat arose when the Makkans planned to besiege Madīnah with an army of almost 10,000 men. Perhaps on the advice of *Salmān al-Fārisī,* a figure surrounded by legends personifying in him the Īrānian element in nascent Islām, a ditch was dug to protect the open parts of Madīnah. To the Makkans, unacquainted as they were with the arts of regular warfare,

[1] *Rasūl Allāh.*

this presented such an obstacle that they did not dare cross it, though their cavalrymen could have done so with ease. Finally inclement weather and failing supplies compelled them to retreat without having achieved their object. The *War of the Ditch* was not a real success for Muḥammad, but he made good use of it as a clear demonstration to the outside world of the impregnability of his city.

Muḥammad could now venture to arrange for the elimination of the last of the Jewish tribes in Madīnah. By a skilful manoeuvre he persuaded the other inhabitants to agree that the men of this tribe should be put to death, the women enslaved and their property apportioned. Muḥammad's share of the spoil was a Jewess whom he took into his ḥarem after a special revelation had authorized him to exceed the number of four legitimate wives permitted to other Muslims. He was to make ample use of this authorization. After remaining monogamous up to the death of Khadījah, he had in the last years of his life no less than ten wives. This is a familiar point of Christian polemic, the more so because there are passages in the Qur'ān which deal with the settlement of internal dissension in the Prophet's ḥarem (Sūrah 66, Verses 1-3). The Muslim is inclined to answer a Christian's astonishment at this fact with the contention that the Saviour of the Christians is reported to have mingled with very disreputable persons, and that that equally is open to slanderous imputation. To anyone who is convinced that the mission of Jesus was directed above all to the "weary and heavy-laden", this argument is naturally unacceptable.

In general, the Prophet's revelations during the Madīnan period became less frequent and ceased to be clad in the religious ecstasy of the earlier Makkan period. Muḥammad evidently now had such a power over himself that he could to a certain extent induce the occurence of trances; and the revelations which were now vouchsafed to him are in reality legal decisions and directions for the life of the community. These show that the Prophet more and more assumed the task of a statesman and that his rôle as a religious leader became correspondingly less important.

ḤUDAYBĪYAH

It was during this time that Muḥammad sought permission to make a pilgrimage to the Ka'bah, of whose significance he was well aware. He set out with a number of his *Companions*; whether he entertained the design of gaining access to the sanctuary by force cannot be determined. At all events, the Makkans were not disposed to permit his pilgrimage and advanced with their army to meet him at *Ḥudaybīyah,* where their sovereignty ended. The Prophet again found himself faced with an unavoidable decision. He could not return without incurring a stigma which might be irreparable, while a fight would have been hopeless. He therefore made sure of the good faith of the participants by shaking hands, and decided to conclude a treaty with the Makkans permitting him and his adherents to perform the pilgrimage in the following year provided that they went unarmed. He also consented to being mentioned in the treaty simply by his own name, and not by the title "Apostle of God".

The believers who accompanied him, including ʿUmar, were indignant at these steps and only acquiesced later when they saw that the reputation of their cause had not, as they at first feared, in any way been impaired. Muḥammad's action is often regarded as an incomparable diplomatic masterstroke, since by it he obtained recognition as a treaty partner of equal status. This is probably an exaggeration; a more tenable opinion is that force of circumstances had predisposed the Makkans to mutual recognition, and that this state of affairs had already been sanctioned by the ransoming of the prisoners after the battle of Badr. With the keen insight of a realistic statesman which he now increasingly displayed, the Prophet extracted himself from a situation which might otherwise have led to a disaster, while gaining certain not inconsiderable advantages which the Makkans feared to refuse him in view of the well-known bellicosity of his followers. He acquired the right to make alliances with the Beduin tribes on the same terms as the Makkans, though he had to undertake to repatriate Makkans of minor age who had deserted to him at Madīnah without obtaining recognition from the Makkans of a similar obligation in the opposite case. In view of the high regard attached by the Arabs to considerations of honour, the treaty must be considered to have been hardly satisfactory. Muḥammad's diplomatic mastery was to be proved less by the conclusion of this treaty than, as he himself realized in the resultant circumstances, by the extent to which he maintained and further swiftly raised his prestige.

THE CONQUEST OF MAKKAH

Muḥammad made full use of the right to conclude alliances (which he had, indeed, already possessed), and began to form a nucleus of Beduin tribes, devoted to his allegiance and in the process of conversion to Islām, whom he could set against the allies of Makkah. He conquered several districts, including the neighbouring Jewish oasis of Khaybar, and undertook various military expeditons. Meanwhile, in 629, he had, as stipulated at Ḥudaybīyah, performed the pilgrimage, which had passed without incident and had, moreover, afforded the first opportunities of contact with the hitherto ill-disposed Makkan magnates. It was becoming more and more clear that Muḥammad's cause would prevail; and the politically discerning among his former opponents, such as his uncle ʿAbbās, and Khālid, the real victor of the battle of Uḥud, deemed it expedient to come to terms with him. An attack on his native city was no longer beyond the range of Muḥammad's daring. He made careful preparations for the event, but kept them secret to the last.

In 630 the decisive blow fell. The city surrendered almost with no resistance after security of life and property had been guaranteed to those who kept to their houses without fighting — a point on which the Prophet insisted. More than this, he brought a sincere good will towards the Makkans. He bestowed such privileges on them in financial matters that his old Companions grumbled and had to be taught by him that the "reconciliation of hearts" (to Islām) by means of money came entirely within the compass of the divinely willed ordinance (Sūrah 9, 60); only all traces of paganism in public and in private homes must be banished.

Undoubtedly one of the most beautiful passages in the Qur'ān is the 110th Sūrah, which was revealed to the Prophet after his victory and contemplates the achievement in these brief and noble words:

"Now that God's help and the triumph is come/ and thou seest mankind entering the religion of God in troops,/Hymn ye the Praises of the Lord and seek forgiveness of Him; for He forgiveth always."

COMPLETION OF ISLĀM: DEATH OF THE PROPHET

Most Makkans now embraced Islām without resistance. The goal of Muḥammad's life had been reached. In the days which followed, further progress was made in the building up of the Muslim state; and some expeditions were sent against Byzantine territory (which, if not failures, gave no practical results) and against the surrounding Beduin.

To the religious structure, finishing touches of great importance were added. While the revelations which Muḥammad now received became even rarer than before, he issued various instructions, and in February 632 laid down rules for the pilgrimage to the Kaʿbah (from which he had stayed away for two years). Earlier he had given the pagans a final choice between submission and extermination and had forbidden them to take part in the ceremonies. The form which the Prophet gave to the pilgrimage in this year — preserving quite a number of the old pagan ceremonies deprived of their original significance — has remained valid for all subsequent ages. All distinctions of birth were now declared invalid, and the degree of an individual's attachment to Islām was set forth as the only standard of his worth (though tribal consciousness could not, of course, be thereby abolished forthwith). This completed the Prophet's lifework; as one of the last Sūrahs expresses it (Sūrah 5, Verse 3): „This day have I (God) perfected your religion for you and fulfilled my favour unto you/ and have appointed Islām as your religion." Shortly after returning from his *Farewell Pilgrimage,* the Prophet was stricken by a fever which rapidly lowered his strength and to which he succumbed on June 8, 632, in the arms of his young spouse *'Ā'ishah,* daughter of Abū Bakr, at the age of about 62. His death took the Believers completely by surprise and left them in great confusion, the more so because Muḥammad, though he had frequently spoken of his decease, had in no way indicated what was then to be done.

THE LIFE OF THE PROPHET

In reviewing the Prophet's life, none can dispute that his coming suppressed or repressed many abuses, such as the custom of burying newborn girls alive (for the Arabs valued male issue most) and the popular obsessions with luck and fame. He placed gambling and wine-drinking under a general ban. The requirements of mutual help and of good treatment of slaves, beggars, prisoners and travellers contrasted advantageously with the practices of earlier times. One's judgement nevertheless wavers before the many facets of his character, which comprised both the Prophet of Makkah and the astute and not always straightforward statesman of Madīnah. His strong sexuality is, in particular, often condemned. For all this, it should not be forgotten that the Prophet himself never pretended to be a pure, sinless man, but always emphasized his possession of personal weaknesses and his human identity with other men. This did not, however, prevent the exaltation of his figure within the Muslim community at an early stage: the attribution to him of sinlessness, infallibility and knowledge of the future, and the formation round his person of a whole cycle of myths, starting from his youth and surrounding every phase of his life. The biography of Muḥammad written by *Ibn Isḥāq* (d. 768) and revised by *Ibn Hishām* (d. 834) already contains much of what is familiar to us as the Tradition of the Muslim community in this respect [1].

This conception of the Prophet had, and still has, far-reaching effects on the development of public life. In consequence of it, Muḥammad's deeds and conduct are viewed as absolute standards, prophetic significance is ascribed to his commands, and efforts are made to regulate everything as he would have done. There thus arose a special science of *Tradition* (*Ḥadīth*), which collected reports of actions and sayings of the Prophet or imagined to have been his with the object of fixing them as universal rules of conduct. They were at first transmitted orally, but subsequently an extensive literature (which will be discussed later) grew out of them.

THE DUTIES OF ISLAM

The legalistic tendency dominating Muḥammad's whole achievement as a founder of religion explains why the so-called "religious duties" or "pillars" of Islām have no close connection either with the individual soul's need for redemption or with moral requirements. They are better described as duties of worship, and they correspond to similar prescriptions in other religions [2]. These requirements are five in number (a sixth, that of Holy War (*Jihād*) against unbelievers, having after much vacillation been dropped), and are in effect rules of worship and ritual; (1) The Profession of Faith in God and His Prophet; (2) the Prayer (*Ṣalāt*) five times daily (the number five was only fixed later, perhaps under Zoroastrian influence); (3) the Fast in the month of Ramaḍān (*Ṣawm*); (4) the "Poor Tax" (*Zakāt*), payable according to a definite procedure; and (5) the Pilgrimage to Makkah (*Ḥajj*), to be performed if possible at least once in a lifetime.

---

[1] Details belong to the sphere of Islāmic religious and doctrinal history. The outstanding study is that of the Swedish Islāmologist, TOR ANDRAE, *Die Person Muhammeds in Lehre und Glauben seiner Gemeinde*, Stockholm 1918.

[2] This subject likewise belongs primarily to the history of religion.

THE "RIGHTLY GUIDED" CALIPHS

ABŪ BAKR: RIVAL PROPHETS

Reverting to political events, we stand at the point where the viability of the young Muslim theocracy was to be put to the test. The Prophet had passed away without designating a successor. (A contrary opinion, to be considered later, is held by one of the great sects of Islām). Whether he was restrained from so doing by preoccupation with the changing course of events, or by confidence in his cause as that of God, can never be known for certain. In any event, the news of his death produced extraordinary confusion, so much so that his mortal remains were left for a whole day before being interred in his dwelling house. Meanwhile influences of every sort had pushed to the surface. The old rivalries between Companions of the Flight from Makkah and "Helpers" from Madīnah, between particular tribes and between individuals, had broken out anew. It was a sign of prudence — Muslims would say, a proof of divine guidance — that on the proposal of 'Umar, the leading "Companions" agreed on the choice of an estimable man, who had been one of the deceased's closest friends — *Abū Bakr,* the father of Muḥammad's favourite wife at the time of his death, 'Ā'ishah. The title which he assumed was *Deputy of the Apostle of God* (in Arabic, *Khalīfah,* whence *Caliph*). We have already come across him as an absolutely honourable and reliable man, enjoying universal respect, who had unqualified trust in the divine revelation vouchsafed to the Prophet, that is in the Qur'ān. Even if not a great statesman, he succeeded by his unfailing steadfastness and tranquil probity in warding off the dangers which threatened young Islām.

The Beduin tribes around now saw the opportunity of cutting the trammels which bound them to the ruling power at Madīnah, or at least, while not rejecting the Faith, of escaping from the Poor Tax. In spite of every danger, Abū Bakr decided to carry on with an expedition against Byzantium which the Prophet had ordered as a last wish in the closing days of his life; and the situation remained critical for two months until the return of the expeditionary force, of whose achievements nothing is known. The danger was increased by the appearance of *Rival Prophets* who, fired by Muḥammad's example, believed themselves called upon to play similar rôles vis-à-vis their own tribes. There was even a woman among them. After hard struggles, they were all eliminated and their followers were dispersed. The hardest was with ***Maslamah,*** contemptuously dubbed by the Muslims with the diminutive form "Musaylimah", whose field of action was the district of Yamāmah in Central Arabia. His followers were finally slain in the so-called "Garden of Death", a walled enclosure into which they had chosen to retreat. After the suppression of these break-away movements, the authority of the government at Madīnah was restored or estabished over the whole of Arabia up to the East Roman frontier; the Persian and Abyssinian spheres of influence in the north-east and south were eliminated; and above all, proof was given of Islām's power to survive.

CAMPAIGNS OF CONQUEST

These achievements also brought about a suitable conjuncture for the great campaigns of conquest, ranking among the mightiest feats of war in history, on which the Islāmic Arabs now embarked. Their previous collisions with Byzantine frontier troops on the edge of the Syrian desert had had no far-reaching significance. Now their attack was launched simultaneously against that empire and against Sāsānid Persia. Two divisions of the army moved north. One, under *'Amr ibn al-'Āṣṣ,* invaded southern Palestine in 633; the other, directed against Mesopotamia, was under *Khālid ibn al-Walīd,* who had meanwhile accepted the religion of the Prophet. In Mesopotamia, the frontier fortress of al-Ḥīrah had already fallen in 633. In Palestine, at a place perhaps called Ajnādayn (the reading and the tradition are uncertain) the East Romans were defeated in the summer of 634, with the help of Khālid who had hastened to the scene in a perilous march across the desert. In several further struggles, the Romans were pushed back to Damascus; and Jerusalem, the holy city of the Christians, was obliged to capitulate, its Patriarch acting as intermediary. Damascus surrendered in the following year. In spite of great exertions and considerable reinforcements, the Emperor Heraclius's brother could not avert disaster. On August 20th, 636, the Byzantines were vanquished in the Battle of the River *Yarmūk,* south of the Sea of Galilee, and forced to surrender the city of Emesa (Ḥimṣ) and the district up to the northern border of Syria. Soon afterwards Khālid was dismissed from the supreme command, though not from all office, in Syria; according to tradition, he had earlier brought down on himself the wrath of the new Caliph at Madīnah.

ʿUMAR

After ruling for two years, Abū Bakr had died at Madīnah on August 22, 634, and been succeeded by *ʿUmar* whom he had recommended on his death-bed. ʿUmar belonged to the circle of old and true friends of the Prophet. In addition to the title *Caliph,* he adopted that of *Prince of the Believers* (*Amīr al-Mu'minīn*). With him, one of the most outstanding statesmen not only of Islām but of world history took over the control of state affairs at Madīnah. He was a man of the utmost will-power, keenest sense of duty and indefatigable energy, and an organizer of the first rank. Of transparent personal simplicity in his bearing, he possessed the gift of exercising absolute command over men. Under him the campaigns in Syria and Mesopotamia, which had hitherto been left in practice to the discretion of the army commanders on the spot, were systematically organized and coordinated. After the conclusion of the conquest of Syria, which he marked by a personal visit to that province and to Jerusalem, the main attention of the central government was claimed by the struggle against the Sāsānid empire.

PERSIA

Following the campaigns of Heraclius and the violent death in 628 of Khusraw II, the Persian empire had been shaken to its foundations. To a large extent no real governmental authority remained in being. In the course of a few years numerous insignificant rulers, including several woman and children, had followed one another on the throne. After the accession in 632 of *Yazdijird (Yezdegerd)* III, though he too was a mere youth, there had indeed been a beginning of recovery, but the defeat at the hands of the Byzantines and the resultant disorders had so gravely weakened the Persian state's capacity to resist that the Arab attack had a success beyond all expectation. The swift advance of the Arabs against the Persians and East Romans is to be explained very largely by the exhaustion of the two latter through their long immediately preceding war.

Another factor was the collapse, some time after 602, of the Arab buffer state of the *Lakhmids* on the Persian frontier, and the decline of the *Ghassānids* who had earlier played an important rôle as auxiliaries of the Byzantines in the Syrian desert. Both these states had known how to keep camel-borne pagan Arab raiders from the peninsula in check at the desert fringe, for they had used similar fighting methods and identical weapons. Neither the Persian nor the East Roman troops, on the other hand, were capable of facing the ferocious onslaught of the Muslim armies, whose martial spirit was inflamed by the ardour of their faith and by their nomads' lust for booty, and whose military backbone was provided by the camel [1].

In the Byzantine lands, strong discontent among the mainly Semitic and largely Jacobite (Monophysite) population against the Orthodox tendencies of the state church as determined by Constantinople was a contributory factor, making the Arabs appear at first as liberators. But in Persia no such factor operated. Nor is there any trace in the records of other — possibly social — discontent at that time. The only explanation left is that of a general state of exhaustion, such as has constantly recurred under initially brilliant dynasties in Persia. Just as the Achaemenid empire was overthrown by Alexander the Great, so in a later age the Ṣafavid empire was destroyed by raiding Afghāns, not to mention several analogous smaller-scale episodes.

The campaigns of the Arabs against the Persians cannot be followed in detail here. After several early successes, the decisive battle took place in the summer of 636 (or 637? — the records vary), near one of the old frontier fortresses named *Qādisīyah*, 21 miles south-west of al-Ḥīrah. After a long and bitter struggle, in which numerous deeds of heroism were performed by day and night and single combats were fought, the capable Arab leader, *Sa'd ibn Abī Waqqāṣ*, vanquished the Persian royal commander Rustam (Rōstahm) who lost his life. This opened the way to the Persian capital, Ctesiphon, which was situated on the middle Tigris — beyond the zone inhabited by Persian-speaking peoples in the midst of an Aramaic or aramaicized population. Immense treasures fell into the hands of the Arabs, a considerable portion of which, including noted works of art, was brought to Madīnah and incorporated into the state treasure. The Persian court held out for some time in the Zagros Mountains on the edge of the Īrānian plateau, but an advance which they made into the plain in 637 was repelled with heavy loss. The situation in southern Mesopotamia (Babylonia) then became temporarily stabilized. Following a conference between the assembled army leaders and the Caliph 'Umar in 637, the district to the north (upper Mesopotamia) was invaded from Syria and conquered in 639/40. In the following year the Armenian frontier districts were also subdued.

[1] Friedrich Wilhelm Schwarzlose, *Die Waffen der alten Araber, aus ihren Dichtern zusammengestellt*, Leipzig 1886; Nikolaus Fries, *Das Heerwesen der Araber nach Tabari*, Tubingen 1921; Leo Beckmann, *Die muslimischen Heeren der Eroberungszeit* ... 622-651, typewritten hesis, Hamburg 1953.

EGYPT

An even more momentous feat of war was a venture which *'Amr ibn al-'Āṣṣ*, the conqueror of southern Palestine (633), undertook reputedly on his own initiative and later carried to fruition with 'Umar's approval and support: the conquest of Egypt. In 639, starting from Palestine, he launched his attack across the Sinai peninsula, along the age-old invasion route of the Near Eastern peoples, and advanced without serious resistance up to the fortress of Babylon (to the south of modern Cairo at the apex of the Delta). By skilful manoeuvres, 'Amr weakened the Byzantine forces to such an extent that the Orthodox [1] Patriarch Cyrus (Kyros) entered into negotiations. Although initially repudiated by the Emperor Heraclius, Cyrus was soon reinstated in Egypt as a result of disorders following the former's death. Meanwhile Babylon had fallen on April 9, 641; and in 642 Cyrus agreed to the surrender of Alexandria also. In addition, Upper Egypt was occupied without any real resistance. In the Nile valley, as elsewhere, the ease and speed with which the Arabs advanced was made possible by religious animosities. After the country had been freed from the Persian occupation about 618, the Emperor had attempted more or less forcibly to incorporate the almost exclusively Monophysite Coptic population into the Orthodox church. This policy had only renewed old antagonisms, with the result that the Coptic inhabitants at first greeted the Muslim Arabs as liberators, though they were soon undeceived. In 645, Alexandria surrendered to an East Roman fleet which unexpectedly appeared, and had to pay heavily for its attitude when reconquered by the Arabs in the following year. From then on, Byzantine influence in Egypt was extinguished for good.

THE FALL OF THE SĀSĀNIDS

In the meantime, after occasionally severe fighting and a few reverses, the Arab conquest of Persia was proceeding to its conclusion. The court of Yazdijird III had withdrawn to the province of Fārs (Persis), in the hope of mobilizing new forces to carry on the defensive struggle there and in the east of the empire. The plan miscarried. After an important victory won by the Arabs at *Nihāvand* in 642, the local feudal lords, though receiving the king with honour, refused him any support. The same lot befell him when he withdrew into the extreme north east of the country, into the province of the Rising Sun (Khurāsān). Its vassal ruler even

[1] In reality, Monothelete.

The spread of Islâm in the 7th and 8th cents.

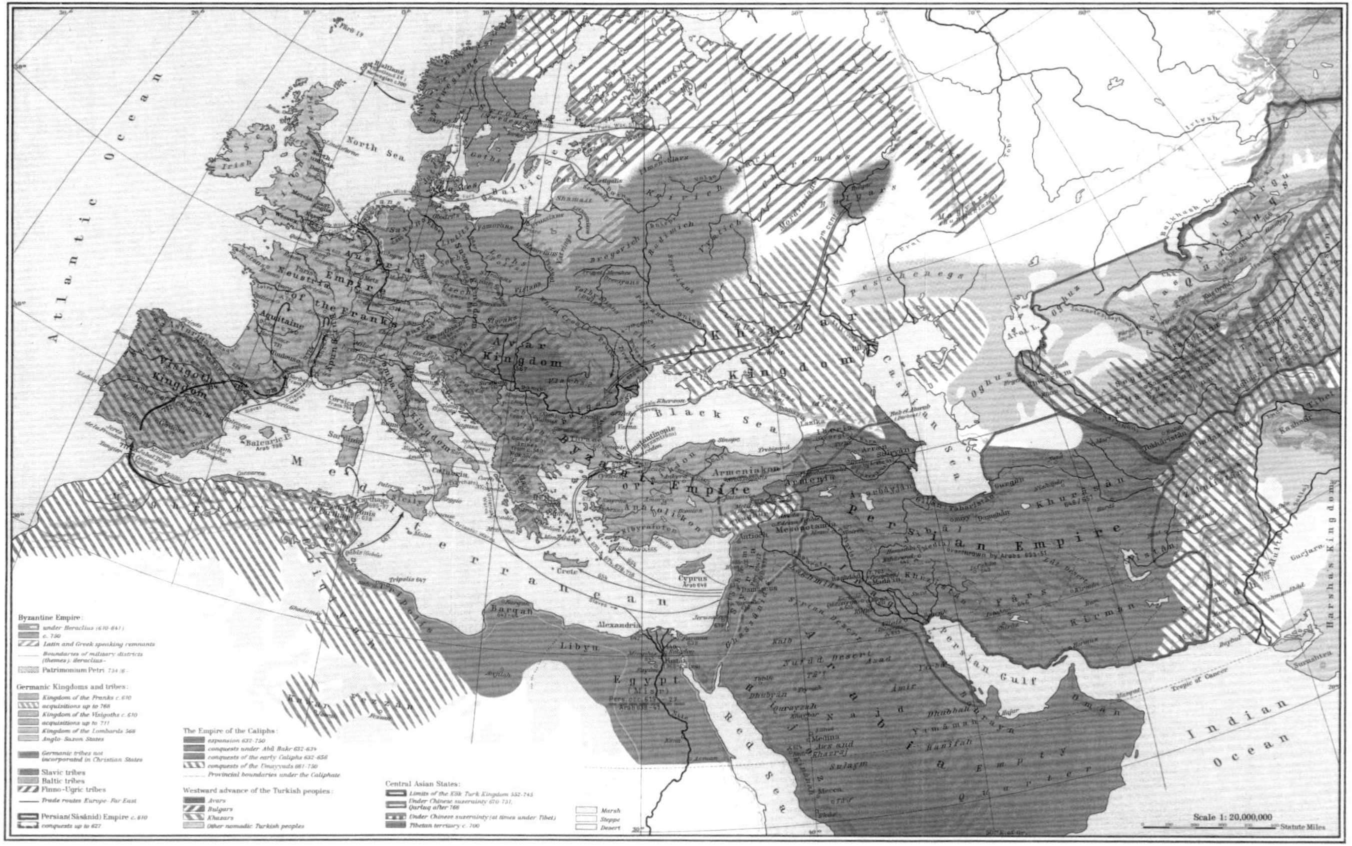

called in the help of the Turks against him. Finally, at the instigation of this prince, he was murdered in 651 in the house of a miller where he was passing the night. The last of the Achaemenids, Darius III, had come to a similar end. Yazdijird's son *Fīrūz (Pērōz)* did not yet give up the struggle. He plotted uprisings against the Arabs, who had meanwhile made themselves masters of one city after the other and for the first time come into collision with the Turks of Central Asia on the Oxus. He even endeavoured to find support in China (whose sphere of influence extended at that time far into Central Asia), despatching several embassies during the following decades to the Son of Heaven. All this was no longer of any avail. The empire of the Sāsānids had finally collapsed.

"PEOPLES OF THE BOOK"

The enormously extensive Arab conquests did more than bring a decisive turn of fate to the countries affected. They also, in the following century, confronted the Arabs with tasks to which they could not have risen equal without assistance, lacking as they did almost all the prerequisites for governing foreign lands. The practical sagacity and realism which Islām has repeatedly displayed both as a religion and in its state organization were evinced by its success in obtaining such assistance, and in so directing those who gave it that they did not set aside the basic ideas of Islāmic theology, even if substantial modifications could not be avoided. Already the Qur'ān had laid down the relationship of Muslims to adherents of foreign religions; and since, for Muḥammad's followers, the Qur'ān is the Word of God, this position has in all subsequent times formed a basis for the attitude of an Islāmic government to a subject population of different faith. The Prophet had distinguished between the possessors of a "holy" (revealed) scripture and mere "pagans", and had promised his government's protection to the former if they submitted and paid a *poll-tax* at a prescribed rate. He had specifically named the Christians, Jews and "Ṣābians" as *"Peoples of the Book"*.

While the adherents of these faiths thus had the right to keep their religion, Islām for its part was in practice disinclined to convert *en masse* the inhabitants of Christian countries which it had conquered. Arabia itself was the only country in which no other religion besides Islām was tolerated and the Christian and Jewish communities were forced to choose between conversion and exile [1]. In Mesopotamia, Syria and Palestine,

[1] The Jewish communities of the Yaman appear to have survived continuously since pre-Islāmic times.

and Egypt, on the other hand, the Christian populations were expected to provide as taxpayers for the maintenance of the Arab-Muslim warrior caste. Under the Caliph 'Umar, the practice was adopted of paying pensions to the troops from state funds to enable them to devote their lives undistracted by other cares to fighting to expand the territory of the realm. For this purpose, and for self-protection against any insurrection among the subjugated inhabitants, the Arab armies, now including recent proselytes and converted tribes, were concentrated in a number of large military camps. Use was sometimes made of already existing fortresses, but more often of new sites, whose choice gave evidence of the military far-sightedness of their founders. In this manner such cities as *Kūfah* and *Baṣrah* in southern Mesopotamia came into being, and a little later *Wāsiṭ* ("The Central") between the two. Similarly, at the head of the Nile Delta, *Fusṭāṭ* (Latin: Fossatum) was founded on a site a little to the north of which, several centuries later, the city of Cairo arose. Today Fusṭāṭ, with the ancient and honoured Mosque of 'Amr, still forms the quarter known as "Old Cairo".

TAXATION

The setting up of these military strongholds, most of which soon developed into foci of learning and economic life, made it possible to assemble larger armies, available for campaigning at any time. It was essential for this purpose that the Arabs should not disperse over the countryside and therefore that they should not settle in the lands which they had conquered. In the first decades of Islām, a stern law forbidding the Arabs to take over house properties and landed estates achieved such a result. Not only the Arabs and Muslims were affected by this law, but also the subject peoples, for whose later destinies its consequences were most far-reaching. Islāmic *theory* distinguishes between territories which submitted to the Muslims without fighting on the basis of a covenant (*ṣulḥan*), and those which were subdued in the normal way after a struggle (*'anwatan*). The inhabitants of the peacefully surrendered territories obtained a contractual right to protection of life and property, which was secured to them in return for their payment of poll tax (*jizyah*) in addition to the land tax (*kharāj*) [1]. The right to practise their religion

[1] Probably a loan word from the Greek χοράγιον. In Egypt and Persia both words were evidently used without distinction at first, and only gradually fixed as technical terms when it became necessary to regulate the financial obligations of new converts in the reign of 'Umar II (p. 46 ff.). In Egypt the word "Kharāj" always included the rental value of the land. (cf. C. H. Becker, *Die Entstehung von 'Ušr und Charāǧ-Land*, in *Islamstudien*, I. 1924, p. 218-233).

undisturbed was also included in the covenant. Conquered territories, on the other hand, belonged as booty to the victors; their inhabitants became slaves, and the land and soil state property disposable at the state's discretion. Ample space might have been available here for free colonization by the Arabs, had not the law expressly forbidden them to settle, and had they not as nomads generally had a distaste for agriculture (which in the early stages was an at least equally important reason). In the circumstances, there was no alternative but to leave the inhabitants of these lands likewise in possession, after confiscating one fifth as state property. It was their manual labour which tilled the soil, and their contribution of its produce which gave it real value to the Muslim-Arab ruling class. The theoretical distinction between territories acquired by covenant and by fighting was thus in fact largely eliminated, except that the tax (*kharāj*) on the latter territories could at any time be arbitrarily raised. In the course of the centuries, certain after-effects ensued which will be considered in connection with the economic and social development of Islāmic society. *In practice*, both in Egypt and in Mesopotamia, the old Byzantine or Persian forms of taxation and other imposts (*leitourgia*), including forced labour and especially in early times the impressing of seamen, were retained for long periods, because of the impossibility of maintaining a well-ordered financial system without making use of the already existing officials and dossiers. Numerous papyri and other documents discovered in the Nile valley enable us to form even today a fairly exact picture of this economic continuity and its gradual modification. A particularly grave political problem which arose during the 8th and 9th centuries was the migration to the towns of great numbers of recent converts to Islām. In consequence of this flight from the land, many areas were left uncultivated.

STATUS OF VASSALS

The conclusion of treaties of surrender involved, as has been mentioned, toleration of the Christian and Mosaic religions among the subject peoples, who at an early date were designated by the old Semitic term "*flocks*" (Arabic plural *raʿāyā*). The Muslims did not think of forcing their own religion on their subjects. Certain restrictions were, of course, imposed. Religious activity outside the churches and synagogues was curtailed, the ringing of bells forbidden, the construction of new church buildings prohibited, and death was the penalty for any proselytizing of Muslims (as also for apostasy from Islām). In their clothing, Christians and Jews were to mark themselves off from the Muslims and from each other; they might only ride asses, not horses. They paid the poll tax and became state-protected vassals of foreign faith (Arabic, *dhimmī*). Their conversion to Islām would naturally have led to the falling away of the poll-tax; and this was the main reason why the Muslims did not at first do any proselytizing, which would only have weakened the state finances by diminishing the revenue and thus have endangered their own pensions. They did not interfere in doctrinal questions and were quite uninterested in the internal affairs of the Churches [1]. They merely held the spiritual leaders (Patriarchs, Bishops and Rabbis) responsible for a loyal attitude on the part of the Christians and Jews towards the Islāmic state, and for this purpose granted to these dignitaries supervision over the civil and juridical, as well as the religious, life of their congregations. The Christian and Jewish communities thus formed states within the state, only connected with the government at their summits. This severance is mirrored in the Christian historical sources, which contain but scanty data on the Muslims and then only on governmental matters; while in the Muslim sources there is virtually nothing about the Christian and Jewish communities. The attitude of the Muslims was in marked contrast with that of the Byzantine period. Then the temporal administration had always assisted the spiritual power and, what was worse, the latter, in its efforts to impose Orthodoxy or at least to effect a compromise over doctrinal differences satisfactory from its point of view, had continually seen fit to interfere in the doctrinal conceptions and national standpoints of the Syrian and Egyptian churches. All this now ceased. The Christian hierarchs, and especially those of the non-Orthodox churches, welcomed the Arab conquest because it actually enhanced their influence, while the anti-Byzantine attitude of the masses probably contributed not a little to the rapid sequence of the Arab victories.

All these reasons help to explain, not only why the Muslims were relatively tolerant, but also why most classes of the Christian populations, and especially the notables and officials as well as the priests, so willingly accomodated themselves to the new régime. With the cessation of Byzantine political pressure, their situation was at first better rather than worse. The Arabs were obliged to leave them in their official positions because there was no other way of ensuring the continuance of an

[1] The alleged translation of the Bible into Arabic as early as 637 is a myth of Jacobite propaganda. The first complete translation was made at the beginning of the 9th century in the reign of the Caliph Ma'mūn. Cf. Ignatiĭ Julianovič Kračkovskiĭ, *O Perevodě Biblii na arabskii yazyk pri chalifě al-Ma'mūn* (On the translation of the Qur'ān into Arabic under the Caliph al-Ma'mūn), in *Christianskii Vostok*, VI (1918), p. 189-196.

organized administration and (more important in the profit-loving Arab's eye) of the continued payment of the taxes. The same applied to the highly developed irrigation systems in Egypt and Mesopotamia, to the coinage and to the notarial system. Greek, Coptic, Persian and to a less extent Aramaic-Syriac remained in use as languages of administration, and the East Roman and Persian coins continued to circulate. Their imprints served up to 697/8 as models for new coins minted by the Arabs, which at first retained Greek captions, portraits of the Emperor and even the Christian cross, or the Sāsānid ruler's portrait and the fire-temple, respectively. This conservative attitude of the Arabs towards the pre-existent officialdom, though based on the necessities of the situation, contributed much to the consolidation of their rule and to the efficient functioning of their state administration. Even the use of the Arabic language was at first forbidden to the new non-Muslim subjects. Proud of their pure Arab descent, the aristocracy wished, in this as in other fields, to avoid any blurring of the line between rulers and ruled.

ṢĀBIANS

Circumstances were somewhat different for those subjects who were not entitled to Qur'ānic privileges, being neither Christians nor Jews. The Qur'ān did, however, place on a par with the two latter the "*Ṣābians*", by whom was probably meant — in so far as the Prophet attached any precise idea to this appellation — one of the numerous Baptist sects in southern Mesopotamia (best known of whom were the Mandaeans, who have survived until today). The vagueness of the term made it seem appropriate to allow the outward adoption of the name Ṣābian by all and sundry of the surviving remnants of ancient pagan cults, even if they were in fact quite unrelated. For instance, the adepts of the ancient star-worship at Ḥarrān (Carrhae) were in later centuries called Ṣābians equally with the Baptist sects. In general, the Muslims left things as they were without enquiring further, and many an ancient survival endured long under this cover.

ZOROASTRIANS

Much graver was the problem of the Zoroastrians in Persia. They too had been mentioned, as "*Magi*" (*Majūs*), in the Qur'ān, but in a very unsympathetic context. The Prophet himself had certainly not counted them among the possessors of a revealed scripture. But the common usage even in his time, and in later times Islāmic jurisprudence also, guaranteed them the toleration of the new state, and all the more readily so because they too could proffer a holy scripture — the Avesta. It has even been contended recently that it was the Muslim conquest which occasioned the final codification and dissemination of manuscript texts of the Avesta, by creating the need to point to a "revealed book" (HENRIK SAMUEL NYBERG). The lack of evidence proving the earlier existence of Avestic texts (unless of a few sacred archetypes), and the fact that the Arabs termed the Zoroastrians "*mumblers*" (because they handed down their holy scriptures by rote and so gave an impression of mumbling) [1], are advanced as proofs in support of this argument. However this may be, the inhabitants of Persia also enjoyed the status of *dhimmīs*. In that country, however, it was not the priesthood (*mōbeds*) who kept their position and became the bearers of the national tradition; on the contrary, they disappeared fairly rapidly and played no part in the Īrānian heritage (except among the Pārsīs in India who belong to a different environment). The reason for this is probably that social relations in Persia were quite different from those prevailing in East Roman territory between the Near Eastern and Egyptian inhabitants and the state. There the Christians were wont to view the state with hostility as the representative of hellenism and Orthodoxy, and had already for centuries grouped themselves as national entities in their churches (though the existence in those days of consciously formed national churches in the modern sense cannot be admitted without important reservations).

In the Sāsānid Empire, the Arabs had destroyed a state which in spite of social and religious upheavals — Manichaeism in the 3rd century, Mazdakism with its communistic tendencies in the later 5th century — was nevertheless the national state, which the individual looked on as his fatherland. Moreover, with the collapse of the state, the entire upper class and higher officialdom were not (as in Byzantine territory) driven out or annihilated. Thus in Persia the social structure, which was feudal in character, remained intact, with the lesser territorial nobility (*dihqāns*) retaining their position as representatives of the sovereign authority. It was they who remained to hand on the national tradition and civilization, and who kept in being a suitable social environment in which the saga of the national heroes and an unbroken artistic heritage could be preserved as the point of departure for a national rebirth. Perhaps one of the most striking instances of this development was the retention of the ancient

[1] Arabic: *zamzamah*. HENRIK SAMUEL NYBERG, *Die Religionen des alten Iran*, German tr. by HANS HEINRICH SCHAEDER, Leipzig 1938.

popular festivals of *Nawrūz* and *Mihragān*, which continued to be celebrated, the one at the beginning of spring (and of the Persian year) and the other in the autumn, in accordance with the old Zoroastrian calendar. [1] In Egypt the Nile Festival was likewise still celebrated. In Persia, however, the Zoroastrian calendar remained in use under the Muslims — possibly, being solar, for economic as well as other reasons. (As late as the 11th century, the traveller Nāṣir-i-Khusraw reckons days and months according to the Zoroastrian calendar — a sure sign that mentally he fixed dates by it). Since there was no longer a king, the year of the reign was counted from that of the accession of the last king, Yazdijird III, in 632. This explains why the Persian era commenced with that date.

THE DIHQĀNS IN ĪRĀN

The local nobility (*dihqāns*), especially in Khurāsān which was then the main cultural centre of Persia, could not maintain their position of governmental authority without making concessions in regard to religion. They did not qualify for the privileges allowed to the Christian and Jewish hierarchs by virtue of Qur'ānic doctrine, nor were they the officially recognized representatives of their compatriots; but they could acquire this position, and escape interference by the central power, through embracing Islām and disseminating it among their tenants. That is one of the reasons why Islām spread so quickly and extensively in Persia, the mōbeds having already lost importance, and also why Sunnite (orthodox) Islām remained predominant among the aristocracy. It guaranteed the superior social status which the dihqāns had retained through conversion. The lower classes, on the other hand, partly out of deep religious need and often also in a spirit of national resistance, gave faith to the most varied forms of dissent, of which more will be said hereafter. (A similar socially conditioned movement of conversion took place among the Bosnian nobility in the 14th-15th centuries).

'UTHMĀN

Such was the situation confronting the suddenly aggrandized empire of the Caliphs, with which only China could vie as the biggest on earth. It was a brilliant and statesmanlike achievement, not only by the Arab

[1] The dates of the festivals, including Nawrūz, were not in fact fixed but varied considerably (up to the end of April or beginning of May). Cf. Bertold Spuler, *Die Zuverlässigkeit sassanidischer Datierungen*, in "*Byzantinische Zeitschrift*", XLIV, 1951, p. 546-550.

aristocracy but also by the "Prince of the Believers" ʿUmar, to have directed the general course, if not the details, of its development on such rational and successful lines. The loss to the empire was thus very great when a Christian slave, for reasons of private revenge, murdered him on November 3, 644; and all the more serious because, as things stood, only an unshaken state leadership could ensure the further advance of the conquests. Such leadership ceased when the assembled council of well-tried Companions of the Prophet chose as Caliph, not the strongest, but the weakest of their number — namely *ʿUthmān*, a member of the aristocratic clan of the Quraysh to which the Prophet had belonged. They made the choice in the hope that their influence and ambitions would thereby be obstructed as little as possible — which soon proved to be the case. But this gave rise to dissensions seriously detrimental to the interests of the theocracy at Madīnah. ʿUthmān, who in his youth had been an elegant dandy and of whom it was alleged that he had joined the Prophet mainly in order to marry his pretty daughter, had grown into a meek and, though personally incorruptible, easily led old man. The influences to which he was subjected were primarily those of his family and of the related Makkan aristocracy, who now thought the time ripe to abase the groups, mostly derived from the lower classes, which had been elevated by early adherence to Muḥammad, and to recover their own previous dominance, albeit under the official banner of Islām to which they owed such great successes abroad and resultant enhanced prosperity. It was at first a question of obtaining influential posts in the administration. One of the leading figures in the party was Muʿāwiyah, who came of the *Umayyad* branch of the house of the Quraysh and was a second cousin of the new Caliph. An attempt to get rid of the governor of Egypt, ʿAmr, failed because he could not be dispensed with; but posts of second rank in provinces whose governors proved irremovable were brought into the hands of the noble families. There was a certain justification for this proceeding in that the aristocratic groups were, in general, the only Arabs possessed of the necessary breadth of mind and adaptability to gain some measure of control over the situation in the newly won territories by compromising between opposing requirements. To a large extent events justified them. This argument could not, of course, be appreciated by the frustrated elements, particularly those whose point of view was religious; they therefore concentrated their indignation on the head of ʿUthmān. He for his part was entirely in the hands of his entourage and willingly let himself be used as a tool of the aristocratic forces.

EDITING OF THE QUR'ĀN

The Caliph was personally unconcerned with self-enrichment, and mainly interested in theological questions. The unsystematic compilation of the Prophet's revelations had inevitably given rise to discrepancies in the sacred text; and different readings now threatened to lead to disputes between various tribes and army divisions. The Caliph decided that the sacred text must be finally fixed, and this task was accomplished, with a precision astonishing for that age, by the Prophet's former secretary, *Zayd ibn Thābit*, and others [1]. For the history of Islām, this editing of the Qur'ān was the most important and fruitful achievement of the reign of 'Uthmān. Abroad, expansion had run its course and come to a natural standstill. At home, the Caliph was no longer capable of intervening to regulate affairs and determine policy. All energies were crippled by the growing discontent in wide circles, which were joined by two eminent Companions of the Prophet, *Ṭalḥah* and *Zubayr*, and also by his widow *'Ā'ishah*. The malcontents in Madīnah contacted disaffected groups in southern Mesopotamia and Egypt, and ultimately a band of insurgents marched from Egypt on the city, which was denuded of troops, all the fighters for the faith being on the frontiers. The Caliph was forced to negotiate. It seemed as if the situation had been saved when the Egyptians, stirred up by treacherous intrigues, mutinied and laid siege to the Caliph's house. Finally they stormed his dwelling and murdered him (656). Tradition relates that, being an old man of 80, he took no part in the fighting, but when the mortal blow fell was reading a copy of the Qur'ān, which was bespattered with his blood.

'ALĪ

This was a momentous deed. For the first time, open rebellion had broken out against the rightful head of the empire and Muslims had raised their weapons against fellow-believers. It was the signal for a civil war which was to ravage the young Islāmic state over long decades to come, and also, since it combined constitutional and doctrinal questions in a characteristically Islāmic way, for a permanent schism in the community of the Faithful. The real instigators of the uprising had expeditiously quit the city, to avoid shouldering the blood-guilt. The deed

---

[1] For recent studies, see article 5 in *Handbuch der Religionswissenschaft*, ed. by GUSTAV MENSCHING, Berlin, 1948, Vol. 9, pp. 73 ff.; RICHARD BELL, *Introduction to the Qur'ān*, Edinburgh 1953.

had brought them no profit, as it was immediately evident that they were agreed on nothing except hostility to the prevailing régime. As soon as *ʿAlī*, the Prophet's son-in-law, had as a matter of course taken over the Caliphate, *Ṭalḥah* and *Zubayr*, and also *ʿĀʾishah* who had long been his enemy, turned against him and demanded vengeance for the murdered Caliph. ʿAlī, though personally brave and honourable, was an inept politician and did not succeed in bringing about a compromise. He was obliged to defend his right by force of arms, and in the fighting which now broke out — called the *Battle of the Camel* after the camel from which ʿĀʾishah surveyed the field — he defeated his opponents. Ṭalḥah and Zubayr fell quite soon after the battle. ʿĀʾishah's rôle in politics had come to an end, but she lived another 21 years before expiring at Madīnah in 678.

ṢIFFĪN

If ʿAlī had thought that the matter was then settled, he was to be sorely deceived. *Muʿāwiyah*, who as a close kinsman of the murdered Caliph was pledged by the Arab conception of honour to avenge him, now took over the leadership of the faction opposed to the new Caliph in the intrinsically plausible belief that ʿAlī was not wholly unimplicated in the murder. ʿAlī had already left Madīnah before the Battle of the Camel and moved his headquarters to southern Mesopotamia — a step which was certainly meant to be provisional, but had the result that Madīnah ceased to be the capital of the empire; no Caliph ever resided there again. The preparations of his opponents in Syria, and in Egypt which was equally restive, compelled him to march north and seek a decision. On the upper Euphrates, in the swampy plain of Ṣiffīn, the hostile forces faced each other for several months, which they passed in skirmishing and parleying; since sections of the same tribes and near relatives were present in both armies, the will to fight was not strong. Among the mass of the warriors, if not among the leaders, a certain horror of shedding the blood of fellow-Muslims was probably also still felt. When finally a decision could not be avoided, and victory was tilting towards ʿAlī, his adversary bethought himself of a sly ruse, said to have been suggested by ʿAmr, the conqueror of Egypt; namely to invoke the verdict of the Qurʾān (instead of the verdict of arms). ʿAlī could not but agree to this proposal.

When after several months the Qurʾānic tribunal assembled, ʿAlī was again outwitted. While he had believed that there could be no question of his ultimate recognition as Caliph, Muʿāwiyah's faction had gained recognition as an equally ranking party to the dispute. ʿAlī naturally could not assent to the verdict that "both pretenders" should renounce their position, when in his eyes there was only one rightful Caliph — himself. For this reason he was compelled to break his pledged word to abide by the award of the arbiters.

SHIʿITES AND KHĀRIJITES

This transaction had far-reaching consequences. As long ago as the days after Muḥammad's death, ʿAlī had put forward claims to the Caliphate; and an ever increasing number of followers were ready to see in him, as the Prophet's son-in-law and father of his grandchildren, the only rightful occupant of that office. Soon they formed an "Alī's Party", which was later simply called "The Party" (*Shīʿah*); and some of the extremists among them attributed to him supernatural powers and a peculiar divine enlightenment. Men with such beliefs formed the backbone of his army. It was they who had forced him to accept the "verdict of the Qur'ān". On seeing however, that he had submitted to a "human arbitrament" — by which he had been tricked — and that he had forgone the arbitrament of God alone — i.e. of God and their own swords, ʿAlī's party split. One section, soon reinforced by further malcontents, deserted from the army's camp and presumably for this reason got the name of "*Khārijites*" ("*Seceders*") [1]; though it is no longer possible to determine for certain what were the circumstances leading up to the formation of this party and the exact moment at which it broke away. The Khārijites stood for the principle that only the most pious might be Caliph, regardless of nationality and social origin; and they elected one of their own number as supreme head. The exact opposite of the Arab aristocracy, this party attracted a large following in subsequent periods of troubles and disorders of religious, social and national character, and seriously threatened the rise of Islām and the consolidation of the state's authority. They forthwith turned against ʿAlī himself, who met them in an exceptionally sanguinary battle at *Nahrawān* on July 17, 658 and, though victorious, failed to suppress them.

The Caliphate of ʿAlī had thus run on the rocks. The Syrians and Egyptians were hostile to him, and even in Mesopotamia he was far from secure. Further fighting was unavoidable, if he were to maintain his position. But an unforeseen event occurred: on January 24, 661, at

[1] This view is upheld by FELIX TAUER in *Dějiny*, I, 42. See also LAURA VECCIA-VAGLIERI (Bibliography, p. 125); ELIE ADIB SALEM, *Political Theory and Institutions of the Khawārij*, Baltimore 1956; W. MONTGOMERY WATT in "Der Islam" 36/3(1961).

Kūfah, the Caliph ʿAlī was murdered by a man of the Khārijites, in revenge for their bloody defeat. This deed put an end to the imminent danger of civil war, since ʿAlī's party for the time had no head; and the energetic and wordly Muʿāwiyah at Damascus found no difficulty in securing general recognition, especially when *Ḥasan,* eldest son of the murdered ʿAlī and grandson of the Prophet, six months later sold away his claim to the succession. Ḥasan never again played any important part and died peacefully at Madīnah in 669. [1]

---

[1] The Twelver Shīʿites, who believe that all the "Imāms" were martyrs, hold that Ḥasan was poisoned (See p. 65-66).

THE UMAYYADS

MU'ĀWIYAH AND THE ARAB ARISTOCRACY

Mu'āwiyah, whose right to be Caliph was no longer contested by any except the Khārijites, came, as has been mentioned, from the noble family of the *Umayyads*; and their name has passed to the dynasty which he founded. His accession signified a decisive shift of power within the new state of the Caliphs. It will be recalled that, with few exceptions, the ruling classes of Makkah had made their way into the Muslim community only at a late hour, when it had become clear to political observers that the victory of Muḥammad would endure and that there was no longer any risk in going over to him. It was evident even then that their motives were political, not religious; and it was readily intelligible that after conversion they did not change character or to any great extent adapt their lives to the requirements of Islām. Apart from a more or less superficial profession of the new religion, they remained what they had been — rich merchant princes, high-spirited Arab noblemen, for whom the quest for terrestrial well-being meant more than did the demands of religion. But since the Prophet himself had treated them with the utmost consideration, they remained virtually unmolested and were able to hand down their way of life to their children who, though brought up in Islām, held on to the old fashions to the greatest possible extent. During the Caliphate of 'Uthmān, also a Qurayshite, members of these families and the Makkan aristocracy in general managed to acquire more and more influence in the government and over policy. Their attitude towards political questions was unquestionably more realistic and flexible than that of the genuinely pious circles, who because of their origin were scarcely fitted to lead and govern and were often more concerned with the salvation of their souls than with wordly importance. They too, of course, had no disdain for the good things of this life; that had not (apart from a few minor restrictions) been the prescription of the Prophet, and it would have been altogether contrary to the Arab love of property.

TRIBAL FEUDS

In the Umayyad state, this gay and mundane aristocracy won the upper hand. Mu'āwiyah conducted the government in the patriarchal style of an Arab nobleman *(sayyid)*. His peers had access to him and shared in consultations on matters of moment. Through a marriage alliance with the great South Arabian tribal confederation of the Kalb, he enjoyed the latter's powerful support. That was of importance because the Prophet's admonitions that Muslims be brothers had entirely failed to eradicate the ancient tribal sentiments of the Arabs. The old tribal groupings still survived, and with them the old tribal laws and, above all, feuds. The significance of this fact cannot be exaggerated; almost everything depended on it. Every governor of a city or province sought to provide for his own kinsmen or at any rate fellow-tribesmen, and deliberately excluded members of other tribes; he could indeed hardly do otherwise, because members of one tribe generally refused to work with members of other tribes, and any attempt to compel them to do so would only have caused disorders and murders, leading in turn to a series of sanguinary vendettas.

PROVINCIAL ADMINISTRATION

In these circumstances, the greatest admiration must be felt for the skill with which the Caliph organized the provinces. An account has already been given of the empire's rapid expansion in the first few years of its existence, to which it need only be added that in 647 Tripoli was subjected to tribute by a force from Egypt. The conquests then ceased in consequence of the civil war; and Muʿāwiyah, during his struggle with ʿAlī, found it necessary to pay tribute to Byzantium to protect his rear. As Caliph, he had first to organize the empire before he could think of an ambitious foreign policy. At that time the number of administrative units was small: Egypt (whose conqueror and first governor, ʿAmr, died there in 664), and the two provinces of Kūfah and Baṣrah in Mesopotamia. The entire Persian hinterland at first belonged to the province of Baṣrah, Khurāsān being administered only by sub-prefects. Gradually the custom was adopted of attaching to the governor, whose main responsibility was for military affairs, a director of finance [1], to whom was assigned the task of collecting the various taxes and so ensuring the pension-payments to the Muslim soldiers and the needs of the court, administration and war-treasury. Between these two authorities, there was constant friction.

Shortly after his accession, Muʿāwiyah placed Mesopotamia and Persia in the charge of *Ziyād ibn abīhi* (*Son of his father*, i.e. of an unknown father), a man of humble origin but great efficiency, whom he shrewdly

[1] *ʿĀmil.*

bound to his interest. Ziyād was kept at his post till his death in 676-77; and he knew how to hold his province, which had been singularly hard hit by the civil war, in a tight rein. In particular, he inflicted repeated defeats on the dangerous Khārijites, forcing them to retreat into the Persian highlands, whence they still menaced Mesopotamia with constant incursions. One extraordinarily fanatical sect among them threatened death to any Muslim who did not, as soon as bidden, profess acceptance of its beliefs; on it the hand of Ziyād fell with special severity.

SYRIANS AND COPTS

Towards the Christians in Syria and Mesopotamia the attitude of the Damascus government was tolerant. They formed the great majority of the population, and most of them spoke Aramaic, though not all the Arabic-speaking Christian tribes had yet been converted to Islām. Since the administration could not be carried on without the participation of Christian officials, they were left at their posts — which was quite in harmony with Islāmic theory. In Syria, the Aramaic (or Syriac) speaking inhabitants and the Arabs had been accustomed to living alongside one another since Roman times.

In Egypt, relations were more difficult. The Copts were, indeed, equally indispensable in the financial and other administrative offices of the districts (Greek, *pagos*: Arabic, *kūrah*), which were retained as they had been in East Roman days; the Egyptian bureaucracy had a past thousands of years old behind it [1]. On the other hand, Coptic national pride was wounded by the coming of the Arabs and by the infiltration of further nomadic tribes. The Copts thus became stubborn and later made repeated attempts to rebel, which were suppressed with much bloodshed. These circumstances did not improve the relations between the two elements, but led many Copts to embrace Islām, for instance around 820 and around 1320 [2].

POETS

As bards and court poets, Christian as well as Muslim Arabs played their part. They served not only to entertain the court, which was much

[1] The system, dating from Byzantine times, by which important functions were exercised by two parallel officials, was kept in being for centuries to come.

[2] Cf. Rudolf Strothmann, *Die Koptische Kirche in der Neuzeit*, Tübingen 1932; Bertold Spuler, *Die Gegenwartslage der Ostkirchen*, Wiesbaden 1948. (Both contain historical chapters). B. Spuler in "*Handbuch der Orientalistik*" VIII/2 (Leiden 1960).

concerned with preserving the traditions of the old Arab aristocracy, but also as writers of panegyrics and invectives for political purposes. The nobility in Madīnah, who had lost almost all political influence when the seat of government was removed to Damascus, began to lead an elegant epicurean life, graced with poets and singing-girls, which gave great offence to the sincerely religious groups dwelling around them. These latter regarded themselves as the élite of the new state and were not to be consoled for their social decline as readily as was the local aristocracy which, in contrast with them, had lost almost nothing of its earlier, pre-Islāmic, privileges.

MILITARY OPERATIONS

For the time being, discontent among the religious groups was only a rumbling below the surface. After organizing the provincial administration, the Caliphs were free to consider a new territorial expansion, which offered the incidental advantage of enabling them to divert the enthusiasm of the malcontents into the struggle for the faith. Asia Minor was invaded repeatedly, almost every summer, and the walls of Constantinople were reached twice. For the first time, a Muslim fleet was created, with bases in the still serviceable ports once used by the East Romans in Syria and Egypt. Cyprus and the Aegean Islands were laid waste; and for seven years the Muslims occupied Cyzicus, on the south coast of the Sea of Marmara, whence they harrassed the Byzantine capital, [1] but a combined land and sea attack against the city failed because of the defeat of the land forces.

In North Africa, under the leadership of ʿAmr's nephew *ʿUqbah ibn Nāfiʿ*, the last remains of Byzantine-Christian rule in the area around Carthage were destroyed in 667. Fighting against the Berbers continued; but as the terms imposed on them (apart from acceptance of Islām) were generally not oppressive, and as many of them were attracted by the prospect of sharing in the spoils of the Muslim campaigns, they soon joined forces with the Arabs and after a few decades formed an integral part of the state of the Caliphs, though keeping a very wide measure of internal autonomy. The Latin and latinized elements largely emigrated to Italy.

In Persia, sections of the Arab tribes now began to settle on the land,

[1] "Corsair" is derived from *cursus*, the term used for surprise attacks by the Muslim sea-rovers. WILHELM HOENERBACH, *Araber und Mittelmeer*, in "*A.Z.V.Toğan Armağanī*", Istanbul 1954, p. 379-396.

especially in distant Khurāsān, to which they were likewise attracted by hopes of booty in the Holy War. Conscripted troops were also occasionally sent to the province. For a time, however, the tribal feuds which they brought with them, and the fighting with the Khārijites in south west Persia, prevented further expansion of the empire in that direction.

KARBALĀ'

A serious crisis faced the state when the Caliph Mu'āwiyah died in April 680 and the question of the succession was posed. During his lifetime he had caused homage to be paid to his son *Yazīd I*, and the latter was generally acknowledged; but two groups, both in Mesopotamia, refused to acquiesce. Although common life at the military settlements of Kūfah, Wāsiṭ and Baṣrah had softened tribal feelings, a pronounced provincial sentiment had arisen among the Arabs of that province; since the death of 'Alī, they had considered themselves to be under alien Syrian rule. Thinking the time ripe to regain a leading rôle, and prompted by agitators, the Kūfans now summoned the Caliph 'Alī's second son, *Ḥusayn*, who lived at Madīnah as his brother had done. Yielding to the pressure of his entourage, he set out. Although warned en route that the government's precautions had placed his supporters at Kūfah in a weak position, he declined — probably from a sense of honour — to turn back, and later, in spite of offers of favourable terms, refused to desist from fighting for his right — the right of the *Family of the Prophet* (*Ahl al-Bayt*). On October 10th, 680 (10th Muḥarram 61 A.H.), at *Karbalā'*, west of the Euphrates on the edge of the Syrian desert, he fell after a brief struggle. For the future of Islām, this was an event of the greatest moment.

THE CLIENTS

The discontent among broad circles in Mesopotamia was further enhanced by this tragic death of the Prophet's grandson. Although the principal consequences of the event were not to be unfolded until several decades later, a dangerous rebellion fomented by various 'Alid pretenders was a warning signal to the government — some of whose supporters likewise grouped themselves on a religious basis. (From among them was formed in later times the Kurdish religious community of the *Yazīdīs*, whose doctrinal evolution was to be wholly pagan). The movement, led at Kūfah by *al-Mukhtār*, was particularly ominous because it coupled religious and social motives and for the first time appealed directly to the ever-increasing class of newly converted Muslims. The Arabs, proud above all of their descent in spite of the specific injunctions of Islām to the contrary, were not disposed to give real recognition as brothers to those of their subjects who professed Islām, or to concede to them an equal status in society. Instead, they required them to seek adoption into an Arab tribe as *clients* (*mawālī*). Such persons received the protection of the Arab tribe concerned, but had to sever their previous national, social and economic connections and were precluded from any corporate representation of their interests. Freedom from such limitations was their ideal. The *mawālī* were not willing to tolerate being treated as second-class citizens; nor could the sense of regional solidarity be eliminated, especially among the talented Persians whose language (in contrast, on the whole, with Aramaic) was holding its own with much success. A considerable population of Persian clients lived in the cities of southern Mesopotamia, and it was they on whom al-Mukhtār chiefly counted. The Persians could not but join a movement directed against the ruling Umayyad dynasty as the vehicle of the Arab spirit of domination; and if religious as well as national and economic motives were involved, such a phenomenon was normal in the East, as already shown by the formation of the national separatist churches. Such factors account for the fanaticism of the ʿIrāqī rebellion against the central government at Damascus, and for the great trouble which the latter had in putting it down (686-87).

CIVIL WARS

But the most dangerous threat to the dominion of the Umayyads did not come from sedition by a group such as this. It came from the unwillingness of the majority of orthodox Muslims to recognize the demise of the Caliphate upon a collateral line of the ruling house, the *Marwānids* (so called after the first sovereign of the branch, *Marwān I*, 684-85). Mesopotamia so far as it was not Shīʿite or Khārijite, Arabia and also part of Syria rallied to *ʿAbd Allāh ibn Zubayr*, son of the Companion of the Prophet slain in the Battle of the Camel. Inter-tribal strife now burst out in all its primitive violence. Although Umayyad rule in Syria was restored in 684 on the field of Marj Rāhiṭ (north of Damascus), this battle, in which the pro-Umayyad South Arabian Kalbites defeated the North Arabian Qaysites, gave rise to sanguinary vendettas which went on for decades and made well-nigh impossible any orderly conduct of affairs. Whenever a provincial governorship was held by a member of one or another tribe, the whole administration passed into the hands of his fellow-tribesmen.

On Persian soil, though tribal sympathies were somewhat differently divided, not only was this rule strictly observed, but pitched battles were fought between the different tribes. This strife caused much devastation, and must have undermined the prestige of the Arabs and also of the ruling house.

The civil war between the two pretenders to the Caliphate dragged on for ten years. The Caliph *'Abd al-Malik,* son of Marwān (685-705), only won the upper hand in Mesopotamia after Makkah had been stormed in 692 and 'Abd Allah ibn Zubayr had fallen in a gallant fight for its defence. With the suppression of a few minor outbreaks in Persia, internal peace was then at last restored throughout the empire. It was upheld by the appointment as governor of Mesopotamia of a man of humble origin, *al-Ḥajjāj ibn Yūsuf.* The inhabitants of the province, with their grievance against the supremacy of Damascus, were still an element of unrest; even the rule of so formidable a pro-consul as Ziyād, in the years 60-70 A.H., had been unable to prevent the spread of Shī'ite and Khārijite ideas among them. Ḥajjāj, too, could not succeed in suppressing them, but his ruthless energy finally brought Mesopotamia under effective Umayyad sway and established order in Persia. In the process, he gave little heed to the interests of the genuinely religious groups. He consequently does not get a good name in the historical works — which were written later with an anti-Umayyad bias — and indeed is commonly represented as the type of the worldly, brutal man, indifferent to the "real" interests of Islām.

ADMINISTRATIVE AND MONETARY REFORMS

The reign of *'Abd al-Malik* (685-705) was one of the most important periods of internal reform in Islāmic history. The defeat of the régime's numerous opponents — who, as has been seen, were often identifiable with alien elements — emphasized the Arab character of the Umayyad empire. Expression was now given to this by arabicizing the administration. By a decree of the ruler, the Arabic language was introduced into the government offices, at the expense of Greek and Persian (*Naql al-Dīwān*). The year 696-7 saw the completion of a definitive monetary reform by which the designs and Christian or Zoroastrian symbols of the coins were replaced by Arabic imprints (the Profession of Faith with the issuer's name and title and the place of minting); though there is evidence from numerous specimens which have been found that this change in the coinage had been initiated earlier with minor alterations in the old Byzantine and Sāsānid designs. A longer period of transition in the government offices must also be assumed from the evidence of papyri discovered in large numbers in Egypt.

THE SECOND WAVE OF ARAB CONQUEST

1. Asia Minor

The final restoration of internal peace permitted a resumption of external political activity in the form of a large scale movement to extend the range of Islāmic power — the last such movement to be undertaken by a unitary empire of the Caliphs. The attack was launched at four points, within an astonishingly short space of time but without that concentrated force which was a temporary feature of the first years of conquest. The war against the East Roman empire only yielded relatively slight permanent results: a few frontier fortresses were captured, such as Tyana in Asia Minor. One force several times reached the Black Sea; and in the years 717 and 718 the capital, Constantinople, was besieged and hard pressed.

2. Central Asia

In 704, the province of Khurāsān in north east Persia was entrusted by al-Ḥajjāj to *Qutaybah ibn Muslim,* who thence organized an offensive against the land of the *Turks* (Turkistān) adjoining to the east and north. Their Central Asian realm had freed itself from Chinese suzerainty in 682, and they had begun to expand westwards, to Samarqand and Bukhārā. After years of fighting, during which Turkish appeals for Chinese help want unanswered, these two cities passed under Muslim sovereignty in 715. From then on Islām began to spread among the Turks, who had hitherto mostly been totemists and fetichists, though Christianity and Manichaeism had gained some influence among them (especially in the important kingdom of the Uigurs) [1].

3. India

The third point where the banner of Islām was hoisted at the beginning of the 8th century was *India.* In 711 the first troops from southern Persia

---

[1] A sketch of the pre-Islāmic history of the Turks of Central Asia is given in the author's article listed under the heading "Turks" in Bibliography, p. 126; see also *Handbuch der Orientalistik*; *Turkologie (Geschichte).*

invaded Balūchistān and the Indus valley. Islām thus began to thrust into India, though nearly three centuries passed before there was any important expansion (of which more hereafter).

4. Spain

711 was also the year in which the Muslims invaded Spain. In North Africa west of Egypt — which the Muslims named *Ifrīqiyah*, later *al-Maghrib* (*The West*) — the forward drive of Islām had almost come to a stop. In the course of the 7th century, the Arabs had advanced along the Mediterranean coast and finally driven the East Romans out of Carthage, but had only penetrated into the interior at a few points; the necessary reinforcements were sent by sea. The Berber tribes, as has been mentioned, were not subjugated but won over to Islām and nominally merged into the empire of the Caliphs, though in practice they largely kept their autonomy and soon inclined to sectarian movements which tended to corroborate it. Khārijism found its way to them at an early date, and still today has one of its refuges in the Mzāb district of Algeria. There will be mention of other religious movements in the Maghrib later on.

As capital of the region, Qayrawān was founded by ʿUqbah ibn Nāfiʿ around 670; and from here the present-day Algeria and Morocco were occupied and, finally, the Atlantic Ocean reached. Subsequently, however, Arab dominion was imperilled by a great revolt, which was only put down with much difficulty in 741-2. In 711, at the bidding of the North African commander, a mixed troop of Arabs and Berbers crossed over into Spain. Their leader was *Ṭāriq ibn Ziyād*, from whom Gibraltar takes its name (*Jabal Ṭāriq* = *Ṭāriq's Mountain*). The Visigothic kingdom of Spain had been rent for centuries by dissensions between the Arian and Catholic Christians, and though a compromise had been reached,was still weakened by internal antagonisms between Germans, Romans and Jews. At this moment, moreover, it was passing through a crisis of leadership. The Arabs thus had no hard task in destroying the Visigothic army at *Wādī Bakkah* [1] and, with the help of quickly sent reinforcements, in constricting the Christian territory within a few years to a narrow strip at the foot of the Pyrenees and in the Asturias. Before long the Arabs pushed into France, where a battle fought between Tours and Poitiers in 732 brought their advance to a halt, but did not prevent them from

[1] The hitherto customary appellation of this battle after Jérez de la Frontera, which lies further north, is erroneous.

holding positions on the coasts of Provence and Languedoc for several decades to come.

THE LATER UMAYYADS

The empire, thus enormously extended by these new conquests, had a spatial articulation and racial diversity which could not but engender fissiparous tendencies, unless the government were in the hands of extraordinarily competent rulers. *Walīd I* (705-715) and *Hishām* (724-743) were in fact capable Caliphs and real statesmen. Immediately after them, however, the collapse of the dynasty began. Their successors were young men, wordly and devoted only to their own amusement; they surrounded themselves with wits and aesthetes, singing-girls and boon-companions, and valued only hunting, gambling and frivolous disputations. Their lack of the manifold statesmanlike qualities befitting the special needs of a theocracy, as represented in the state of the Caliphs, brought to pass within a few years the total collapse of the Umayyad empire of Damascus.

PERSIAN DISCONTENT

Before this catastrophe is related, it will be necessary to understand the changed internal conditions on which the later Umayyad rule was based, and to learn about the spiritual and religious trends which served as a background for the rise of new forces. It has already been emphasized that Islām did not, in the first decades of its existence, see fit to call for conversions, because the state finances were largely based on the poll-tax on non-Muslims; the legally prescribed and graduated pensions of the military were in particular mainly paid from these funds. Yet voluntary adhesions to Islām could obviously not be discountenanced; and the pious circles, congregated mostly in Madīnah and Makkah, urged with increasing emphasis that conversion to Islām, and therewith salvation for eternal life, should be placed within reach of the masses. The ideological and political offensive which had now been launched against Byzantium worked in the same direction. Though the state's leaders long remained hesitant over the problem of winning souls for Islām, many of their subjects now adopted the religion of the victors, if only because of the financial pressure of the poll-tax. It has already been said that in so doing they acquired the status of *clients*; but contrary to the real meaning of the law, they did not gain exemption from the tax liabilities, since the state could not forgo this important source of revenue. The motives which led such great masses of the inhabitants to forsake Christianity and Zoroastrianism so relatively soon can only be conjectured. There is, strangely, an almost complete lack of real controversial literature between Islām and the other religions: of a literature which, in the course of apologetics or polemics, might have depicted the relations between the various religious communities and made known to us what were the motives of a conversion, the main points of debate or the doctrines which aroused keenest interest [1]. Its absence adds weight to the conclusion, already reached on other grounds, that among the masses in Syria, Mesopotamia and Persia as well as Egypt and North Africa motives for conversion were only to a minor extent of a religious character; that there was not any dynamic proselytizing quality in Islām, but that the main motives were economic — the desire to evade onerous taxation and be free of diverse restrictions which in the aggregate were oppressive. Various indications in later centuries, which cannot be detailed here, also support this view. There was of course, another contributory factor, namely the relative simplicity of Islāmic doctrine. It drops many of those essential dogmas of Christianity which must have caused difficulties to the minds of ancient and medieval men (and not in the orient alone), such as the Trinity, the Incarnation and questions concerning the nature of the Saviour. Islām knew nothing of such problems, because for it the Prophet was in the beginning just a man, with all the sins and weaknesses of a man. His transfiguration into a saintly and radiant being of an almost supernatural nature was only in its initial stage during the later Umayyad period; and it doubtless owed much to the conversion of Christians and Zoroastrians to whom such ideas were familiar.

In these circumstances, the continuance of the early privileges of the Arabs, and especially of their social status as a military aristocracy, became intolerable from both the religious and the political standpoints. The number of non-Arab converts to Islām had grown to such an extent that they could no longer be almost entirely excluded from any share in the life of the state, especially as the talented and culturally advanced Persians were clearly indicating that they were no longer disposed to

[1] Examples such as exist include: the "*Epistle for Refuting Christians*", by the littérateur al-Jāḥiẓ (circa 770-869), text published by OSKAR RESCHER in *Excerpte... aus... Ǧaḥiẓ*, I Stuttgart, 1931, pp. 40-67; CARL BROCKELMANN, *Arabische Streitgedichte gegen das Christentum*, in *Mélanges Galthier*, 1937, pp. 96-107; M. PERLMANN, *Notes on anti-Christian Propaganda in the Mamlūk Empire*, in *Bulletin of the School of Oriental and African Studies*, X, (1940/1942), pp. 843-861 In this connection, cf. ERDMANN FRITSCH, *Islam und Christentum im Mittelalter*, Berlin, 1932 (*Breslauer Studien zur historischen Theologie*, 17); B. SPULER in "*Handbuch der Orientalistik*" VIII/2 (Leiden 1959).

acquiescence in a subordinate rôle. They were moreover suffering much from the constant feuds between different Arab tribes in their homeland. Their increasing participation in ʿAlid movements must certainly be regarded as a sign of this disaffection. These movements were centred in the cities of Kūfah and Baṣrah, where Persians were in permanent contact with Arab elements and where the lot of the unprivileged was much in evidence. It is also significant that Īrān was becoming the refuge of Khārijism, whose supporters could there express their feelings openly, and whose doctrine of the equality of believers regardless of nationality or colour must have especially appealed to the Persians as long as the Umayyad régime denied them such equality. Inasmuch as the Persians inclined to both of these so divergent movements, it followed that the movements themselves should become representative of Persian interests in order to win over the Persians more effectively; the mutual interaction of the two elements is easy to envisage. It thus came about that these once purely Arab ideologies, especially the Shīʿah, gradually approximated in their outlooks to Persian conceptions.

MURJIʾITES

Recent converts were not the only Muslims who voiced discontent with the course of affairs. Similar attitudes were also held among the Arabs, by no means all of whom (aside from tribal feuds) fully shared the standpoint of the aristocracy in Damascus. The classes genuinely devoted to Islām viewed the conduct of the ruling circles with mounting disgust, seeing in it disrespect for the divine revelation and for the Prophet's clear injunctions. The centre of this movement was Madīnah, where joyous living and religious zeal then coexisted in odd antithesis. Between the rigorists and worldly-minded stood a quite large middle group, whose members rejected the extremist opinion that the Umayyad régime ought to be combatted because of its impiety; they considered on the contrary that its trial and the condemnation of its upholders were God's prerogative and must therefore be "postponed" until the Day of Judgment (whence the name *Murjiʾites*, i.e. "*Postponers*"). In the long run this moderate position could not hold out against the onset of the extremists.

THE TAX LEGISLATION OF ʿUMAR II

For the above-mentioned reasons, further continuance of the Umayyad system with its dependence on the Arab element was now unacceptable.

Some modifications had already been introduced during the reign of ʿAbd al-Malik, who took the religious duties incumbent on him as Caliph seriously in that he frequented the company of theologians and sometimes led the Friday prayer. But the first really to think in theocratic terms was *ʿUmar II* (717-720), who took much pride in his descent through his mother from the great ʿUmar I. This ruler was inclined to draw logical inferences from his standpoints towards problems which had been taking shape over many years but had been left in abeyance. It was thus that the new Caliph decreed that equal pay be given to clients who fought in wars for the faith and that converted peasants be henceforth exempt from the poll-tax. Muslims apparently had still to pay the land-tax (D. C. DENNETT [1]), because otherwise the tax-revenue would have been too seriously impaired. It also appears that the very ancient principle of collective liability for taxes was retained, and that the burden of the payments by Muslims fell onto the shoulders of their fellow-countrymen who remained Christians or Zoroastrians, etc.

ʿUmar II's decrees are often judged solely by their unfortunate effects on the government finances and without taking into account the religious motivation of his policies. It was his sense of self-righteousness as against the transgressions of his predecessors which made him respect the rights of the Christians, in the sense of the Qurʾānic prescriptions. What he really had in mind was only an adaption to the changes which had been taking place for decades: an adaptation which might well have been the basis for a reconstruction of the Umayyad state to meet the needs of the time. His successors did not follow up this path in their internal policies, but preferred to maintain the old system of Arab domination. While exempting new converts from the poll-tax (now and subsequently known by the single name of *jizyah*), they exacted the land tax (now uniformly *kharāj*) from everybody. This stubborness of the ruling class lay at the root of a large-scale process of internal disintegration which set in after the death of Hishām in 743. In the course of the following years, one prince after another was swept from the throne; and finally a revolt among the client population of Persia and Mesopotamia led to the overthrow of Umayyad rule in the Near East.

---

[1] See Bibliography, p. 125.

THE ʿABBĀSIDS

ABBĀSID PROPAGANDA

During the first half of the 8th century, the internal unrest in Īrān had been steadily mounting. The Persian nation had found itself again after the Islāmic conquest, notwithstanding its wide acceptance of the religion of the conquerors, and was making demands which could not be satisfied within the frame of the Umayyad state. Here in the east, propaganda for a new ruling house fell on fertile soil; and the cancellation of ʿUmar II's taxation scheme for clients may have contributed to its rich harvest. Attention was focussed on the "Family of the Prophet", who might be expected to carry out more thoroughly the Qur'ānic prescriptions on equal treatment for all Muslims; though the question of detailed prospects under its rule was left discreetly in the background. The main propaganda no longer emanated from the ʿAlids, whose political fortunes had not proved happy in the repeated uprisings of the last decades, but from the descendants of *ʿAbbās,* an uncle of the Prophet. This ʿAbbās had, indeed, only embraced the Prophet's cause a short while before the fall of Makkah; but a skillfully retouched picture of his religious attitude towards the Prophet was spread abroad, and his son was represented as having been an outstanding transmitter of Muslim Tradition[1]. Three brothers belonging to this family, who lived in virtual hiding in the Jordan district, guided the campaign on these deliberately vague lines with an eye to winning over the partisans of the ʿAlid house, who notwithstanding their many disappointments still possessed religious and political importance. Thanks above all to the extraordinary shrewd propagandist activity of an agent of Īrānian origin, *Abū Muslim,* they gained great numbers of supporters among the population of Khurāsān. This support was undoubtedly an expression of the political discontent prevailing in that province, as already described.

ABŪ MUSLIM

In 746 rebellion broke out in Khurāsān. In a comparatively short time, the rebels under Abū Muslim, whose task was made easier by continuing

[1] On ʿAbbāsid-Shīʿite connections, see article *ʿAbbāsids* in *Encyclopaedia of Islam*, 2nd ed. (by Bernard Lewis).

feuds among the Arab tribes, forced the Umayyad governor to evacuate the province. In 749 Abū Muslim was able to march into Mesopotamia, which was in a very disordered condition, having shortly before been the scene of a civil war and simultaneous Khārijite uprising. Here, on the *Greater Zāb*, a left-bank tributary of the Tigris, the decisive battle was fought from January 16 to 25, 750. It resulted in the defeat of *Marwān II*, Caliph since 745 and personally a brave and capable man, who was reduced to headlong flight through Syria and Palestine to Egypt, where he met his end in August of the same year.

In the meantime, the real, but hitherto concealed, leaders of the enterprise had made their appearance. They were the two brothers *Abū l-ʿAbbās* and *Abū Jaʿfar al-Manṣūr*, the third brother having meanwhile died in prison. On November 23, 749, they received homage at Kūfah, thereby demonstrating that the ʿAbbāsīd house had attained to sovereignty. The ʿAlids, who had long since given up hope that their cause would profit, were baulked once again. In spite of the wide sympathy which they enjoyed among the population, especially in Madīnah, Mesopotamia and Persia, and which was expressed in continual and sometimes (as in 762) quite dangerous revolts, they never succeeded in reversing this verdict of history, because at critical moments they always lacked competent leaders. The Khārijites, too, still sought to make their influence felt, and had some success in Kirmān and Sīstan; but their importance was now dwindling and they no longer constituted a real menace to the state. Nor did any danger threaten from the Umayyads, for Abū l-ʿAbbās hunted down the members of the former ruling house with a relentless severity and had most of them put to death. A few pro-Umayyad generals, notably at the city of Wāsiṭ in southern Mesopotamia, were soon forced to submit; and the pro-Umayyad religious party (the Yazīdīs), which had been forming since some time back (p. 39), never achieved anything remotely approaching the importance of its counterpart, the Shīʿites. But one scion of the fallen dynasty succeeded in evading its general doom, by name *ʿAbd al-Raḥmān*. In 755/6 he reached Spain and founded in that land a new Umayyad empire, which took over the brilliant cultural heritage of the court of Damascus. Such distant rivals, however, could never endanger ʿAbbāsid sovereignty, even when they later (from 929 onwards) raised claims to the Caliphate (p. 107).

THE ʿABBĀSIDS AND ISLĀM

The ʿAbbāsid victory brought to power a régime which, by and large, met the requirements of contemporary public opinion. This was to be proved by its long duration and by the fact that its final overthrow in 1258 would not, like that of the Umayyads, be the work of an internal rebellion. In contrast with the Umayyads, the ʿAbbāsids acknowledged the principle that public life should be regulated by Islām, even if in practice they often let affairs take their natural course and themselves disregarded many an injunction of the faith, such as the ban on wine-drinking. They welcomed in principle the work of the private theologians who had now begun to elaborate and systematize the Law of Islām (*Sharīʿah*), mainly on the basis of real or purported *Traditions* of the Prophet (p. 17). Moreover, except during a brief period under al-Maʾmūn and his successors (p. 64), they avoided entanglement in the theological controversies within Sunnite Islām and only took a stand against Shīʿites, Khārijites, Carmathians and other "heretics" (though they hardly concealed their dislike of extreme Sunnite tendencies such as Ḥanbalism). This normally impartial policy allowed untrammeled freedom of development to the various Sunnite religious movements of the age: to theology in its several forms, to mysticism and its outgrowth into darvīsh orders, and finally to the orthodox-mystic compromise effected by al-Ghazzālī (p. 83). In contrast with Christianity under the Byzantine empire, whose Church Councils excluded Nestorians, Monophysites etc. from the fold, Sunnite Islām under the ʿAbbāsid Caliphate was to preserve its unity.

Sunnite Muslims could thus, in general, view the ʿAbbāsid realm as "their" state. The contrast between temporal and spiritual power, which thanks to Christian history has always been apparent to Christian minds and has long pre-occupied Western theology, only became apparent to Muslim minds in late medieval and modern times, when one Muslim territory after another fell under non-Muslim rule. The recent lifting of colonial rule has led present-day Muslims, particularly in Pākistān, to ask "What is an Islāmic State?". Such a question could hardly have been asked in ʿAbbāsid times. It is a modern problem, to be considered in the light of recent Muslim history.[1]

ADMINISTRATIVE CHANGES

With the enthronement of the ʿAbbāsids came a complete change of system. Control over the reconstruction of the state passed inevitably to those who, by their opposition to the old ruling house, had contributed so much to the outcome of the revolt. With the end of Umayyad rule, an

[1] Sir HAMILTON A. R. GIBB, *Modern trends in Islam*, Chicago 1947; WILFRED CANTWELL SMITH, *Islam in modern history*, Princeton 1957; B. SPULER, *Islamisches Selbstbewusstsein*, in *Die Welt als Geschichte* XVIII/I, 1958, I. 14-25.

end was also put to the claims of Syria and Damascus to hegemony within Islām; the ʿAbbāsids settled in Mesopotamia and in 762 began to lay out a new capital near a small Christian village called Baghdād. The name was assimilated to Persian (*Bāghdādh* = *"Gift of God"*) but is mentioned as early as the 18th century BC. [1]. Persians, always influential in Mesopotamia, now as protagonists of the ʿAbbāsid movement demanded and obtained equal rights with other Muslims, not merely in status but also in the handling of state affairs. The ʿAbbāsids were quite content to grant them such influence, notwithstanding certain apparent indications to the contrary. The Caliph *al-Manṣūr*, who acceded in 754 after the early death of his brother *Abū' l-ʿAbbās al-Saffāḥ* (the *Shedder of Blood*, i.e. of the blood of the Umayyads), treacherously put Abū Muslim, the real organizer of the revolution, to death; but his motive was distrust of an individual who had become too powerful and therefore dangerous. An increasing number of official posts, both executive and subordinate, continued to pass into the hands of Persians, such as the family of the *Barmakid* wazīrs from Balkh, first of the ministerial dynasties so conspicuous in early medieval times, who soon acquired an almost complete authority over the government departments. This came about because the Caliphs now assumed more and more of the status of the earlier Persian kings. They surrounded themselves with an immense court built up on the lines prescribed in the old Persian books of ceremonies, and increasingly shut themselves off from intercourse with their subjects: hence the management of affairs had to be left to a confidant, the *wazīr* [2]. A carefully planned administrative system of Persian model, with separate departments (*dīwāns*), particularly for the army, finance and taxes, postal communications and the provinces, was set up and gradually elaborated in the course of the 9th and 10th centuries. Government revenue, and to a lesser extent expenditure, were subjected to strict regulation and audit — soon, however, to be largely replaced by the ruinous practice of tax-farming, whereby the government procured massive but ephemeral funds and abandoned the tax-payers to every sort of arbitrary exaction by the concessionaires. The postal system, which had been in existence since the days of its Achaemenid founders, was reorganized and supplemented with a carrier-pigeon service and a network of semaphore towers stretching as far as Morocco; and its provincial directors served not only as postmasters but also as intelligence agents and

---

[1] C.f. *Encyclopaedia of Islam*, 2nd ed., I/14 (1958), p. 894.

[2] This word was previously thought to be Persian, but has now been declared Arabic, on strong grounds, by SALOMON DOV GOITEIN (*"Islamic Culture"*, XVI, 1942, pp. 255-263).

inspectors for the central government. Finally, the post of court executioner was instituted at this time; and before long this functionary (unknown to the Umayyad régime) found wide scope for his activity and came to symbolize the changed relationship between ruler and subject. Very detailed and intimate information about all these matters has come to us in a series of histories of wazīrs and histories of government offices, which have been edited and published in recent decades and give a vivid picture of the ʿAbbāsid age.

ECONOMIC PROSPERITY

These changes broke the power of the old Arab aristocracy. So complete was its supersession by the new Persian bureaucracy that the following words were put into the mouth of a Caliph: "The Persians ruled for a thousand years and did not need us (Arabs) even for a day; we have been ruling for one or two centuries and cannot do without them for an hour." Another symptom was that Persian culture, and the Persian way of life with its attendant luxury, made their way into the court of the Caliphs. High officials, and private persons too, built sumptuous, splendidly appointed palaces. The means for such extravagance came from trade, which was steadily expanding; and Baghdād soon became its centre. From Baṣrah, Sīrāf in Fārs and other seaports, Muslim commerce reached distant lands such as Zanzibar, India, Ceylon, and China (where Arabs had rioted in Canton as early as 738). The Mediterranean trade, too, was now recovering; it was carried on partly by protected foreigners and also by Western pilgrims, and yielded good profits, as well as considerable customs revenues which formed the subject of frequent official regulations. This trade in turn helped to revive many renowned Eastern industries which had been temporarily crippled by the wars of conquest: Egyptian linen and wool weaving (almost exclusively carried on by Copts) and papyrus manufacture; Persian cotton production and carpet and tent making; and the glass industry, which flourished again in Syria (famous for its glass in ancient times) and in Egypt and Mesopotamia. These, together with perfume and pottery manufacture, soon became the chief industrial activities; and they made possible the development, not only of a refined luxury centred at Baghdād or Sāmarrā, but also of new artistic styles which acquired a certain unity of trend throughout all the Muslim lands. (This uniformity was accentuated by the restrictions — which cannot be discussed here — imposed by religious inhibitions on artistic creativity). Mining, other than of precious metals and stones, remained, however, within modest limits; mineral oil, for instance, was used mainly as an embrocation, being supposed as in ancient times to have healing properties. Although this prosperity swelled the public revenues, wide scope remained for private initiative, many fields being left entirely to its care. To the general opinion of that age, poorhouses and hospitals, baths and resthouses, and even bridge-building, hardly seemed to be matters for a public welfare, hygiene or traffic policy; they were almost exclusively the responsibility and property of private trusts, including (it appears) trusts founded by the Caliph as a private person, and provided openings for both charity (as *waqfs*, i.e. *pious foundations*) and capital investment.

URBAN LIFE

Thanks to this commercial prosperity, large fortunes were amassed and urban centres grew rapidly. The cities were administered by government officials (*qāḍis*[1], *muḥtasibs*[2], postmasters etc.), who possessed very extensive powers. Municipal self-government such as had existed in Greco-Roman antiquity is not found in the Muslim period (except occasionally in Spain — p. 106), though in fact the leading families, especially in provincial towns, enjoyed considerable freedom of action. Side by side with great poverty, wealth and luxury became features of city life, and much of the material culture of antiquity was taken over: baths, banquets (often with the forbidden wine), singing-girls, gambling games, horse races etc. Concerning the admissibility of many of these things, the theologians held long disputations, but even when agreed on their inadmissibility, they could not stop them altogether; and concerning quite a number of them, the different schools of Law *(madhāhib)* held different opinions.

The small shopkeepers and artisans generally offered their wares for sale in the bazaar where, as in medieval Europe, each single trade would congregate in a single street. They were usually grouped into *guilds* (*aṣnāf*), which performed both economic and social functions and served to represent the various trades and professions. Subject to more or less close supervision by the *muḥtasib*, the guilds fixed "just" prices, controlled standards of quality and regulated apprenticeships and admissions of newcomers. There was a tendency for guilds to assume a role as security squads (*aḥdāth*, i.e. *youth brigades*) whenever the official authority grew weak, and also for them to assume humanitarian functions, in which they joined or coalesced with the later *Futūwah* (p. 98). Parallel with this, an

[1] Judges of the Islāmic law-courts.
[2] Censors of personal and commercial morality.

increasingly important role was played by religious groups — by mystics (*ṣūfis*) with their bands of followers and later by *darvīsh* orders. The phenomenon may perhaps have had some connection with the exclusion of women (or at least of respectable women) from social life. [1]

PERSIAN INFLUENCES

In another field, that of thought, increasing Persian penetration could also be remarked. The religion of Zoroaster did not, any more than Christianity, vanish without leaving traces in Islām. There were centres of resistance such as Yazd, Kirmān and Fārs, where a quite large percentage of fire-worshippers long sustained their defence of the ancient Persian way of life; though in 717 a number of the followers of the old faith migrated overseas to India, settling in Gujarāt and the Bombay region where their descendants, the Parsīs, today hold an honourable place in society, notably as leading merchants. But even where Zoroastrianism gave way before Islām, many of its ideas passed into the new religion. Some of them were generally adopted, such as the five-fold arrangement of the daily prayer and various ritual practices and popular notions, mainly concerning impurity and burial. Other Zoroastrian conceptions, though they failed to gain general acceptance in Islām, were not forsaken by the Īrānian Muslims. This led in time both to the formation of new sects and to a certain fermentation within the body of orthodox (*Sunnite*) Islām. The belief in a principle of light, issuing from God and transmittable hereditarily or at will to different men, and to a lesser extent dualistic notions and beliefs in the transmigration of souls, formed starting points for new speculations. Such ideas were an ancient heritage of the Persian and Mesopotamian lands and had had their outcome in various gnostic groups and in the doctrines of the Zoroastrians and Manichaeans (who both believed in dualism but held diametrically opposed tenets as to its source). On these foundations several sects arose. In Khurāsān around 776, a man appeared who became known as the *Veiled Prophet* [2], since he wore a veil to hide his countenance — which for his followers would have been sinister to behold because of its "shining light". His claim was that he be looked upon as the incarnation of prophethood and fulfiller of the work of the murdered Abū Muslim. He

---

[1] Gustav E. von Grunebaum, *The structure of the Muslim town*, in *Islam*; *Studies in the nature and growth of a cultural tradition*, London 1955; Claude Cahen, article *Aḥdāth* in *Encyclopaedia of Islam*, 2nd ed., Leiden, 1955; Reuben Levy, *The social structure of Islam*, Cambridge 1957, p. 53-134; Louis Gardet, *La cité musulmane*, Paris 1954, p. 258-263. For material on contemporary industry, agriculture and mining, see the maps in the present volume.

[2] *Al-Muqanna*ʿ.

gathered a quite numerous body of supporters among the Persians, who were openly dissatisfied with this latest turn of ʿAbbāsid policy, and only after a long struggle was defeated in a desperate fight for his own castle, wherein he cast himself into the flames [1]. From the remnants of this man's followers, from surviving advocates of the Mazdakism of Sāsānian times (p. 28) and from economic malcontents, another sect was formed in *Āẕarbāyjān* in 816-817 under the leadership of *Bābak (Pāpak)*, a Persian; its members were called the *Khurramites (Joyful Ones)*, and some of the principles which they advocated were communistic, while they were also relatively tolerant as regards religion. It may be presumed that in this movement also there were national and social undercurrents, although in the indigenous sources nothing is stated to that effect. It was easy for the Khurramites to get support from neighbouring Caucasia, and they were particularly dangerous to the Caliphs because they cut communications with the east along the ancient silk route south of the Caspian Sea. After a long siege, Bābak was compelled to abandon his mountain fortress and flee with his brother to Armenia, whence he was extradited. In 838 both were executed at Baghdād. His victor, the Turkish prince (*Afshīn*) of Usrūshanah in Transoxiana, was later put to death in 840 on charges of alleged Magian (?Manichaean) leanings and of assuming privileges traditionally belonging to a ruler.

THE SHUʿŪBĪYAH

In all these stirrings, Persians were giving vent to their reluctance to submit unconditionally to Arab ideas. The same attitude found expression in the *Shuʿūbīyah*, a movement among the men of letters advocating the equality, and indeed superiority, of things Persian over things Arab. The writings of this school, which long evoked vehement — and not merely literary — polemics, more or less openly drew logical conclusions from the changed position of the Persians vis-à-vis the state of the Caliphs, and justified on theoretical grounds the practical equality of status which they had obtained.

SUNNITE THEOLOGY

In the face of all these tendencies, the ʿAbbāsids could only hold fast to orthodoxy, since recognition by public opinion and approval by the

[1] Aleksandr Jur'evič Jakubovskiĭ in *Sovetskoe Vostokovdenie*, V, 1948, pp. 35-54, regards this movement as essentially social.

theologians were the strongest props of their régime. Of necessity they were much concerned with the strict performance of religious duties. They regularly led the Friday prayers, and also exercised influence over the development of doctrine, as the forms which it took could not be a matter of indifference to them if their prerogatives were to be safeguarded. Unlike the Shīʿites, whose hopes they had frustrated by occupying the throne, they upheld the school which believed itself to possess the correct *Tradition* of the Prophet and to have preserved the *Custom* of the Islāmic community (in Arabic, *Ahl al-Sunnah waʾl-Jamāʿah,* whence the name, henceforward in general use, of *Sunnites*). While many doctrinal questions (such as those raised by the Murjiʾites) remained over from Umayyad times, the most important present task was to establish, or reestablish, the rightful Tradition of the Prophet as the vehicle of their claims. This became the point of departure for Muslim theology, which furthermore had soon to seek solutions to problems inherited from classical antiquity, and also from Christianity. It was the enquiring spirit of the Persians which did most to bring these problems home to the Islāmic world [1].

THE PROFANE SCIENCES

In the religious field, influences from outside could only gain surreptitious entry. The wide field of the profane sciences, on the other hand, was to receive a lasting stimulus from the activity of Christian (especially Nestorian) translators from Syriac. Mainly through this channel, Greek knowledge of the natural sciences, mathematics, astronomy, geography and medicine found its way to the Muslims. In respect of medicine, important contributions were also made by the academy of *Jundīshāpūr (Gondēshāpūr),* which dated from Sāsānian times, and by the activity of Jewish and Christian physicians. Not being barred by religious sanctions, acquisition of the new knowledge could proceed freely, often by direct learning; and it thus came about that the Arabs were the first to transmit to medieval Western Europe a large part of the hellenistic legacy — in the form of Latin translations (chiefly made in Spain and southern Italy) from Arabic versions of works of Aristotle, Euclid, Galen, Claudius Ptolemaeus and others. An equal stimulus was given to

[1] Cf. JOSEPH SCHACHT, *The Origins of Muḥammadan Jurisprudence*, Oxford, 1950; also the exposition of Sunnite theology in MENSCHING's *Handbuch* (ref. p. 31 above, footnote); RUDI PARET, *Der Islam und das Griechische Bildungsgut*, Tübingen, 1950 (*Philosophie und Geschichte*, 70); DE LACY O'LEARY, *How Greek Science passed to the Arabs*, London, 1948; BERTOLD SPULER, *Hellenistisches Denken im Islam*, in *Saeculum* V/2 (1954), p. 179-94; JOHANN W. FÜCK in *Bibliotheca Orientalis*, X/5, Leiden 1953, p. 196-198.

Arabic literary composition — an art which was extensively practised by Persians. (The question whether *al-Fārābi* or *Ibn Sīnā (Avicenna)* were Turks rather than Transoxianan Persians is indeterminable and immaterial, what matters being the cultural environment in which they grew up). Without this hellenistic leaven in Islāmic culture, the philosophy of *Yaʿqūb al-Kindī* or *Ibn Rushd (Averroes)* would have been unthinkable. These questions belong to the history of Muslim science and Arabic literature and cannot be gone into here; but mention will be made of one incidental circumstance. The spread of the manufacture of paper (*kāghidh*) from flax reduced the need for papyrus, which was very costly, and almost completely ousted it by the 9th-10th centuries. This had been made possible by the Arab capture, in an encounter with the Chinese on the Talas in 751, of some persons acquainted with Chinese methods of paper production; they continued to prosecute their industry in Persia, whence it quickly spread throughout the Islāmic lands.

FOREIGN POLICY

During this period when the empire was undergoing momentous internal transformation, foreign affairs receded almost entirely into the background. Fighting continued on the East Roman marches in Asia Minor and in Armenia, as well as in eastern Īrān and Transoxiana and on the Balūchī border. The Muslim hold over Crete and other islands of the Aegean Archipelago was threatened by Slavs expelled from Spain (see p. 106), and soon exposed to increasing danger from the Byzantines. All these events were of only temporary and local significance, and had no lasting effects.

INTERNAL CONDITIONS

Internally, however, the ʿAbbāsid state reached the summit of its glory. The Caliph al-Manṣūr (754-775) had been succeeded by his greater son *al-Mahdī* (775-785), and he in turn, after a brief interregnum, by his son *Hārūn al-Rashīd* (786-809), who shines so resplendently in legend. He is one of the chief figures of that treasure-house of Arab, Persian and Indian lore [1], the Thousand and One Nights, which began to take shape during this period but was not finally compiled until the 14th-15th centuries, in Egypt. He probably, however, did not possess quite the importance

[1] Baron Carra de Vaux, *Les Penseurs de l'Islam*, I, pp. 359-370, believed that there are also Jewish themes. Cf. Enno Littmann in "*Encyclopaedia of Islam*", 2nd. ed., I, 358-64.

as a ruler with which he is clothed in indigenous accounts, because these ascribe to him many characteristics which really belonged to one or other of his predecessors and successors.

A serious jolt was given to the internal structure of the empire by the sudden and violent overthrow of the talented and enlightened *Barmakid* wazīrs in 803. Most of the members of the family were incarcerated and stripped of their private wealth; confiscation (*muṣādarah*) was now to become the usual practice in such cases. The report that Hārūn entered into diplomatic relations with Charlemagne is not mentioned in oriental sources; it may perhaps be assumed that, as frequently occurred, a party of travelling merchants represented themselves as an official embassy for the sake of netting bigger profits.[1]

AL-MAʾMŪN

Hārūn took a very dangerous step over the succession to the Caliphate. He wished to divide the empire between his two sons, *al-Amīn* and *al-Maʾmūn*, both of whom had been born in 786-7, the former of an ʿAbbāsid princess, the latter of a Persian slave-woman, and in addition to give to al-Amīn a certain right of supervision over the other half. But al-Maʾmūn had much the more impressive personality and the advice, it appears, of better wazīr. In any event he swiftly mastered the eastern half of the empire, which was his share under the division and in which his mother's national origin helped him with the Irānians. In 813 he was able to eliminate his brother; and after a few years of unrest and disorders he moved his residence to Baghdād.

Al-Maʾmūn was, to all appearance, the most significant ruler of the dynasty. He was a capable organizer and, with his father Hārūn, deserved the real credit for building up the administrative system. Yet during his reign tendencies appeared which in the following period were to ruin the administration and the unity of the state. The most serious was the separatism of certain provinces. Inaccessible Caucasia's connection with Baghdād was growing weaker; but it was mainly in four regions, Persia, Arabia, Egypt and North Africa, that such centrifugal forces were to be felt, and to a lesser extent in Syria and northern Mesopotamia. For an understanding of the changes which occurred in the next decades, a glimpse at the destinies of these provinces will be necessary.

---

[1] For information from Western sources, see FRANCIS WILLIAM BUCKLER, *Hārūnuʾl-Rashīd and Charles the Great*, Cambridge (Mass.) 1931 (*Monographs of the Mediaeval Academy of America*, 2).

THE RELIGIOUS SITUATION IN PERSIA

Hārūn al-Rashīd's resolve to assign the eastern territories of the empire to his son al-Ma'mūn may partly have been based on a recognition that the Persian people could no longer be ruled directly from Baghdād. The principles of the Shuʿūbīyah movement (p. 55) were beginning to find application in Īrānian demands not merely for equality, but also for self-government. This was particularly the case in the geographically isolated province of Khurāsān. In the ensuing centuries, that region and the neighbouring Transoxiana were to become the principal centres of Īrānian culture — a function for which their importance in Sāsānian times had already fitted them. In the circumstances of the age, it is not surprising that the intellectual rebirth of Īrān should have begun in the east. It may be presumed moreover that, following the Arab invasion and the frequent disorders which resulted, for instance from the repeated influx of fugitive Khārijites, a population shift had occurred in the sense that part of the Īrānian inhabitants of western Persia had been pushed eastwards. In Khurāsān and Transoxiana the Irānians, inasmuch as they largely followed the lead of their territorial nobility in adopting Sunnite Islām at a quite early stage, soon joined in the common cultural and social life of the state of the Caliphs. The important southern province of Fārs, on the other hand, did not become a centre of intellectual life until later; probably the main reason for this was that here, as in the remote regions of south-eastern Persia, Zoroastrianism held out longer, and indeed went through a last recrudescence in the 8th and 9th centuries. The religious writings of that faith dating from this period could not, of course, find a place in Islāmic culture, and they debarred their devotees from the fruitful process of mental intercourse within the polity; they thus contributed nothing whatever to the further growth of the Persian intellect, which was now Islāmic in outlook. Another probable reason was that Fārs was at that time suffering too much from Khārijite and other disorders to be able to develop an intellectual life. Finally, the early rooting of the Shīʿite form of Islām in central Persia, for instance at Qumm, may have formed an obstacle to vigorous interaction with the main body of Muslim civilization. [1]

THE ṬĀHIRIDS

That Persian life was developing on its own lines was a fact of which

[1] Cf. Francesco Gabrieli, *Al-Ma'mūn e gli ʿAlidi*, Leipzig 1929 (*Morgenländ. Texte und Forschungen*, hrsg. von August Fischer, 11).

al-Ma'mūn was already aware through his mother and was to become increasingly cognisant during his long stay in the east. When the trusted general, *Ṭāhir*, whom he had appointed governor, proceeded to form a separate state in Khurāsān and in 821 discontinued the mention of the Caliph's name in the Friday sermon *(khuṭbah)*, thus proclaiming himself sovereign, al-Ma'mūn raised no objection; and this was the wisest course he could take. After Ṭāhir's death not long afterwards, al-Ma'mūn confirmed his son *Ṭalḥah* as his successor and so, in form, as plenipotentiary of the Caliph. The Ṭāhirid state which thus arose in eastern Persia was the first effectively independent realm in Īrān since the conquest, apart from certain border districts in the east (in the present Afghānistān) and others on the south shore of the Caspian Sea, where various families of native rulers, many of them still hostile to Islām, had been able to hold out in the inaccessible jungle region throughout this period. One of the rulers in that region, *Māzyār (Māhyazjār)* actually attempted, in conjunction with *Afshīn* (p. 55), to recreate a Persian Zoroastrian state on a new social (agrarian) basis, but was soon discomfited (840).

THE ṢAFFĀRIDS

Al-Ma'mūn's restraint towards the Ṭāhirids was not a matter of choice; first, because it was essential to avoid clashes between the two powers, whose outcome would have been exceedingly dubious when the Khurramite rebellion (p. 55) was still raging in Āẕarbāyjān, and other disorders (to be mentioned later) had broken out in Mesopotamia; and secondly, because Ṭalḥah's brother *'Abd Allāh* was commander-in-chief of the Caliph's troops and as such held a very strong position: Baghdād lay virtually at his mercy. (In 828 he succeeded his brother in Khurāsān). The importance of the Ṭāhirid state was solely political. It constituted the first grouping of Muslim Persians in any large number on their own soil, and redirected Persian energies to their ancient task of keeping guard on the flood gates of Central Asia. No particular cultural policy was developed by this dynasty; the times were doubtless too disturbed for such a thing. It was only now that the last Khārijite uprisings in Khurāsān were suppressed; and a keen rival to the Ṭāhirid régime appeared in a new state structure which was taking shape further south in eastern Persia, in Sīstān (Sijistān). In that district also, Khārijism was not yet extinct and had even acquired a degree of social respectability, though undeniably still maintaining certain connections with roaming robber-bands. In the self-defence measures taken by the local inhabitants, a man named *Yaʿqūb ibn Layth,* who had originally been a coppersmith (*ṣaffār*), earned outstanding distinction. His success was such that he could soon assemble a large army which, thanks to the iron discipline maintained by its puritanical leader, proved most efficient in battle. He invaded Fārs several times (869, 871, 875), gradually overran the southern areas of the Ṭāhirid realm such as Harāt (867) and finally captured its capital Nīshāpūr in 873, putting an end to its existence as a state. He was unable, however, to defeat the army of the Caliph and suffered a severe reverse near Baghdād in 876. The government at Baghdād was nevertheless ready to compromise, and conceded its formal recognition of the coppersmith's *de facto* authority. Before a final understanding had been reached, Yaʿqūb died on June 4, 879. He was followed by his brother *ʿAmr* who, after a youth likewise passed in humble employment, now proved to be a worthy successor of the deceased, whose righthand man he had been. In the long run, however, he failed to maintain the original high promise of the Ṣaffārid state; he had to sustain long and involved struggles with other aspirants to power, and after having been finally overthrown in 900 by the *Sāmānids* (p. 76 ff.), was executed at Baghdād in 902 by command of a newly acceded Caliph.

DECLINE OF THE CALIPHATE

These developments, whether or not they were intrinsically desirable, were certainly most unwelcome to the Caliphate, because the increasingly impecunious court at Baghdād received much less in the way of tribute and "donations" from Persia than it had previously drawn from taxation or farming out the taxes. A Caliph's sanction of such a development was therefore hardly likely to be given with a good grace. Events in Mesopoamia were the main reason why the Caliphate, till lately so powerful, became completely devitalized and was reduced to a puppet in the hands of one war-lord after another. To this turn of events consideration must now be given.

SOCIAL REGROUPINGS: THE TURKS

The social transformation resulting from the overthrow of the Umayyads had not only displaced the Arab aristocracy from the control of government affairs, but had at the same time altered the composition of the armed forces. The Arabs were not able and certainly were not willing to be the sole bearers of the burden of military preparedness, whatever its prospects of booty, when they had been deprived of their leading position in public life. It therefore became necessary to reconstruct the military power of the state on another basis. The inhabitants of Mesopotamia, and also the Persians — in contrast with their distant ancestors — at that time no longer displayed military prowess; nor have the Persians often done so since. There could be no question of their forming the nucleus of the army. In Central Asia, however, the Arabs had come into hostile contact with the Turks and had found them to be the most stubborn of fighters, both as enemies and when employed in the Muslim forces after being taken prisoner. At the beginning of the 9th century the government took in hand the planned formation of a standing Turkish army, in which after a short while Turks were also commissioned as officers. Use was thus made of the soldierly valour of the Turks (a quality which has persisted till today); and at the same time a substitute of equal or greater military value was obtained in place of the Arab tribes. [1] The transposition was complete by 833, when the pension payments and other benefits previously granted to the Arab tribes were withdrawn. The sequel was to be a phenomenon which, from the nature of the case, is always induced by an organized foreign mercenary soldiery; a pretorian guard, like those in the Roman and other empires, came into being which tyrannized the native inhabitants and soon reduced the ruler to complete dependence on its will, especially when, as happened after the death of al-Ma'mūn, the Turks influenced the choice of occupant for the throne. The "Commanders of the Faithful" played scarcely any part in politics during this century; they virtually confined themselves to conferring titles and robes of honour [2] — till the 19th century the oriental equivalent of decorations and medals — and to theological disputations, which the Turks gladly left to them. No difference was made to this state of affairs by the removal of the capital from Baghdād to Sāmarrā, a short distance to the north. From 838 to 883 the seat of the empire was at that city, which contemporaries often renamed *"Surra man ra'ā", "the Eye's Delight"*.

At this time too, simultaneously with the elimination of the old Arab aristocracy and doubtless under the influence of ancient Near Eastern and Persian ideas which made headway in the East Roman empire also, the status of women in public life underwent a decline. While the public appearance of singing-girls and actresses became more

[1] Sidki Hamdi, *Die Entstehung und Entwicklung des türkischen Einflusses im Abbasidenreiche . . .*, Thesis, Tübingen 1954.

[2] Arabic *khil'ah*, whence the Spanish *gala*.

and more of a scandal, married ladies were increasingly relegated to the women's quarters, the *ḥarem*, and were now obliged to veil their faces in public. A correlated development was that it became the general practice, even among the highest classes, to give equality of status to children by slave women, who were usually of foreign origin. In all this it seems legitimate to discern a second manifestation of the decay which set in under al-Maʾmūn.

THE REBELLION OF THE ZUṬṬ (JĀT)

A third remains to be described. The importance of the Turkish mercenaries was enhanced by the fact that not only were they involved in operations in provinces such as Persia, but that Mesopotamia itself now also became the scene of dangerous rebellions which made these pretorians wholly indispensable. Although a certain compromise had been reached between the two leading nationalities since the beginning of the ʿAbbāsid régime and much ill-feeling had thereby been removed, among the working classes who were mostly of non-Arab and non-Persian origin and partly drawn from the indigenous Aramaean population acute and varied social tensions had arisen. These were partly due to the disappearance of the household economy and the formation in its place of closed corporations or guilds of craftsmen with collective liability. The most pressing immediate problem, however, was presented by a race of Indian origin akin to the Gypsies, namely the *Jāts* (Arabic, *Zuṭṭ*), who had been settled in the marshes of southern Mesopotamia since pre-Islāmic, probably Sāsānian, times; in the last years of the Caliphate of al-Maʾmūn they started a dangerous rebellion which cut communications between Baghdād and the sea and was only put down after prolonged fighting in 834-35. The Jāts were then made to emigrate.

THE ZANJ REBELLION

A few decades later, in 869, the negroes working as slaves in the great salt extraction works near Baṣrah broke into rebellion. They were known as the *Zanj* (a word akin to Zanzibar). Their leader was a pretended or real ʿAlid, who however stood for Khārijite, not Shīʿite, principles and promised his followers the status of lords. The rebellion spread dangerously: Baṣrah city was several times given over to massacre and the sack; traffic throughout southern Mesopotamia was crippled, the country up to the outskirts of Baghdād became insecure and the stability of the régime was imperilled. Thanks, however, to the energy of the Regent *al-Muwaffaq* [1], brother of the insignificant Caliph then reigning and one of the most illustrious representatives of the house of ʿAbbās, the Zanj were successfully thrown back before the gates of Baghdād, and after tedious preparations finally annihilated in August 883 in their last almost unapproachable refuge amid the tangle of reeds and swamp on the lower Euphrates. One of the main reasons why the struggle was so prolonged was that al-Muwaffaq had simultaneously to conduct a defensive campaign against the Ṣaffārids, who have been discussed above. Yaʿqūb the Coppersmith refused, however, on religious grounds to consider proposals by the Zanj for an alliance. Had he taken a different attitude and accepted the rebel slaves as allies, the ʿAbbāsid Caliphate might then have met its downfall.

THEOLOGICAL CONTROVERSIES: THE MUʿTAZILITES

Spiritually, also, the empire was sorely convulsed. The unquestioning simplicity with which orthodox Islām expounded its doctrines had failed to satisfy the educated classes, which comprised numbers of newly converted Persians. Many such men had reverted to the teachings of their ancestors and often joined Manichaean cells. Even when lengthy persecutions by the Caliphs al-Mahdī and al-Mutawakkil around the years 780 and 850 had largely driven this religion from public view, Manichaeism was still spoken of in the late 8th and early 9th centuries as a secret creed of educated men. Against this background, a new religious movement arose, partly derived from Greek thought, yet genuinely Islāmic. It sought to harmonize Islām with the higher ideas about the concept of God prevailing among the educated. Starting from previous discussions of the relationship of the divine omnipotence to the free will of the human individual, the *Muʿtazilites*, as the followers of this movement were called, proceeded during the 9th century to apply their minds and powers of logical reasoning to the analysis of the Prophet's teachings and elaboration therefrom of a system of doctrine. Though the opinions of the Muʿtazilites must be studied within the framework of the religious history of Islām, a mention of their rise is necessary here because the Caliphs intervened in the controversy between them and the "orthodox". Al-Maʾmūn pronounced himself in favour of the Muʿtazilite views and, with the energetic support of the theological groups who shared

[1] Cf. Walther Hellige, *Die Regentschaft al-Muwaffaqs*, Berlin 1936 (*Neue Deutsche Forschungen*, 87).

his standpoint, persecuted their orthodox opponents[1] as zealously as the latter had earlier persecuted the former. For several decades the Muʿtazilite teachings were the official doctrine of the state, until in 847 they were repudiated by another Caliph, *al-Mutawakkil*, and replaced by absolute orthodoxy; they later gradually became extinct and to-day are completely excluded from the official theology of Islām. It was mainly in Central Asia that they held out for any length of time, as late indeed as the 13th and 14th centuries; and they had a real influence on Shīʿite ideas. Egypt however, where the mass of the population had never been effectively hellenized, was untouched by the controversy. The interference of the Caliphs in this matter was a fourth reason for the decline of the Caliphate, over and above the external, internal and military factors. Their attitudes placed them in the same position within the Sunnite party as they had previously occupied in relation to the Shīʿah and the non-Islāmic religions. (Khārijism by now had ceased to be of any significance in the east). They were no longer backed by the whole Sunnite community; they only had the backing of the school of thought uppermost at the time. The religious authority of the Caliphs was thus also on the wane.

SEPARATIST TENDENCIES IN THE PROVINCES

In these circumstances, it is no wonder that separatist tendancies and bids for autonomy made headway in other parts of the ʿAbbāsid empire besides the east. In the west and south also, spiritual forces, by no means of a Sunnite temper, were at work clearing the ground for breaches with the Caliphate at Baghdād. Most important among them were the Shīʿites, who notwithstanding oppression had succeeded during the previous century in spreading their doctrines ever more widely among the population. Their success impelled the Caliph al-Ma'mūn to name as his successor an ʿAlid, the "*Imām*" *ʿAlī al-Riḍā*, who however was eliminated after a few years, supposedly by poison. The Caliph's publicly expressed hope had been that this settlement of the succession would win him the loyalty of the very widespread groups of Shīʿite partisans.

SHĪʿITE ACTIVITIES

The Shīʿite communion suffered from a weakness which has beset it throughout its history and still characterizes it to-day. It has tended to

[1] Notably the fundamentalist theologian and Traditionist Aḥmad ibn Ḥanbal (p. 50), imprisoned by al-Ma'mūn and his successors but favoured by al-Mutawakkil.

split into sundry sub-denominations, which engage in more or less vehement mutual strife. This is to some extent a corollary of the Shīʿite theory based on recognition of the Prophet's descendants through his daughter *Fāṭimah's* marriage with the Caliph *ʿAlī*. The ʿAlids had already become extraordinarily numerous, as they have remained till the present day; and disputes soon cropped up on the question which prince was the legitimate successor. Shīʿite hearts were at odds over this question, so vital for every one of them. All of the three main persuasions which thus arose cherished the belief that the series of successors ended with a specific pretender who, in their commonly accepted credence, lived in concealment and directly or through an agent gave signs to his faithful followers; who was biding his time until, perhaps not before the end of the world, he should return as an eschatological redeemer and fulfiller of God's rule on earth, to gather in his flock and convert mankind, both Muslims and non-Muslims, to the creed of the Shīʿah. In regard to the place in the above-described series held by the "*Imām*",[1] that is the descendant of the Prophet legitimately entitled to have reigned, the three main Shīʿite persuasions separated from one another, and are designated "*Fivers*", "*Seveners*" and "*Twelvers*".

In the politics of these early centuries of Islām, the Twelver Shīʿites counted least, though the number of their adherents was considerable. Probably the main reason for this was that their pretenders, after being removed from Madīnah, lived obscurely at Baghdād or nearby as pensioners of the Caliphs, with the single exception of the ephemeral heir-apparent during al-Maʾmūn's reign (p. 65). The twelfth of the line — as to whose having existed at all there is no testimony beyond the consensus of Shīʿite opinion — vanished as a small child in a cellar at Sāmarrā in 873 and is thought to be living in concealment as "*Lord of the Age*" (*Ṣāḥib al-Zamān*); he is therefore envisaged as the saviour who will come at the end of time to redeem the world, and deemed worthy of a virtually divine reverence by those who believe in him. This creed only acquired political importance in later times, and then primarily in Īrān; for the past four and a half centuries that country and ʿIrāq have been the strongholds of the Twelver Shīʿah.

ZAYDITE STATES

In the 9th and 10th centuries the other two persuasions, Fivers and Seveners, were those which acquired political importance. Of all the

[1] See the table on p. 117. The world *imām* means literally *leader*.

three, the *Fiver* Shīʿites were the closest to the Sunnites in belief and the most moderate in politics; the chief qualifications which they required of their Imāms were doctrinal knowledge and political ability. They were named *Zaydites* after an ʿAlid, *Zayd*, who had rebelled in Mesopotamia during the later Umayyad period and whom they acknowledged as the fifth Imām (739). Their political successes were modest, but in part very enduring. To South Arabia, where the aristocracy, heirs to the ancient civilization of the Minaeans and Sabaeans, had kept the old social structure in being under Islām, Zaydites gained admittance as mediators between contending factions and between the Muslims and the Christians still subsisting in the district of Najrān. In the land of the Yaman, known to the ancients as Arabia Felix, they were able in 897 to found a small Zaydite state; and this formed the nucleus of a Zaydite community which maintained itself through countless struggles against sundry local potentates, and against the rulers of Egypt and the Caliphs, before finally winning independence under its Imāms of the Family of the Prophet. The Prince Yaḫyà, who ruled from 1904 to 1948 and resumed the title of "*Imām*", held out against the Turks from 1905 onwards and in 1920 secured recognition of his country's formal independence. Another state was founded by Zaydites in Ṭabaristān, on the south shore of the Caspian Sea, in 864; it collapsed after a short and disturbed life in 928, but left an enduring mark in history by winning the district for the Shīʿah, and indeed by first really winning it for Islām in any guise. The Caspian region became a hotbed of Shīʿite ideology in Īrān, though ultimately a different form of this ideology was to prevail in that land.

THE ISMAʿĪLITES

Doctrinally the Sevener Shīʿites were the reverse of the Zaydites; and politically they represented the most radical and most dangerous type of Shīʿite belief. They were known as *Ismāʿīlites* after the ʿAlid, *Ismāʿīl*, whom they recognized as their seventh Imām. (The Twelver Shīʿites regarded his brother as the seventh Imām and perpetuator of the legitimate line). This Shīʿite denomination soon came under the influence of dualistic and speculative theories and of ideas bearing the stamp of various oriental faiths; and as a result it took on the form of a secret sect. Its members were initiated into its secret lore in seven, later nine, different stages and (except for the real organizers) were kept in the dark as to the structure of the movement and even as to the identity of its supreme guides — most of whom have, indeed, remained unidentified.

Another outstanding feature of the Ismāʿīlites was their practice of the rule of *taqīyah,* that is of dissembling one's religious affiliation before outsiders, especially in times of peril; but the principle, in varying degrees of intensity, is common to all Shīʿites.

THE CARMATHIANS[1]

The Ismāʿīlite movement in its turn split into various branches deriving from quarrels over pretenders; and it begot one very strange sect, which was permeated even more deeply than the others with gnostic speculations, philosophical notions of hellenistic origin and Christian and Mandaean-Baptist ideas. The members of this sect were known as *Carmathians,* after their leader *Ḥamdān Qarmaṭ.* (The name *Qarmaṭ* may perhaps be an Aramaic word meaning "teacher of secret knowledge"). They succeeded in establishing a realm of their own in the remote district of al-Baḥrayn in eastern Arabia, whence for several decades they prevented the movement of pilgrims to Makkah; and in 930 they carried off the black stone of the Kaʿbah from that city, which had long been convulsed by revolts under ʿAlid and other flags. A quarter of a century passed before the stone was recovered. In another, more dangerous, thrust, they penetrated into southern Mesopotamia, which the recent Zuṭṭ and Zanj rebellions had left in much disorder; and although they did not stand for any radical social reform and indeed depended on slave labour, in the years 890 to 906 they beset the Caliphate (now back at Baghdād) with grave difficulties. One result was that in the course of the next century (between 951 and 968) ʿAlid pretenders were able with comparative ease to make themselves masters of central Arabia, including the holy cities; and under two lines, bearing the title of *Sharīfs,* their rule was to last over 200 years.

EGYPT AND THE ṬŪLŪNIDS

There was another region in which non-Sunnite independence movements won success, namely North Africa. The only country whose separatist tendencies were not interwoven with sectarian differences was Egypt. The Nile valley, though troubled in the 8th and 9th centuries by Coptic revolts (p. 37) and also by epidemics of the plague, had remained loyal to the Caliphs and achieved complete economic recovery during the period. The decline of the papyrus industry was offset by the cultivation of two new crops introduced by the Arabs, rice and sugar.

[1] WILFERD MADELUNG, *Fāṭimiden und Baḥrainqarmāten,* in "*Der Islam*" XXXIII/3, Sept. 1959.

(Cotton was grown only in Persia, where it was indigenous). On account of the lack of valuable minerals, the population was overwhelmingly agricultural [1]. Food-supply and taxation were the subject of strict regulations, about which we are precisely informed in numerous surviving records; a government wheat monopoly with large granaries ensured the sustenance of the inhabitants even in times of dearth. In commerce, negotiable documents analogous to cheques and bills of exchange were in use. The administration was headed by governors, who after 750 were often ʿAbbāsid princes and after 856 Turkish generals. The latter, however, sometimes preferred to stay with the court at Sāmarrā or Baghdād in the hope of safeguarding their influence, and to leave deputies behind in Egypt. One such deputy, *Aḥmad*, son of a Turkish slave *Ṭūlūn*, succeeded in so entrenching himself on the spot that from 868 onwards he never relinquished his post, though summoned to do so by the Caliph and the wazīr, and he even brought about the recall of the director of finance attached to him. While still acknowledging the formal suzerainty of the Caliphate by having the Caliph's name mentioned in the prayers and by despatching presents, he was able to rule the country in *de facto* independence till his death in 883 and to give it considerable prosperity through his wise taxation policy and army reforms. His son *Khumārawayh*, in spite of a reverse, kept command of the bridgeheads (sought by Egypt since ancient times) which his father had occupied in Palestine and Syria; but after his sudden death at Damascus in 896 the country was rent by clashes over his succession and fell into such confusion that the Caliph's troops were able to recover control of it in 905.

NORTH AFRICA: THE AGHLABIDS

The subsequent destinies of Egypt were to be determined in North Africa. Berber resentment against the pretensions of the Arabs to social as well as religious superiority had early opened the way for the spread of Khārijism with its racially and socially equalitarian tendencies, and had led to the establishment of several ephemeral Khārijite States, including that of the *Ibāḍites* (*Abāḍites*) which maintained itself for 130 years at Tāhert in the Algerian Atlas (c. 761-908). The district of Mzāb in the northern Sahara, and the land of ʿUmān (Oman) in Arabia with its former dependency Zanzibar, have remained refuges of Khārijism till to-day.

---

[1] DIETER MÜLLER-WODARG, *Die Landwirtschaft Ägyptens in der frühen Abbasidenzeit*, in "*Der Islam*" XXXI-XXXIII (1954/57).

A more important political rôle was played by the dynasty of the *Aghlabids*. From the old provincial capital of Qayrāwān and from their newly built city of Raqqādah nearby, they extended their power over a wide area during the early years of the 9th century and only accorded nominal recognition to the Caliphs at Baghdād. Their dominion soon stretched far to the west, and they had occasional collisions with the Spanish Umayyads. For the future of civilization, the most important feat of the Aghlabids was the conquest of *Sicily*. This began with their capture of Palermo in 831; and over the next decades they occupied about one third of the island and harassed the coasts of Italy, twice threatening Rome itself, in 846 and 849. At Taranto and Bari they held their positions for considerable lengths of time (between 841 and 915).

In 875 the Muslims took Syracuse, and after composing their internal dissensions they remained masters of the island till 1060, when the Normans occupied it. The last hundred years of their rule was a notable period of peace and cultural brilliance, which has found a classic historian in MICHELE AMARI (1806-1889). It opened in its sequel a channel, second in importance only to that through Spain, for the inflow of eastern and Arab-hellenistic intellectual riches into Western Europe. One need only recall *al-Idrīsī*'s geographical manual with its map of the world, which he dedicated to King Roger II. The old administrative arrangements were also taken over by the Normans, and many traces of the Arab age (which cannot be detailed here) remained in evidence up to and during the reign of the Hohenstaufen Emperor Frederick II (1215-50).

THE FĀṬIMIDS

It was a Shī'ite movement which undermined and finally destroyed the power of the Aghlabids in North Africa. Here too, Khārijism was displaced from its rôle as the chief opposition party within Islām by Shī'ism — though in the long run the latter did not endure. The movement was led by a dynasty purported to descend from the Prophet and designated "*Fāṭimid*" after his daughter. Its founder's son *'Ubayd Allāh*, who in the light of recent research [1] appears only to have been the deputed "*imām*" ("leader") and not a scion of the hallowed family, came from Syria to North Africa in circumstances whose details are largely obscured by tendentious legends, and with the help of a Berber tribe which he won to his cause was able to overthrow the Aghlabids and establish him-

[1] By BERNARD LEWIS, *The origins of Ismā'īlism*, Cambridge 1940, whose conclusions are rejected by VLADIMIR IVANOW in his *The alleged founder of Ismā'īlism*, Bombay 1946.

self in their capital Raqqādah in 909. Soon afterwards he founded a new capital, al-Mahdīyah, on the coast. After various changes of fortune, he succeeded in consolidating his power and also in eliminating the *Idrīsids* of Fās (Fez), another Shīʿite dynasty which had been ruling the Moroccan area since around 800 and was now enfeebled through apportionments of its domain among the family. The power of the Spanish Umayyads remained unimpaired.

The rise of the Fāṭimids created a new situation. Being convinced *Sevener Shīʿites*, they did not acknowledge the suzerainty of the ʿAbbāsid Caliphate even in theory, but proclaimed themselves possessors of the legitimate title to leadership of the Islāmic community. This being their attitude, they could not remain content with their position in North Africa, but were obliged to contemplate war against the "usurping" ʿAbbāsids and, if possible, the destruction of the latter and the acquisition for themselves of their authority as Caliphs. ʿUbayd Allāh therefore launched attacks in 914 and 921 against the Nile valley, which since the fall of the Ṭūlūnids was again under the direct control of the ʿAbbāsid Caliphs. For the time being, the Faṭimids could not hold their ground in Egypt and remained confined to North Africa. Meanwhile the governor of Egypt, *Muḥammad ibn Ṭughj*, a descendant of the old Turkish princes of Farghānah, had assumed autonomous powers since 935 and induced the Caliph at Baghdād to confer on him his family's ancient title of *Ikhshīd* and thus distinguish him from the general run of provincial governors. (The rulers of Egypt in the 19th century took the title of *Khedive* for the same reason). When he died in 946, his agent, the Abyssinian eunuch *Kāfūr*, at first ruled as guardian of his two sons, but after their death was invested with the governorship of Egypt.

THE FĀṬIMIDS IN EGYPT

Meanwhile the power of the Fāṭimids in North Africa had greatly increased. By 969, the fourth "Caliph" of this house, *al-Muʿizz*, was strong enough to mobilize an army which, under the command of a former Greek slave [1], conquered the whole of Egypt in the same year without encountering any vigorous resistance. As a monument to his triumph, the Fāṭimid ruler built a new capital near the site once occupied by the ancient Babylon of Egypt and the later Fusṭāṭ, and on this he bestowed in 973 the epithet of Mars, planet of victory: *al-Qāhirah* (Cairo).

[1] IVAN HRBEK, in "*Archiv Orientální*" XXI (Prague 1953), p. 560-71, considers this commander, *Jawhar*, to have been a Slav.

Here too, and at the same time, he founded *al-Azhar* college as a centre for propagating the Ismāʿīlite faith in Egypt and the Near East, and also the *Dar al-ʿIlm*, a sort of academy. Egypt was thus finally detached from its previous, albeit nominal, allegiance to the ʿAbbāsid Caliphate and restored to independent statehood. The Fāṭimids, on the other hand, never came near to destroying the rulers of Baghdād, even though they continued their political and religious offensive against them (p. 82) and for one brief spell during the next century even enjoyed nominal recognition in Mesopotamia itself.

THE GEOPOLITICAL SITUATION OF SYRIA

The Fāṭimid conquest of Egypt reestablished a state of affairs which had characterized the whole of antiquity down to the Arab conquest, with only a few exceptions such as the Achaemenian period: namely that the Mesopotamian region (as a rule politically united with Persia) and the Nile valley formed separate political entities. During the five and a half centuries down to the Ottoman conquest of 1517, this state of affairs again determined the political picture of the Near East; and the spatial interrelation of the two regions is such that tensions were bound to result. For whenever Mesopotamia and the Nile valley confront each other as two independent states, they never fail to contend for the possession of Palestine and Syria, each regarding those countries as a necessary *glacis* for its own defence[1]. That is what actually happened in the following centuries, and as in antiquity the process took three forms determined by the above-mentioned geopolitical factors. Syria became an outer bastion either of Mesopotamia or alternatively of Egypt; or thirdly, the two latter might reach an equilibrium, in which case Syria became more or less independent and almost invariably split up into several local principalities. In the middle ages, as in ancient times and in the modern period, Syria's occupancy of one or another of these three alternative positions depended on the distribution of power in the whole Near Eastern-Egyptian area and on whether Mesopotamia or Egypt happened to be preponderant.

THE INTERNAL SITUATION IN MESOPOTAMIA

The positions of both countries in the 10th and 11th centuries will be intelligible in the light of two considerations: first of the developments

[1] For Mesopotamia, access to the Mediterranean has economic importance also.

in Mesopotamia during the time when the outer territories, as already related, were becoming autonomous; and secondly of the interplay of forces between Mesopotamia and Egypt. The evolution of the Caliphate has been followed to the point at the end of the 9th century where the rebel movements had been suppressed (Zanj 883, Carmathians 906) and the ʿAbbāsid power had recovered some importance. This recovery was originally due to the energetic leadership of the Regent al-Muwaffaq; and it did not last long. The position of the individual Caliphs (whom it would be profitless to enumerate) lost all importance, having been sapped by constant palace revolutions and garrison revolts in favour of different pretenders. The real authority belonged at first to the wazīrs. They frequently changed, and their subordinates generally changed with them; but they sometimes were in power for several terms and in the period of the ministerial dynasties (p. 51) often bequeathed their office to relatives. One such family was that of *Ibn al-Furāt*, which held fiefs extending as far as Persia and Transoxiana. The practice of granting fiefs to the military, instead of pay, became usual during the 10th century, with the result that even in the residue of the empire power to dispose of landed property slipped out of the hands of the rulers, and their cash revenues fell off accordingly. Before long, the position and influence of the wazīrs in public life passed to the generals, who during this period — from 936 onwards — bore the title *Amīr al-Umarāʾ* (*Chief Amīr*). The period has been vividly described in the works of ALFRED FREIHERR VON KREMER and ADAM MEZ, and impressive early accounts of it have come down to us in a number of histories of wazīrs and histories of government offices (*Hilāl as-Ṣābiʾ* and *Ibn Miskawayh*; *al-Ṣūlī, Ibn Jaḥshiyārī*). Literary activity at Baghdād, in a wide range of fields, was notably vigorous at this time; the *"Catalogue"* (*Fihrist*) compiled by *Ibn al-Nadīm* in 987 gives an idea of the profusion and variety of the literature then circulating.

THEOLOGICAL PROBLEMS

Political instability was not the only factor disturbing the public life of Mesopotamia during the period. Theological controversies had of course not been resolved with the suppression of the Muʿtazilites; the trains of thought set in motion by that school went ahead, with far-reaching effects. The most significant outcome was the effort of *al-Ashʿarī* (d. 941) to apply the dialectical methods which had been used by the Muʿtazilites, and some of their theses, to the task of constructing an intellectual framework for orthodox theology. This initiative brought down on him much hostility at first, but his system won increasing acceptance during the next decades and then became an established component of orthodox doctrine. The mass of the people were more affected by the growth of mysticism culminating in the 9th and 10th centuries. The mystic *(ṣūfī)* martyr *al-Ḥallāj* was executed in 922. Further information about these important subjects must be sought in works on the religious history of Islām.

THE BŪYIDS

During this period of internal and external instability, western Persia after the fall of the Ṣaffārids was for half a century the scene of exceedingly confused faction-fighting, in the course of which a prince of Ṭabaristān, *Mardāvīj*, gained most prominence. He openly strove, like Māzyār in an earlier age, to restore the Zoroastrian Persian civilization, and by 928 had amassed a formidable strength; but his murder in 935 put a sudden end to such endeavours, as his brother *Vashmgīr* did not maintain his standpoint. Increasing forces now gathered round a Shīʿite family originating from the district of Daylam on the south shore of the Caspian Sea, who had seized Karaj (south east of Hamadān) and Iṣfahān and expanded from these bases, constituting a dynastic power of their own since 932-34. Rayy and Shīrāz soon passed under their control, and when the disorders in Baghdād reached their climax in connection with a famine, *Aḥmad Būyeh* (or *Buwayh* — this being the family's name) decided to invade Mesopotamia. The city of Baghdād was occupied in December 945. This created a singular situation, not so much because the conqueror arrogated power to himself as Chief Amīr — a practice which had become normal — as because a Persian Shīʿite now exercised the supreme authority in the state of the Caliphs, Commanders of the Sunnite Faithful. The Būyids remained strong during the first generation, because Aḥmad, the conqueror of Baghdād and former ruler of Kirmān, lived on good terms with his two brothers; the Caliph, by what was becoming the convention in such circumstances, honoured him with a title, *Muʿizz al-Dawlah* (*Fortifier of the Empire*); and after he had repelled attacks by the Sāmānids of Khurāsān (whose turn for mention will come soon) and had subjugated and, by means of forced migrations, pacified and Islāmized the frontier regions of Kirmān and Baluchistān, nobody in Īrān could seriously contest his power.

After the death of the three brothers, good relations were not maintained among their successors. Wars broke out between them, but did not lead to the collapse of the Būyid authority since one of them, *'Aḍud al-Dawlah,* who came to power in 949 and was perhaps the most outstanding of his line, was able to defeat his rivals in 976 and gather the whole inheritance into his own hands. After his death in 983, however, the Būyid state fell asunder for good. Several petty principalities took its place, until the eastern half was conquered by the *Ghaznavids* in 1029 and the rest by the *Saljūqs* in the years from then till 1055.

THE ḤAMDĀNIDS

In view of the severe strains caused by their internal quarrels, it is not surprising that the Būyids found little time to defend the empire against external enemies. During the period of their supremacy, the state of the Caliphs had no direct contacts with non-Muslim lands. The Byzantine frontier had been held since 890 by the *Ḥamdānids,* Beduin Arabs by origin, who had built up a dynastic power centred on the cities of Mardīn and Mosul (al-Mawṣil) and were on varying terms with the Caliphate. The Ḥamdānid *Ḥasan,* whose rule began in 929, subjugated the whole of northern Mesopotamia and northern Syria and then forced the Caliph to recognize his authority and confer on him the title *Nāṣir al-Dawlah* by which he is known to history; but the Būyids were in a position to compel him to acknowledge their suzerainty after 945. In 968 he was deposed by one of his relatives whom he had mortally offended by his arbitrary tyranny; he had also ruined his subjects by excessive taxation. Eleven years later his descendants had to submit outright to the Būyids, and in 990 they were supplanted by another ruling family, the *'Uqaylids.* These latter were masters of the area for over a century (till 1096).

BYZANTINE ENCROACHMENTS

Nāṣir al-Dawlah's brother *Sayf al-Dawlah* fared better in northern Syria, with headquarters at Aleppo (Ḥalab), and won distinction as a defender of the faith in the war against the East Romans. This consisted, as in earlier times, of well-nigh annual raids or *razzias* (from the Arabic word *ghazw*), conducted by the professional frontier troops described on p. 38 who were called *Ghāzīs* (from the same Arabic root), or on the Byzantine side *Akrites* (frontier guards). Under competent leadership they were capable of presenting an impressive military performance. To secure his rear, Sayf al-Dawlah after initial dissensions combined with the Ikhshīdids of Egypt (p. 71). He had every need to do so, because during this period the East Romans became active again and inflicted many reverses on him (in 931-40 and from 949 onwards). They occupied his capital Aleppo — except the citadel — for a short time in 962-63. Sayf al-Dawlah nevertheless succeeded on the whole in safeguarding his domain, though in the Armenian borderland the enemy effectively pushed back the confines of Islām. During this period Crete and Cyprus, after a century and a half of Muslim domination, also fell back into Byzantine hands, in 961 and 965 respectively.

After the death of Sayf al-Dawlah, his son *Saʿd al-Dawlah* had to face a grave situation, which not even an alliance with the recently acceded Fāṭimids of Egypt and a profession of the Ismāʿīlite faith for their benefit could alleviate. In the same year 969 in which the latter overran the Nile valley, the Byzantines captured Antioch; and shortly afterwards they took Aleppo. Saʿd al-Dawlah was obliged to declare himself a vassal of the Byzantines and to cede to them the cities of Antioch and Laodicea (Lādhiqīyah) with a coastal strip stretching nearly to Tripoli. In an incursion into Palestine, which proved to be only a passing episode, the East Roman Emperor [1] reached the gates of Jerusalem. The Ḥamdānid dynasty was so weakened by these setbacks that a major-domo was able to displace it in 1002; and he too submitted to Fāṭimid suzerainty.

The Ḥamdānids were important as patrons of art and science. The poet *al-Mutannabī* (d.965), one of the last great figures of classical Arabic literature, and the philosopher *al-Fārābī* (d. 950), author of a Utopia and advocate of the superiority of philosophy over religious revelation, lived and worked for many years at their court.

THE SĀMĀNIDS

While the Ḥamdānids did much to encourage intellectual life among the Arabs, the Būyids failed to render any corresponding service to the Persians. Their principal aim was to consolidate their political position; and as members of an Īrānian tribe scarcely touched by higher civilization, the Daylamites, they took little interest in anything except military matters [2]. Another possible explanation may be that conditions in western Persia (described on p. 59) were still unfavourable for the growth of a new civilization, and that it was no fortuitous accident when the rebirth of Persian culture began in the Sāmānid realm of Khurāsān and Transoxiana.

[1] John Tzimiskes.
[2] Some of the Būyid princes patronized Arabic authors and Twelver Shīʿite theologians.

The *Sāmānids*, who took their name from a village in the vicinity of Balkh and were descended from an old Persian priestly family, had gained influence during the first half of the 9th century as provincial governors for the Ṭāhirids (p. 59 f.) and sometimes also for the Caliphs in the eastern parts of Īrān, mainly in Khurāsān but also at Bukhārā and Samarqand in Transoxiana. This family influence reached a point where four brothers held high administrative posts in the area. The most important of them was *Aḥmad*, governor of Transoxiana, whose son *Naṣr* became for all intents and purposes an autonomous prince (*Amīr*) after 874-75, when the ascendancy of the Ṭāhirids was overthrown by the rising power of the Ṣaffārids. Though the Sāmānids nominally recognized the suzerainty of the Caliphs at Baghdād, they were in fact independent rulers in eastern Persia, and their importance steadily grew inasmuch as the Caliphs claimed their help against the Ṣaffārid peril. In 903, Naṣr's brother and successor *Ismāʿīl* (892-907) virtually annihilated the Ṣaffārids, who proved incapable of resistance except in their homeland, Sīstān, where they long maintained themselves as a local dynasty. Command over the larger part of Īrān, subject to the nominal supremacy of the Caliphs, passed for several decades to the Sāmānid house, until counterbalanced by the rise of the Būyids in the west.

THE CIVILIZATION OF THE SĀMĀNID REALM

The Sāmānid state, which comprised Khurāsān and Transoxiana and for a time also encompassed Sīstān and Kirmān together with Jurjān, Ṭabaristān and Rayy, had great historical importance in several respects. The linking of eastern Persia with the borderlands of Turkistān for the time being protected the Īrānian-inhabited region from inroads by Turks. At the same time, these latter were exposed to the parallel influences of the Islāmic religion and Persian culture, both of which prepared the ground for the incorporation of the mass of the Central Asian Turks into the body of Near Eastern Muslim civilization; and that civilization, as yet unshaken by outside pressure, was reaching its perfection during the period. These achievements of the Sāmānid state would have been impossible had it not formed the centre of the Persian national renascence.

It has already been suggested (p. 59) that north-eastern Īrān had become the main gathering place of the country's national and cultural forces; and these received generous encouragement from the Sāmānid house. Another reason was the fact (to which allusion has already been made) that in eastern Īrān the social structure had undergone little or no modification; the leading position of the local nobility (*dihqāns*) had been preserved, and in this milieu the national traditions, which they carefully cherished, had remained very much alive — particularly in art and the legends of the kings. This state of affairs was not disturbed by the Sāmānids, who had firm support in the existing social order. They gave the provinces of Īrān a new era of peace and security, and made it possible for the Persian intellect to regain full consciousness and develop and express itself in freedom. At their court lived *Rūdakī* (d. 940/41), the first important poet of the modern Persian language, and *Balʿamī*, who in 963 finished his Persian version of the voluminous annals of al-Ṭabarī (839-923). There too were composed the works of *al-Jayḥānī* (c. 900), who did much to promote the rise of geography and to give a definite shape to this branch of learning; hitherto it had consisted of manuals for the postal and other governmental services, but it was to grow into a special and highly valuable department of Islāmic literature. For scientific, as well as theological and philosophical works, such as those of the physician-scientist *Ibn Sīnā* (*Avicenna*; 980-1037), the language in use long remained Arabic, whose status resembled that of Latin in medieval Western Europe.

SĀMĀNIDS AND QARA-KHĀNIDS

The service rendered by the Sāmānids in promoting the sciences and Persian poetry was imperishable. At the bottom of it lay a stable economy and a sedulous attention to agriculture, which in view of the need for very careful maintenance of the irrigation system was particularly liable to disaster in the event of unrest [1]. Sāmānid policy, however great its merits, was necessarily limited by this fact. Soon after the death of *Naṣr II* (913-942; d. 943), the most glorious representative of his house, internal difficulties arose. The nobility (*dihqāns*) became more and more unruly; and the increasingly numerous and influential Turkish officer class sometimes conspired with malcontent elements within the state, and sometimes joined hands with the *Qarluqs (Karluks)*, a powerful Turkish people who since 840 had been pressing in from the Tʿien Shan, and with the dynasty of the *Qara-Khānids* (or *Ilig-Khānids*) who were gaining ascendancy over them. The organization of these latter was based on a plurality of juxtaposed rulers, each with his own function and title,

[1] Irrigation depended mainly on underground canals (*qanāt*). cf. WILHELM BARTHOLD, *Kistorii orošeniya Turkestana* (A historical study of irrigation in Turkistān), St. Petersburg 1914.

The Near East c. 1020, showing agriculture, stock raising and mineral production

MAP 2

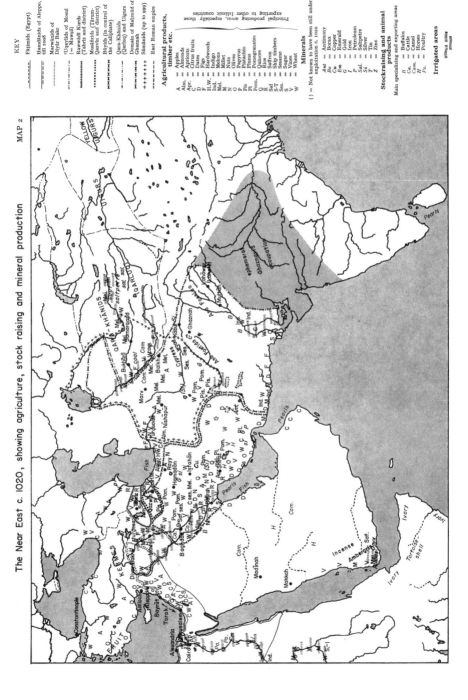

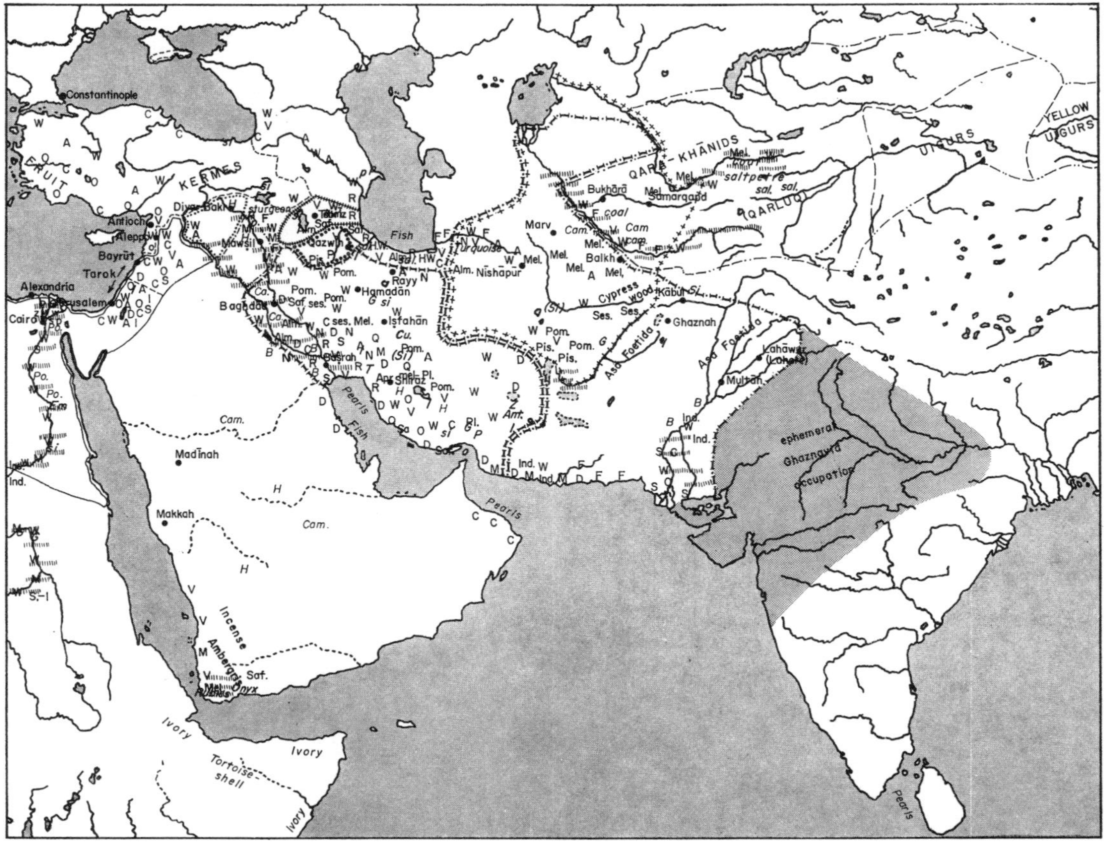

KEY

- Fāṭimids (Egypt)
- Ḥamdānids of Aleppo, till 1008
- Marwānids of Diyār Bakr
- ʿUqaylids of Mosul (= Mawṣil)
- Rawwādī Kurds (Tabrīz and district)
- Musāfirids (Ṭārum-Qazvīn and district)
- Būyids (in control of the Caliphate)
- Qara-Khānids (Qarluq) and Uigurs
- Domain of Maḥmūd of Ghaznah
- Sāmānids (up to 999)
- East Roman empire

Agricultural products, timber etc.

Principal producing areas, especially those exporting to other Islāmic countries

A = Apples
Alm. = Almonds
Apr. = Apricots
C = Citrus fruits
D = Dates
F = Figs
H.W. = Hardwoods
Ind. = Indigo
Mel. = Melons
M = Millet
N = Nuts
O = Olives
P = Papyrus
Pis = Pistachio
Pl = Plums
Pom. = Pomegranates
Q = Quinces
R = Rice
Saf = Saffron
S-T = Ship timbers
Ses. = Sesame
S = Sugar
V = Vines
W = Wheat

Minerals

( ) = Not known to have been still under exploitation c. 1020

Ant = Antimony
Bo = Borax
Cu = Copper
Em = Emerald
G = Gold
I = Iron
P = Petroleum
Sal. = Saltpetre
Si = Silver
T = Tin
Z = Zinc

Stockraising and animal products

Main specializing and exporting areas

B = Buffalos
Ca. = Cattle
Cam. = Camel
H = Horses
Po. = Poultry

Irrigated areas

recalling the apportionment of functions and territories between contemporaneous Augusti and Caesars in the reconstruction of the later Roman Empire under Diocletian and his successors. Recent research has for the first time elucidated the constitution, social structure and titles of the Qara-Khānid state [1]. To these difficulties of the Sāmānids were added conflicts between members of the family; the reigns of *Manṣūr I* (961-976) and *Nūḥ II* (976-997) were mainly occupied with such struggles and with others against disaffected clans of noblemen. When no longer able to see any other means of warding off the growing dangers, the Sāmānid ruler called to his aid the *"Sulṭān" Subuktigīn (Sebüktigin)* and his son *Maḥmūd*, Turkish slave-soldiers by origin, who had risen to power in the second half of the 10th century in the governorship of the present-day Afghān territory on the Indian frontier, with their seat at Ghaznah. (The term *Sulṭān* — really an abstract noun meaning *sovereign authority* — began to be used during the 10th century to designate rulers). The Sāmānids received help from this quarter; but their helpers were not content to leave it at that. They demanded and obtained various provinces from the Sāmānids, and finally dislodged them in 999. The Sāmānid territories south of the Oxus were incorporated in the new realm of Ghaznah, while Transoxiana was added to the Qara-Khānid sphere of influence.

THE GHAZNAVIDS

The destruction of the Sāmānid State was not such a severe blow to the renascent Persian civilization as might have been feared. It has already been pointed out that the Sāmānid régime contributed much to the dissemination of the Īrānian intellectual patrimony and the Muslim religion among the Turks. In the cultural field, the dynasty of the *Ghaznavids* (as Subuktigīn's descendants were named, after their capital city) largely carried on the task bequeathed by the Sāmānids. In the religious field, they proved to be zealous champions of Sunnite orthodoxy. All the Turks, indeed (with the single exception of those of Āẕarbāyjān, among whom Persian influences remained dominant over the centuries), continued to be Sunnites, right through to the present day, and spurned the never very important Shīʿite movements which, on rare occasions — for instance in early Ottoman times — were to arise in their midst. In this

[1] cf. Omelian Pritsak, *Karachānidische Studien*, *I*-X (typescript dissertation, Göttingen 1948). (Turkish translation by the "Türk Tarih Kurumu", Ankara, in preparation). Parts have been printed in *Oriëns*, 111 (1950), p. 209-228, and in the *Zeitschrift der Deutschen Morgenland-gesellschaft*, 101 (1951), p. 270-300.

respect they contrasted with the Persians, from whom they acquired their culture.

Partly as a result of this rigid orthodoxy, the Turks did not much appreciate the ancient pre-Islāmic traditions of the Persians. No surprise need therefore be caused by the famous story of the niggardly recompense which *Maḥmūd of Ghaznah,* Subuktigīn's successor since 997 and an outstandingly gifted and energetic military and political leader, thought fit to grant to the foremost poet of Īrān. It was under Maḥmūd's patronage that the Persian national epic — and one of the greatest classics of world literature — took shape in the *Shāhnāmeh* (*Book of the Kings*). After the premature death of another poet to whom some 1000 of the opening verses are due, the composition of the book was taken over by *Abū' l-Qāsim Manṣūr,* whom the Persians styled *Firdawsi* (*"from Paradise"*) — whether after his reputed birthplace at Firdaws, near Ṭūs, or on the score of his poetical achievement, is still debated. He lived from perhaps 934, or 939, till around 1020. For every verse, according to the story, Maḥmūd had promised him one gold piece, but when the work was completed, gave him a silver piece only — with some reason, indeed, considering that the verses amount to 20,000 and that payment of the promised sum would have meant a deep inroad into the public funds, for which Maḥmūd doubtless contemplated other uses. He may also have seen fault, and his Turks must have found nothing attractive, in the virtually complete absence of Islāmic preconceptions from the epic with its unmixed fabric of legends dear to the Persian nobility. Recent research has shown that Firdawsī very largely depended for his material on the Book of the Kings of the ancient Persians, as known in Arabic versions by *Ibn al-Muqaffa'* and *al-Tha'ālibī* [1]. The poem depicts the legendarily idealized history of the Persians before Islām; its heroes are Zoroastrians and Sāsānids [2]. Linguistically, it marks the final elevation of modern Persian to the rank of a language of culture within Islām, and consequent emergence among the literary vehicles of the modern age. From Firdawsī's day onwards, intellectual production in this language never stopped, though Arabic influence became increasingly important, especially on the vocabulary, until very recent times.

Maḥmūd also patronized other literary talents, notably the celebrated

---

[1] Theodor Nöldeke, *Das iranische Nationalepos*, Strassburg 1896, 2nd ed., 1920.

[2] There are English versions of the Shāhnāmeh by J. Atkinson, London 1832 and reprinted 1886, 1892 (abridged); A. Rogers, London 1907 (fairly complete); and A. G. and E. Warner, London 1905/15. Excellent German translations of large parts of the poem were made by Friedrich Rückert and Adolf Friedrich, Count von Schack. There are French and Italian translations by Jules Mohl, Paris 1876-78, and Italo Pizzi, Turin 1886-88, respectively.

traveller and investigator *al-Bīrūnī* (d. 1048), whose Indian researches are of especial interest; and he interested himself in the embellishment of his capital Ghaznah (in the east of what is now Afghānistān).

THE CONQUEST OF NORTH WESTERN INDIA

Maḥmūd's chief concern, however, was with the military expansion of his realm and resultant dissemination of Islām (p. 77). Fighting took place against the Turkish Qara-Khānids, who only gradually embraced Islām and were masters of the Transoxianan half of the Sāmānid heritage, but it was never on a large scale; and the conquest of certain Būyid districts in central Persia in 1028, during which a Būyid prince was taken captive, did not give rise to any serious complications. Maḥmūd could therefore turn his main attention to campaigns in India. Islām had penetrated into that country as long ago as 711 (p. 42), but had so far made no significant advances: it first gained ground as a result of Maḥmūd's almost annual campaigns in the Panjāb. Besides that province and Multān, parts of Gujarāt passed under Ghaznavid rule. At the Indian city of *Lahore* (*Lahāwur*), the dynasty maintained itself for a hundred and fifty years. In Persia, meanwhile, its power had collapsed.

THE RISE OF THE SALJŪQS

The collapse occurred quite soon after Maḥmūd's death in 1030. One of his sons, *Masʿūd*, after overthrowing a brother whom their father had designated to be successor, ruled efficiently till murdered in 1041. During his reign, however, fighting broke out with a family of chieftains heading the *Oğuz (Ghuzz)* Turks (in Arab parlance, the *Türkmen* tribes), who around 970 had made their way from the modern Kazakhstan (Qazāqistān) to Bukhārā. These were the *Saljūqs (Selcük)*, scions of a Turkish chieftain of that name. (The Arabic term Saljūq is generally applied in Islāmic, and hence in Western, writings to the posterity as well as to the eponymous ancestor). At Bukhārā their influence grew alongside that of the Qārā-Khānids. The main founders of their might were the brothers *Ṭughril* (*Toğrul*) *Beg Muḥammad* and *Chaghrī* (*Çağrī*) *Beg Dāʾūd*, who apportioned the realm among the princes of the house in accordance with the same feudal and hierarchical principles which were customary among other Turkish tribes, for instance the Qara-Khānids. In a decisive battle at *Dandānqān* in 1040 the two brothers wrested Khurāsān from the Ghaznavid Masʿūd, and soon expelled his descendants, who were much weakened by family strife, beyond the bounds of Persia, confining them to India. They also, in a series of swiftly following victories, occupied central and western Persia, drove out the Būyids who till then had kept control of that area against the Ghaznavids, fixed themselves at Iṣfahān and ultimately, in 1055, destroyed the 110 year-old Būyid hegemony over the Caliphate. This must have been welcome to the Caliphs, in spite of their continued impotence, because the Saljūqs were Sunnites and an end was thus put to the paradoxical situation in which the Caliphate had been controlled *de facto* by Shīʿite potentates. A Turkish officer in the service of the last of the Būyids, by name *al-Basāsīrī*, placed himself under the suzerainty of the Fāṭimids of Egypt (p. 72) and attempted further resistance, but was soon disposed of (1060).

ADMINISTRATION AND CULTURE IN THE SALJŪQ PERIOD

After more than two centuries of confusion, the Saljūq régime once more brought the eastern part of the empire of the Caliphs under a single administration, firmly reuniting the Īrānian lands with Mesopotamia. Northern Syria, too, was added, its Egyptian rulers being driven out in the course of the next decades. The empire was apportioned among the princes of the Saljūq house; but this did not prove dangerous as long as the seniors were strong men. Such, without question, were Ṭughril Beg and his nephew and successor, *Alp Arslān* (1063-1072). The Saljūqs kept order within the lands which they ruled. Any local revolts, like those which had been such a constant feature of the preceeding century, were suppressed almost without exception; public security was restored, the administration was regulated, tax-incidences were fittingly graduated and, above all, intellectual life received vigorous encouragement. In the execution of these policies, indispensable service was rendered by the wazīr *Niẓām al-Mulk* — one of the greatest ministers whom the East has known. His very real administrative abilities were epitomized in what may be called a "Model Statesman's Manual", the *Siyāsat-nāmeh*, of which he is the reputed, but perhaps was not the actual, author. Niẓām al-Mulk continued to hold sway under the Saljūq Amīr *Malik Shāh* (1072-1092), who succeeded his murdered father Alp Arslān while still a minor and in spite of certain efforts could not evade the tutelage of so towering a personality.

Islāmic science owed much to the favour shown to it by this wazīr. He sponsored the establishment of an observatory [1], and also of several

[1] Among the workers at the observatory was *ʿUmar-i-Khayyām* (d. 1123), the author of the partly freethinking, often very pensive and religious, quatrains made famous by EDWARD

colleges *(madrasah)* on lines perhaps suggested by institutions existing in the eastern territories (the Buddhist) *vihāra)*. The most renowned and important of these was the *Niẓāmīyah* college at Baghdād, founded to be the headquarters of Sunnite erudition in opposition to the Ismāʿīlite college, al-Azhar, at Cairo. Instruction at the Niẓāmīyah was based on the ideas of al-Ashʿarī (p. 73), with the result that these finally won the upper hand and all others came to be regarded as more or less heterodox. [1]

At this college was spent part of the teaching life of the last great theological thinker of Islām, *al-Ghazzālī* (1058-1111). A native of Khurāsān and first professionally active at Nīshāpūr, he in his early career defended the Ashʿarite principles in a number of brilliant works. Then, under the impact of various personal experiences, he attacked the Ismāʿīlite and Shīʿite ideas and turned above all to the study of Islāmic mysticism. From this study he concluded that the goal of the mystic is entirely consistent with the doctrines of Islām, and further that mystic intuition has every right to a place in the theological system of the Sunnah. He therefore devoted the last years of his rather short life to advocating the integration of *ṣūfī* mysticism in the Islāmic doctrinal structure; and so illuminatingly did he expound this thought that his teaching met with general approval.

FOREIGN POLICY: THE CONQUEST OF ASIA MINOR

Besides fostering theology and the exact sciences [2], the Saljūqs and their Amīrs were eager to pursue a vigorous foreign policy. Their principal achievement was to overpower for good and all the Byzantine line of defence against Islām in Asia Minor. Mention has already been made of the fighting which continued intermittently on this front for hundreds of years, and of the northeastward expansion of the East Roman border since the middle of the 10th century as far as the Upper Euphrates (p. 75 f.). The Saljūqs not only halted this movement, but definitely reversed it in favour of Islām. After many years of skirmishing, and after Armenian resistance had been thrust aside, Alp Arslān won the decisive

---

FITZGERALD's English rendering. He was partly responsible for the introduction (mainly for fiscal purposes) of the solar year, in 1079; this did not, however, gain acceptance in place of the *hijrī* year.

[1] See J. RIBERA, *Origen del Colegio Nidami de Bagdad*, in *Homenaje a D. Francisco Codera*, Saragossa 1914, p. 3 ff.; ASʿAD ṬALAS, *L'enseignement chez les Arabes*, *La Madrasa Nizamiyya et son histoire*, Paris 1939; A. S. TRITTON, *Materials on Muslim education in the Middle Ages*, London 1957.

[2] See MARTIN PLESSNER's chapter on "*Die Naturwissenschaft bei den Muslimen*" in the "*Handbuch der Orientalistik*", additional volumes.

battle of *Manzikert* (*Malazjird*), north of Lake Vān, on August 26, 1071. In its effects, this victory was one of the most far-reaching, not only of Near Eastern, but also of world history. The East Roman army was crushingly defeated and the Emperor [1] taken prisoner. Asia Minor lay open to raiding Muslim bands, which pushed as far as the Aegean Sea and brought the whole central and eastern part of the peninsula under their control. To a large extent it was lost forever to the Byzantines and to the Christian cause. The year 1071 is the starting point of the turkicization of Asia Minor (which will be discussed presently), and the date on which were laid the foundations of Turkish, though not of Ottoman, statehood in Anatolia.

EGYPT UNDER THE FĀṬIMIDS

The Saljūqs had to hold a second front, on the borders of the Fāṭimid empire. It will be recalled that the Fāṭimids belonged to the Ismāʿīlite Shīʿah (p. 70), and that as guardians of its secret lore they set out after conquering Egypt in 969 to propagate this faith in other lands. In Egypt itself they did not, in spite of certain endeavours, impose it at all widely. The population stayed predominantly Sunnite. At times the Fāṭimids showed a preference for the Copts, who were now distinguished only by religion from their Muslim compatriots; during the 11th and 12th centuries the former almost entirely abandoned the Coptic language for Arabic [2], as the latter had earlier done in consequence of increasing miscegenation with immigrant Arabs. Although the Fāṭimids did not follow any consistent policy in favour of the Copts, and so indirectly to the detriment of the Sunnite element, the minor and middle-grade officials were preponderantly Christians, with some Jews. They still proved indispensable in the government offices with their carefully devised systems of records (known to us in code-books preserved since the 11th and 12th centuries) and especially in the irrigation department, where traditional techniques and exact knowledge were essential, and in the closely linked revenue administration.

As under the previous régime, a breach with past methods, always so perilous to ancient river-valley civilizations, was carefully avoided. Even the integration of the former districts into provinces (*aʿmāl*), which took place under the Fāṭimids, was carried through only by stages. It was the Mamlūk régime in Egypt, and the Mongol régime in Mesopotamia, which allowed the irrigation systems to break down and thus

---

[1] Diogenes Romanus.

[2] For details see *Encyclopaedia of Islām*, Vol. 2, Leiden and Leipzig 1927, article "*Ḳibṭ*"

helped to bring about the long-lasting economic ruin of those two lands. The military organization, however, was kept strictly separate from the civilian departments and remained always in Muslim lands.

AL-ḤĀKIM AND THE DRUZES

The reign of the third Fāṭimid of Egypt, *al-Ḥākim* (996-1021), was a time of much unrest. Highly capricious in character and, as his year advanced, evidently unsound in mind, this ruler in all his proceedings rushed from one extreme to another. At one time he gathered around him scientists such as the noted mathematician *Ibn al-Haytham* (d. 1039), at another he cast them into dungeons; Christians he now favoured, now persecuted furiously; and after first giving licence to the utmost profligacy, he sought to restore public decorum by stern morality-laws. Above all, he reverted more and more to the extreme Ismāʿīlite religious standpoint and began to view himself as the living incarnation of the supreme being. Finally he proclaimed himself such. This was perforce highly repulsive to the strongly Sunnite and monotheistic Egyptians; but in Syria, then a Fāṭimid possession, where pagan ideas had preserved some existence through the years under Christianity and Islām in remote mountain districts, men still lived whose minds were ready to admit such an apotheosis. A group of tribes in southern Syria were attracted by al-Ḥākim's extraordinary doings; and at the instigation of a missionary, *al-Darazī*, from whom they take their name, they combined into the community of the *Druzes* and made the deification of al-Ḥākim the central point of their doctrine. This must have been helped not a little by the latter's mysterious and never explained disappearance in 1021. The Druze community, which sets neither Muḥammad nor ʿAlī at the centre of its doctrine of salvation, can hardly be regarded as Muslim; and it has furthermore absorbed a number of ancient pagan traditions. It has survived till to-day as a separate community, probably in part because it originally constituted the residue of some ancient national entity.

This is only one instance of the way in which Syria has become a patchwork of the most varied faith-groups. Besides the numerous Christian communities (whose history cannot be related here) and the Sunnites, the people still comprise Druzes, Twelver Shīʿites, Ismāʿīlites and in a far corner the already mentioned Yazīdīs (p. 39); then finally, in the district round Lādhiqīyah, men who view ʿAlī as an incarnation of God and call themselves *ʿAlawites*. Previously these latter were generally known as *Nuṣayrīs*, apparently because having assimilated various

Christian rituals in their cult, they were derided as *"little Christians"*. They too are essentially non-Islāmic, but have maintained their existence into the present age.

THE LATER FĀṬIMIDS

Al-Ḥākim's successors (after 1021), while keeping within the Ismāʿīlite fold, chose more moderate paths. They had to combat the same lawlessness of their Turkish mercenary troops as did their ʿAbbāsid rivals at Baghdād. Order was reestablished by an Armenian wazīr during the long reign of *al-Mustanṣir* (1036-1094), and the country then enjoyed further economic and cultural prosperity, though the number of foreign soldiers in the service continued to increase, most of them being Turks and negroes. For their benefit the government increasingly abandoned the old system of letting out lands of the state domain against prepayment of the appropriate taxes (*ḍamān*), and adopted one of granting fiefs (*iqṭāʿ*), whereby the untaxed income of an estate was left to the occupant. In foreign affairs, reverses were suffered at the hands of the Saljūqs, who took Jerusalem in 1071 and Damascus in 1076.

ISMĀʿĪLITES AND ASSASSINS [1]

The Fāṭimids not only conducted a political and military struggle with the Saljūqs, but made their presence felt as champions of the Ismāʿīlite cause as far afield even as in Persia. The means by which they did so were the same as those which had led to their success in North Africa and to the upsurge of the Carmathians (with whom, however, their relations were mostly hostile): a mysterious interpretation of the Qur'ān, party organization on secret society lines and strict internal discipline. They were able to gain a footing in Persia and even to win over the Sāmānid ruler, Naṣr II (p. 78) Numbers of dwellers in that land made pilgrimages to their court at Cairo, including the poet *Nāṣir-i-Khusraw* (d. 1038) whose *Safar-nāmeh* (*Travel Diary*) gives a detailed account of his journey. A token of Ismāʿīlite activity in Mesopotamia has been preserved in the *Rasā'il Ikhwān al-Ṣafā* (*"Letters of the Sincere Friends"*), dating from around 983. The most important figure, however, is *Ḥasan al-Ṣabbāḥ* (d. 1124). Although he belonged to a separate persuasion, differing as to the identity of a hereditary recipient of the supernatural grace, he nevertheless served a useful purpose in sapping

[1] See M. G. S. Hodgson, *The Order of the Assassins*, The Hague 1955.

the Saljūq might in Persia. He succeeded in ensconcing himself in the inaccessible mountain country south of the Caspian Sea, where he made his hill-fortress *Alamūt ("Eagle's Nest")* the centre of a religious order. Complete libertinism is said to have been the rule among the leaders of this order; but its lesser members were trained into a mood of absolute and fanatical readiness to sacrifice themselves for their spiritual superiors and systematically exploited as instruments of political murder. In their minds, of course, it was a question of religious murder, directed against the enemies of the true Imām. To ensure their complete pliancy to the will of the leaders, prospects of the joys of paradise were fluttered in a no longer explicable manner before their eyes, perhaps with use of a narcotic distillate of hemp, ***hashīsh***, from which the sect got its name and the French and English word *"assassin"* is derived. As early as 1092, a *fidāʾī* ("one ready to sacrifice his life") murdered the minister Niẓām al-Mulk when the latter refused to comply with the sect's demands.

SALJŪQS AND ATABEGS

This murder dealt a critical blow to the Saljūq state. Niẓām al-Mulk was engaged at the time in carrying out an internal reform. In 1087 he permitted the Turkish officers to retain the gross income of their fiefs in lieu of pay, which was discontinued; hitherto they had — at least formally — been entitled only to the net income remaining after deduction of the taxes due to the state. Under the new plan it was hoped that they would no longer extort all they could from their estates and then exchange them for others. Although Niẓām al-Mulk's reform only marked the end of a long process, the system became generally prevalent in the subsequent period and was taken over by the Ottomans. Any planned reconstruction of the social order was ruled out, however, when his sovereign pupil, Malik Shāh, died a few weeks after him [1]. The resultant succession troubles showed that the apportionment of the empire among different princes with varying degrees of eligibility for the throne was not capable of ensuring peace to the land.

The next thirty years saw the kaleidoscopic rise and fall of various pretenders and several break-away movements in different provinces, none of which can be detailed here. During these struggles the Fāṭimids were able to recapture part of their lost territories in Palestine; Jerusalem once more fell into their hands, in 1098.

---

[1] Felix Tauer, in *Dějiny a Kultura islámu*, II,45, thinks it probable that he was poisoned by Assassins.

With the accession of *Muḥammad,* a younger son of Malik Shāh, in 1105, peace was restored in the land and the Saljūqs could again gather strength. They directed their energies chiefly against the 'Abbāsid Caliphs, who had attempted to intervene actively in the disputes among the rival aspirants to power, and later also against the Assassins, who had been growing ever more obnoxious. By 1118 the Assassins were on the verge of losing their main base at Alamūt, when Muḥammad suddenly died, perhaps poisoned by them.

From now on the Saljūq empire began to split into separate principalities. In Persia alone the process was held up for some decades by the forceful rule of the regent *Sanjar.* Within the principalities, the Saljūq princes were overshadowed and finally supplanted by *Atabegs* (*guardians* of minors, later major-domos), who became a characteristic feature of the period.

THE CRUSADES

Before this process is traced further, another development, of particular interest to us Westerners, must be examined: namely the Crusades. It is not possible here to consider what was the significance of these military expeditions in the history of Western Europe and the Byzantine Empire, or how important was their contribution to the intellectual and economic growth of Western civilization; but an allusion may be made to their effect on the knightly orders and the feudal system, to the borrowing of oriental military methods, arms and armorial bearings, to the introduction of textiles such as damask, muslin, and blouses (from Damascus, Mosul and Pelusium), and finally to the complete change in the West's attitude towards the East which becomes apparent from then on. Scientific progress, however, owed much less to the Crusades than to Spain and Sicily. The influence of Islāmic culture on Western courtly refinement and its much disputed, but recently reasserted, effects on the minnesingers and the troubadours [1], also came primarily from the western Mediterranean.

THE SIGNIFICANCE OF THE CRUSADES FOR THE EAST

Viewed as an episode in the sequence of contacts between the East and the West, the Crusades appear as the first counter-stroke of the Occident

[1] R. A. Nykl, *Hispano-Arabic poetry and its relation with the old Provençal troubadours*, Baltimore 1946; Henri Pérès, *La poésie d'Andalousie et ses relations possibles avec les troubadours*, in *L'Islam et L'Occident*, Paris, 1947. For older studies see "*Orientalische Literaturzeitung*", 1941, esp. p. 41-44.

to the forward march of Islām. Orientals, however, unlike Europeans, have always included in this sequence the Spanish *"reconquista"*, that is the gradual conquest of the Iberian peninsula by Christian states, and they date the beginning of the Crusades from the loss by Islām of Toledo in 1085 (p. 108). It must not be forgotten that the community of Muḥammad was attacked simultaneously there and in the east and that on one occasion a crusading army was purposely directed to Spain and took part in the capture of Lisbon in 1147. The events in the east only receive first consideration here because the course and outcome of the clashes in Spain merit separate attention. The results of the two offensives were very different; the one led to the definite expulsion of Islām from Spain, while the other was only transitory in its effects, both political and cultural, on the East. It cannot be too strongly emphasized that the Crusades had no such fundamental significance for the East as they did for Europe. For the East they were a side-show, running solely in Syria, Palestine and on the coast of Egypt, which even at its height meant little or nothing to Mesopotamia and the Caliphate, let alone to Persia or Central Asia or even to Middle and Upper Egypt. The political evolution of these lands was in no way affected and their inhabitants had no contact whatever with the Crusaders.

BYZANTIUM AND THE CRUSADES

The Crusades can therefore be only briefly discussed here, as an episode in the history of a small part of the whole Muslim world. Their proximate cause was the forward drive of the Saljūqs, which in two respects had consequences alarming to Western Europe. One, and evidently the less disquieting, was the overthrow of the Byzantine sway in Asia Minor. It has been seen how after the battle of Manzikert in 1071, not only the tracts in eastern Anatolia and on the Syrian coast which the Byzantines had reconquered in the 10th century, but also the central and southern parts of Asia Minor, had fallen into the hands of the Muslims. Western Europe had indeed hitherto cared little about the fate of East Rome, in view of the violent doctrinal controversies which had led in 1054 to the definite breach between Western and Eastern Christendom; it was not yet clearly seen that there was nothing but Byzantium in the south east to shield the Occident and its civilization against Islām. Nevertheless, when the East Roman Emperor then reigning appealed for help, his call did not pass unheard. But this, as already said, was not the main consideration. Much more important, it seems, was the fact that the Saljūqs, after their capture of Jerusalem in 1071, had subjected the still quite numerous Christian pilgrims to various annoyances the like of which had not been experienced under the Fāṭimid régime. It will be recalled that the Fāṭimids, on account of their uneasy relations with their Egyptian and Syro-Palestinian subjects of Sunnite faith, as a rule treated the Christians in their domain comparatively mildly.

The reaction in the Occident to the changed relations in the holy places resulting from the Saljūq occupation was, as is well known, vigorous; and it found expression at the Council of Clermont in 1095. A host of French, Norman, and Brabançon knights then set out on their way eastwards to liberate the holy land. They had apparently not heard the news that in Jerusalem, meanwhile, the status quo ante had been restored by the Fāṭimid recapture of the city in 1098.

THE POSITION OF THE KINGDOM OF JERUSALEM

During the Crusade in Asia Minor (1097-98), the Saljūqs were thrust to the rear, and the holy city fell on July 15, 1099. This led to the formation of a small Kingdom of Jerusalem, to which were attached several Western Christian feudal principalities lying to the north — Antioch, Edessa, Tripoli and others. The Westerners never controlled more than a coastal strip. Facing them stood a number of Syrian Muslim Amīrates, which occupied the hinterland. Such a fragmentation of Syria and Palestine into small states was, it has been suggested (p. 72), a normal state of affairs when the influences of Mesopotamia on the one hand and Egypt on the other were in approximate equilibrium.

Soon all sorts of alliances and coalitions were formed between the different small states, as well as various cross-connections between Christians and Muslims and also with the East Roman Empire. All this, however, left the balance of power in the Near East quite undisturbed, for the cross-connections counterpoised one sphere of influence against another and were thus quite neutral and harmless in relation to Islām as a whole. The fighting, or as some have said bickering, which took place in the course of these manoeuvres was no more important than that which had been seen in the east for centuries since the break-up of the unitary power of the Caliphs. The fact that Christian states were involved was of no great significance in this land where more or less considerable Christian communities had been a factor all along, and it gave rise to few serious misgivings among the Muslims. The Christians, moreover, were split into a number of mutually distrustful, if not antagonistic, denominations.

On the denominational, as on the political plane, an equilibrium was reached between the various forces — Western Christians ("Latins"), Orthodox Christians, Jacobites, Maronites and Copts (the Nestorians being a negligible factor in this area), or Sunnites, Twelver-Shīʿites, Ismāʿīlites and Nuṣayrīs. There was never any risk of a common movement to one religion. World politics, and especially the church history and cultural evolution of later ages, were profoundly affected by the rift between the East Roman empire and Western Europe, which the Crusades so enlarged that it could never again be patched up (as it always had been in the past). The Byzantines now held once more both the northern and, since around 1100, the southern borderlands of Asia Minor, as well as a broad strip in the west; but they necessarily took it for granted that not only the reconquered territories in Asia Minor, but also those in Syria and Palestine, should revert to them as the rightful Christian rulers. The Crusaders, however, were altogether unwilling, for denominational, economic and other reasons, to cede any of their conquests. Their attitude deeply aggrieved the Byzantines and thus prevented the formation of a united Christian defence front — which at that time might well have been organized by the Byzantine government, then greatly increased in strength under the dynasty of the Comneni. This misunderstanding was the indirect cause of the fairly rapid collapse of the Christian enterprises, and explains why their outcome was so different from that of the struggle in Spain. The armies there had behind them the compact might of a league of geographically adjacent and religiously associated states; in the Near East, the natural supporting power, Byzantium, was deliberately debarred from a share in the undertaking.

THE RISE OF THE AYYŪBIDS

The Crusader states were able to hold out as long as fragmentation continued in the Muslim territory alongside them. The first formidable opponent whom they encountered was *Zangī* (*Zengi*), the Turkish guardian (*Atabeg*) of a Saljūq prince in Mosul. Since 1127 he had been methodically extending his authority, and had largely displaced the *Artuqids* and the *ʿUqaylids*, lords of the land between Mārdīn and Kharpūt and around Raqqah on the Euphrates respectively, whose internecine feuds had cramped the fighting strength of the Muslims. As these two dynasties were at the same time hard pressed by the Byzantines, now again on the offensive (p. 95), Zangī was able to expand his dominion far to the west. In 1144 he captured from the Christians the city of Edessa, which was so situated as to constitute a simultaneous threat to the Crusaders and to the East Romans. Two years later Zangī was murdered and his inheritance was divided between his two sons; but the younger and more energetic, *Nūr al-Dīn*, while not intervening in the elder's realm in Upper Mesopotamia, followed up the father's successful career. He gathered together the Muslim forces in Syria and, though he could not drive out the Crusaders who with their command of the sea had a safe supply line for reinforcements from Europe, threw them onto the defensive. His power was firmly based on a just and frugal system of government, heedful of the welfare of its subjects; and it was to be greatly expanded by the impending collapse of the Fāṭimid empire.

SALADIN

In Egypt, two wazīrs of Armenian origin, father and son (p. 86), had on the whole kept good order during their years of office from 1073 to 1121. Thereafter, owing to the ineptitude of the contemporary Fāṭimid Caliphs, power had fallen completely into the hands of rival generals, none of whom contrived to endure for long because even when capable men they soon fell victim to other contestants. In these circumstances, the young Fāṭimid monarch *al-ʿĀḍid* felt obliged to request the intervention of Nūr al-Dīn, especially as the "Frankish" Kings of Jerusalem were also starting to intervene. Nūr al-Dīn entrusted this assignment to a Kurdish general in his service, *Shīrkūh*, who after several vicissitudes succeeded by 1169 in establishing a firm position for himself at Cairo as wazīr. When he was murdered shortly afterwards, his authority was transferred to the son of his no less valiant brother *Ayyūb* (from whom the family received the name *Ayyūbid*). Two years later this son, *Ṣalāḥ al-Dīn*, known to the Franks as *Saladin*, did away with the Fāṭimid dynasty. With its fall, the Ismāʿīlite doctrine, which had never had any following outside certain court circles, also disappeared from the Nile valley. The Sunnite faith of the natives now triumphed in full strength, as the proportion of Copts in the population had meanwhile fallen to around a tenth, that is to about the same percentage as they still form to-day. Egypt has been a stronghold of Sunnite Islām ever since and was to become a haven of Islāmic science and theology, with the Azhar college, first closed, then after 1250 transformed into a Sunnite establishment, as their centre.

The Nile valley, which was then in a flourishing economic condition,

Europe and the Near East c. 1100 (after the First Crusade)

MAP 3

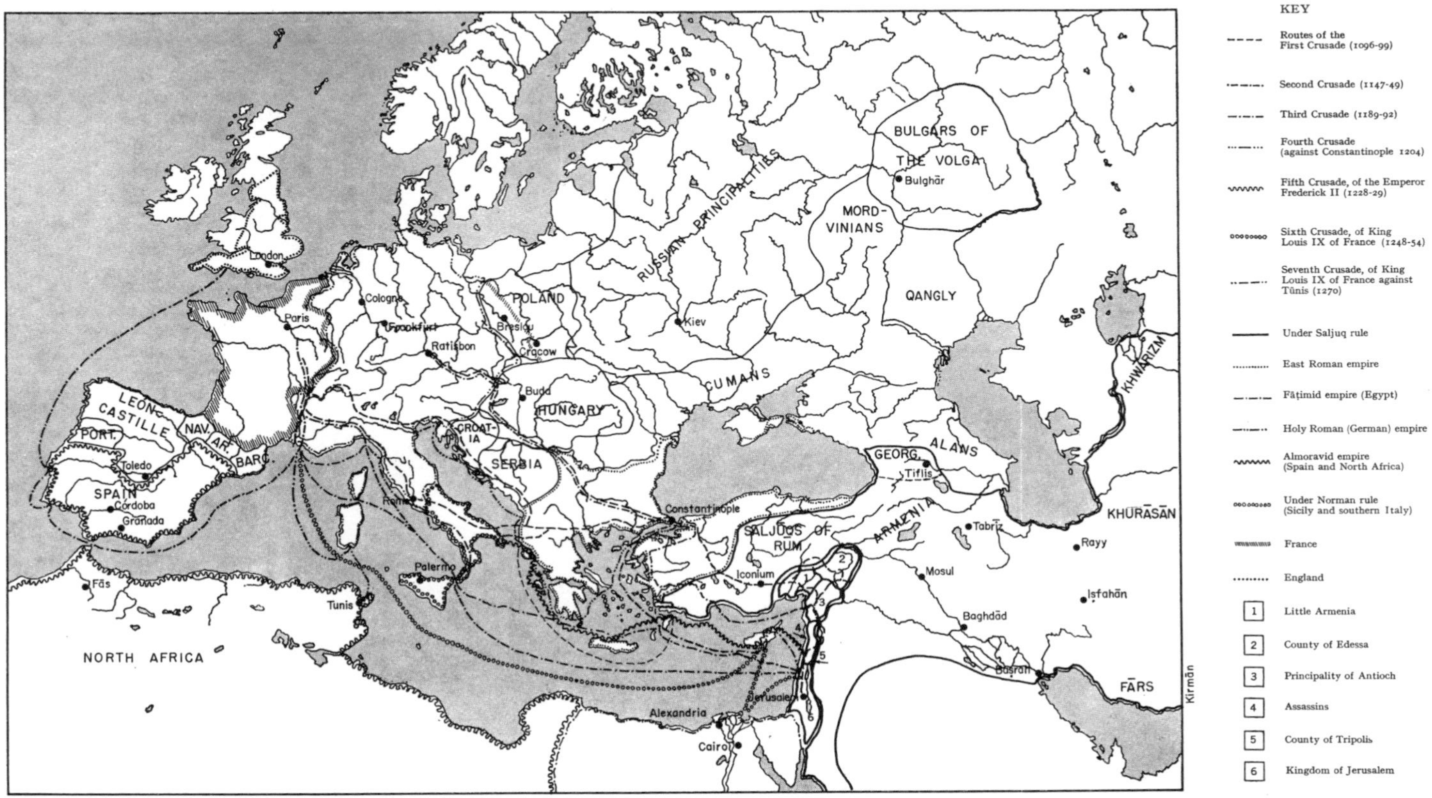

formed a base for Ṣalāḥ al-Dīn's successful offensive against the Crusader states. This he undertook both for deeply felt religious motives and with the political purpose of turning Palestine and Syria into a forward defence zone for the security of Egypt. The prestige of the Baghdād Caliphate remained as low as ever, while northern Mesopotamia was now partly in the hands of Ṣalāḥ al-Dīn's cousins and partly in those of other dynasties, none of them in a position to interfere with his plans. His former feudal overlord, Nūr al-Dīn, had died in 1174, and he soon eliminated the latter's son. Among his preparatory measures for the offensive was an understanding with the head of the Assassins of Syria, famed in the history of the Crusades as the *"Old Man of the Mountain"* (*Shaykh al-Jabal*). The Ismāʿīlites had stretched out their tentacles from Persia to Syria and succeeded in lodging themselves in the area west of the city of Ḥamā, whence they sent out emissaries who were a standing menace to Christians and Muslims alike. Ṣālāḥ al-Dīn also gained a foothold in South Arabia, at the city of Ṣanʿāʾ, and thither dispatched a branch of his family who ruled till 1228 and for a time extended their jurisdiction over the Sharīfs of Makkah (p. 68; the Sharīfate had been reestablished by *Qatādah*[1] around 1200). Finally, in 1187, he launched his assault against the Crusaders and at a favourable site near *Ḥiṭṭīn*, west of the Sea of Galilee, beat the King of Jerusalem who had advanced to meet him. A few months later he took Jerusalem, where Muslim worship was duly reinstated.

This event seemed likely to result in a new threat to his domain, in that it gave occasion to the Third Crusade under the powerful leadership of the Holy Roman (German) Emperor, Frederick Barbarossa; but the military potential of that expedition was much reduced by the Emperor's death in Asia Minor. Ṣalāḥ al-Dīn was thus able to keep possession of Jerusalem; and when peace was made in 1192, he only had to hand back a few coastal tracts to the Crusaders, who all along had held onto their main ports. Shortly afterwards, on March 4, 1193, he died, leaving behind him a realm which included Egypt, Syria and Palestine with the exceptions indicated, and Upper Mesopotamia almost to Mosul. Its dimensions were thus typical of the Egyptian empires which have appeared in the course of history, whenever the Nile valley has attained to political preeminence in the Near East.

---

[1] Ancestor of the King of Jordan and of the late King of ʿIrāq.

THE LATER AYYŪBIDS

Ṣalāḥ al-Dīn did nothing to ensure the continuance of his empire, but apportioned it before his death among his sons and brothers; and a series of civil wars naturally ensued. From these, however, his brother *al-Malik al-ʿĀdil* emerged in 1200 as virtually master of the former whole, controlling Egypt, Palestine and most of Syria and northern Mesopotamia, and receiving allegiance from branches of the family in Aleppo and South Arabia. Such being the circumstances, the Muslims were fortunate in that crusading enthusiasm in Western Europe had meanwhile worn off, and that the Franks did not make use of their coastal fortresses as points of departure for new incursions. They only chose to attack the Egyptian Delta city of *Damietta* (*Dimyāṭ*), on the correct view that their principal enemy must now be sought out in Egypt. Their forces seized, but could not long hold, the city; it never, indeed, proved possible until quite modern times to occupy Egypt from the sea (as the British did in 1882). Only a year later (1221), the Muslims expelled the Franks from this base on the Egyptian coast; and they were again fortunate in being able to do so, because Al-ʿMalik al-ʿĀdil, heedless of previous experience, had also divided his realm among his sons before his death in 1218. This had again led to fighting, in which one of them, *al-Malik al-Kāmil*, sought help against a hostile brother from Frederick II, Emperor of Germany and also King of Sicily. Although this brother had died before Frederick appeared on the scene, the Ayyūbid ruler ceded the city of Jerusalem, together with Bethlehem and Nazareth, to him in 1229.

Al-Malik al-Kāmil's death in 1238 was the signal for a complete disintegration of the Ayyūbid empire. As usual, rival contestants warred for the throne; and it was not thanks to them that Jerusalem fell once more, and for good, into Muslim hands in 1244 (p. 99), or that the Franks were driven off in 1249 after they had again seized Damietta, this time under the leadership of King Louis IX of France. This fratricidal strife made an end of the Ayyūbid régime, which all considered had been a time of economic well-being and thriving scholarly activity for both Egypt and Syria. The Sunnite faith, moreover, consolidated its hold on the Nile valley during the period.

In 1250, the Turkish and turkicized Caucasian troops who over the centuries had increasingly been recruited — or *"bought"*, whence the Arabic name *Mamlūks* — were able to seize control of Egypt. A new phase in the history of the Nile valley then began.

THE SALJŪQS IN ANATOLIA

Fissiparous tendencies like those seen in the Nile valley became conspicuous in other Islāmic territories also; and the protracted civil wars which they engendered were to weaken the military strength of the Muslim world in a degree which soon proved disastrous. Asia Minor may be taken as the first instance. When the unitary Saljūq empire disintegrated early in the 12th century (p. 87), one branch of the family emerged as an independent dynasty in Anatolia with the title *Sulṭāns of Rūm* (i.e. of the East Roman or "*Romaic*" lands). After the failure of an attempted intrusion into southern Armenia and the mountain borderland of northern Mesopotamia, their territory consisted mainly of the central Anatolian plateau, on which lay their seat, the city of Konya (Iconium). Successive rulers, especially *Qïlïj* (*Kïlïc*) *Arslān I* and *II* (1092-1106/7 and 1156-1192 respectively), built up quite a considerable power and also did much to foster cultural progress. They began systematically to intersperse the area with Turkish nomads, who gradually became sedentarized, and they vigorously promoted Islām and therewith the Turkish way of life. The result was manifest, though few details of the process are available [1]: a large part of the population of the area was alienated from Christianity and later from the Greek tongue also.

DEVELOPMENTS IN ASIA MINOR

During this time the Saljūqs of Rūm were involved in frequent hostilities with a second Muslim state, which had come into being round Malatya under the *Dānishmand* family and maintained its existence for several decades, though progressively on the decline. They also had many difficulties with certain small Greek principalities and still more with the Kingdom of Little Armenia, formed by fugitive Armenians in Cilicia. (Caucasian Armenia from the 7th to 10th centuries had generally been under nominal Muslim suzerainty, but had at times been partitioned into Muslim and Byzantine spheres of influence - in which case it was usually devastated by warfare between those two powers and among the native grandees). In these circumstances, the Saljūqs were incapable of preventing the gradual reoccupation of the southern margin of Asia Minor by the East Romans. Little Armenia and in 1137 Antioch passed under Byzantine control; and the domain of the Rūm-Saljūqs was thus

---

[1] See ALBERT HUGO WÄCHTER, *Der Verfall des Griechentums in Kleinasien in 14.* Jh., Leipzig 1903. Cf. OSMAN TURAN in "*İslâm Ansiklopedisi*" ,VI (1955), p. 613-663, 681-707.

practically cut off from the sea. They did not regain much freedom of movement till 1176, when the East Romans, having embarked on an offensive against the Turks, met with a crushing defeat near Myriokephalon on the *Chardak* (*Çardak*) *Pass*. From then on the Byzantine empire decayed steadily until in 1204, after the 4th Crusade, it was supplanted by the Latin empire, whose authority was virtually confined to Constantinople. The Rūm-Saljūqs conquered the south coast of Asia Minor in a number of campaigns and henceforth held it firmly in their possession. Sinop(e) on the Black Sea coast also fell into their hands, while in Trebizond (Trabzon) a separate Greek empire came into being. The Dānishmand state was finally overthrown in 1180; but Little Armenia held out, with the status (after 1198) of a vassal kingdom owing allegiance to the Holy Roman (German) Emperor.

At this period the might of the Rūm-Saljūqs reached its apogee. With the clearing of the south coast, Mediterranean commerce had access to their realm. Here too, however, as in the Ayyūbid empire, rapid disintegration set in when the country was apportioned among different princes. The Saljūq army, never too strong numerically in face of the indigenous Greek and Armenian elements, was much weakened by fratricidal struggles and degenerated into a rabble, still capable of subduing one insurrection of native malcontents but not of rising equal to the Mongol invasion in 1243.

QARA-KHITAI AND KHWĀRIZM-SHĀHS

This is the first mention of the nation which in the 13th century became the scourge of the Near East and embodied the last and most important westward thrust of the forces of Central Asia. In its elemental ferocity, the Mongol irruption undoubtedly came as a surprise; but foretastes had not been lacking. An account has already been given of the preceding immigrations of the Oğuz, the Qara-Khānids and the Saljūqs from Central Asia.

It has been seen how the Saljūq empire broke up at the beginning of the 12th century and how two independent Saljūq states were formed in northern and central Persia and at Kirmān. The last named of these never had more than local importance; but the remaining Persian lands were reunited into a compact state by the Saljūq prince *Sanjar*, who reigned from 1097. This wise and energetic ruler was the last significant representative of the Saljūq house in these parts; for several decades he succeeded in maintaining order throughout the extensive territory under his control. He was obliged, however, to admit the authority of a purported descendant of the Ṣaffārids in Sīstān (p. 77) and to recognize a former governor of Khwārizm, *Muḥammad*, as a more or less independent ruler in that province with the title of *Khwārizm-Shāh*. The attitude of the latter, and still more of his son *Atsïz* (1128-1156), towards Sanjar was for the most part unfriendly. To free himself from the bond of Sanjar's overlordship, Atsïz finally called in a Mongolian tribe, the *Qara-Khitai*, from Transoxiana where they had settled after being expelled from China. (The Khāns of the *Khitai* under the name of "*Liao*" had ruled northern China from 916 to 1125). In 1141, on the far side of the Oxus, this tribe inflicted a grave defeat on Sanjar.

The triumph over the forces of Islām in the east thus won by a non-Muslim chieftain (whose fellow tribesmen were in part Nestorian Christians) received added colour from various romantic fables and from a misinterpretation of the title *Gürkhān* borne by the heads of the Qara-Khitai, and so gave rise to the legend of "*Prester John*", the imaginary Christian potentate in Central Asia who would clear the way for the downfall of the Muslims in alliance with the West. This legend will be re-encountered later.

From their seat at Balāsāghūn, the Qara-Khitai built up a powerful empire, stretching from the Yenisei to Balkh and eastern Turkistān: and the Khwārizm-Shāhs were now obliged to submit to their suzerainty.

KHWĀRIZM-SHĀHS AND GHŪRIDS

Although Sanjar succeeded in rallying from this blow, he suffered another defeat in 1153 at the hands of the Turkish Oğuz tribe, who had burst upon north eastern Īrān in flight before the Qara-Khitai. They took him prisoner, and shortly after he had regained his liberty he died. This virtually ruined the authority of the Saljūqs in Persia; Sanjar's successors, who reigned till 1194, were puppets in the ensuing clashes between a number of different states. The new Khwārizm-Shāh, *Īl Arslān*, whose reign began in 1156, enjoyed effective independence; and a hill tribe, the *Ghūrids*, in 1150 drove the Ghaznavids from the last remnant of their Īrānian domain to the accompaniment of shocking atrocities, Ghaznah being completely destroyed and its inhabitants massacred. Thenceforward the Ghaznavids were confined to north west India (Vol. II, chapter 6). The Ghūrids were soon overtaken by their own doom. They sought to intervene in a civil war in Khwārizm, but were defeated in 1174; and in 1204, on their retreat after another reverse, they were almost completely wiped out by the Qara-Khitai.

The western half of Persia could now breathe more freely. It was in the power of the Khwārizm-Shāh *Takash*, who had definitely gained control in 1193 and was succeeded by his son *Muḥammad II* in 1200. But the pause vouchsafed to Īrān was of short duration. In addition to civil wars, Muḥammad undertook an offensive against the dynasty of Atabegs in Āẕarbāyjān, who had held the reins in that province for close on 100 years and were now represented by a highly efficient prince named *Özbeg*. Meanwhile the ʿAbbāsid house, after several centuries of political inanity, had again produced a scion with a measure of aptitude for statecraft. This was the Caliph *al-Nāṣir* (1180-1225). He contrived to raise central and southern Mesopotamia to a position of some importance under his sceptre and then proceeded to intervene in the western borderland of Persia and later also in Āẕarbāyjān.

THE CALIPH AL-NĀṢIR

The resultant clashes were of little military consequence, but are interesting because both sides looked for support from the Shīʿite elements which had taken root in Persia and to some extent elsewhere during the past centuries. While the Assassin state of Alamūt, though still in existence, was no longer of much importance, Twelver Shīʿism had now definitely emerged as the strongest Shīʿite denominational grouping. The Caliph could only use an indirect approach in his attempt to win the support of the Shīʿites in Mesopotamia, where from the outset they were always numerous, especially in the south. He attempted to exploit for his own purposes a fraternity called the *Futūwah*,[1] which had apparently originated among the frontier troops and displayed conspicuous Shīʿite tendencies. Its members not only practised secret initiation and dedication ceremonies, exchanged widespread mutual hospitality and held convivial gatherings, all highly reminiscent of the freemasonry of a later age; they also, in their initial phase at least, cherished an ideal of piety modelled on the personality of ʿAlī. These societies did not, however, develop into real military orders. Subsequently, in the 13th and 14th centuries, they spread most widely in Asia Minor, where they later merged with the Janissaries, the Bektashi *darvīsh* order and the guilds. While the Caliph could only make indirect use of Shīʿite movements, the Khwārizm-Shāh had a counter-Caliph of the Family of the Prophet installed in 1217 and took steps to prepare for a military reckoning with Baghdād.

[1] Meaning roughly *chivalry*.

This clash never actually occurred. According to later and not necessarily accurate accounts, the hard-put Caliph addressed himself to one of the tribes then newly arrived in Central Asia, thus following a course already taken by several Muslim potentates before him and notably by the Khwārizm-Shāhs against the Saljūqs. This time, however, the attack launched by the particular Central Asian tribe was to have consequences far surpassing anything that had previously been experienced. Destiny now confronted Islām with a nation whose impact on the evolution of the Muslim lands was to be absolutely fundamental: namely, the Mongols.

THE DOWNFALL OF THE CALIPHATE

Once again, however, a breathing space was granted to the Caliphate. The first sweep of the Central Asian conquerors only hit eastern and northern Persia (1218-22) and then veered past the eastward end of the Caucasus to southern Russia. Jingiz Khān's death in 1227, and the internal reorganization of the Mongol empire which then became necessary, secured a forty years' respite for the countries of the Near East. The Caliphs, however, no more thought of looking around for allies against the impending danger from the east than the Russian princes had thought of forming a defence league after the defeat of their own and the Cuman armies on the Kalka in 1223. The Khwārizm-Shāh, chief opponent of the Caliphs, was overthrown by the Mongol advance; and his son *Jalāl al-Dīn Mangubirdī* (*Mengüberdi*), after an adventurous but not really formidable career as a guerrilla-leader against the Mongols, was finally murdered by a Kurd in 1231.

The feeble Caliphs who followed al-Nāṣir after 1225 thought that they could safely content themselves with a contemplative life. Neither the surrender of Jerusalem to the Emperor Frederick II in 1229 (p. 94), nor the forced submission of the Saljūqs of Asia Minor to Mongol overlordship in 1243, nor the seizure of Jerusalem by remnants of Jalāl al-Dīn Mangūbirdī's troops in 1244, disturbed them from their complacency. The Caliph *al-Mustaʿṣim*, who succeeded in 1242, was thus wholly unprepared for the doom which awaited him. In 1253, a redoubtable army began to assemble in Transoxiana under *Hūlāgū* (*Hülegü*), a grandson of Jingiz Khān and a brother of the Great Khān *Möngke* (*Mangū*) who reigned in China from 1251 to 1259. Reinforced from all parts of the Mongol empire, this army pushed irresistibly through Persia; the only delay experienced was in the reduction of the Assassin fortress of Alamūt. By 1257, Mesopotamia was directly threatened. Such was still the religious prestige of the Caliphate that Hūlāgū, notwithstanding the fanatical insistence of his learned Shī'ite adviser *Naṣīr al-Dīn Ṭūsī*, endeavoured to reach an amicable accord with the Baghdād government. The Caliph, dazzled by the brilliance of the past and ill counselled by his staff, would not hear of an agreement; nor was he willing to let his treasures be used to finance the recruitment of a large army. Events thus continued along their fated course; after a short siege Baghdād fell into the hands of the Mongols on February 10, 1258. The Caliph was compelled to disclose the secret whereabouts of his treasures; then, ten days later, he was done to death by envelopment in a carpet. The shedding of sovereign blood was thereby avoided. The Mongols, who were themselves Shamanists or Nestorian Christians, proceeded against the city's inhabitants with the utmost severity; plunder and rapine stalked the streets, and only the Christians and the Shī'ites — at the behests of Hūlāgū's Nestorian wife Doquz and the Shī'ite Naṣīr al-Dīn respectively — were spared to any extent.

Thus fell the once mighty 'Abbāsid Caliphate, after a span of 500 years. The symbol of the unity of Sunnite Islām was destroyed; but so far advanced was the decomposition of the Muslim commonwealth into separate states that in the confusion of the Mongol inrush nobody raised a hand to fight for the 'Abbāsids. In Egypt the Mamlūks, persistent and unbeaten adversaries of the Mongols, did indeed make a pretence of continuing the dynasty so that they might pass off as legal heirs to the rights of the Caliphate; but this had little effect beyond the frontiers of the country. Islāmic unity under the Princes of the Believers was dead, and would never be resuscitated in that form. A page in the history of the Islāmic East had been turned.

SPAIN

THE SIGNIFICANCE OF SPANISH ISLĀM

A land lying on the periphery of the Muslim world, which led a distinct existence and was in general but loosely involved in developments affecting the rest of the Islāmic domain, will now again receive attention; and assuredly Spain presents a most fascinating picture. Together with adjacent Portugal, which first took shape as a separate state during the Islāmic epoch, Spain is the only country of the Roman-German world (in the phrase of LEOPOLD VON RANKE) which — at least in great part — experienced several centuries of government by Muslim rulers and whose present culture displays significant traces of Islāmic influence. In Sicily, the one territory comparable with Spain in this respect, no such surviving after-effects are visible today. During this epoch, moreover, Spain was the chief centre of intellectual exchange between the medieval Christian and the oriental civilizations — the meeting place of two worlds [1]. This seems a sufficient reason to make a general view of its history desirable for the student of Western as well as of Islāmic mental development. Spanish Islām found a classic historian in the Netherlander REINHART DOZY (1820-1879); his fruitful researches have formed a starting point for all subsequent investigators, outstanding among whom are EVARISTE LÉVI-PROVENÇAL (1894-1956) and, notably in the field of intellectual life, the Spanish savant MIGUEL ASÍN PALACIOS (1871-1944). To their writings everyone interested in the story of Western Islām must refer without fail.

SPAIN AFTER THE MUSLIM CONQUEST

The second great wave of Muslim expansion, set in motion at the beginning of the 8th century, covered Spain and spread far beyond, to central France, Provence and certain points in Italy. Though the vanguards of the conquest were repulsed, the greater part of Spain remained in firm occupation as a domain of Islām on European soil (p. 43 ff.).

---

[1] Cf. UGO MONNERET DE VILLARD, *Lo studio dell'Islam in Europe nel XII e XIII secolo*, Vatican City, 1944 (*Studi e testi*, 110); E. S. PROCTER, *The scientific works at the court of Alfonso X of Castille*, in the *Modern Language Review*, XL (1945), p. 12 ff.

Communication with the then capital of the empire of the Caliphs at Damascus was insecure and nearly always depended on the land route through North Africa, command of the sea being generally held by the Byzantines and by Westerners of various nationalities. The internal troubles which soon beset the Umayyad empire, and the various Berber risings in North Africa, helped to detach Spain from the practical control of the Caliphs and to put her on her own feet. The Iberian peninsula, known as a whole to the Arabs as *al-Andalus* after the Vandals dwelling in the south, was colonized by both Arabs and Berbers. Their numbers were certainly not large; but among them, significantly, were certain sections of the South Arabian tribes loyal to the Umayyads. It is therefore no matter for suprise that when that dynasty had been overthrown in 750, one of its few surviving princes fixed his gaze on the west and after a brief sojourn in what is now Morocco made his way to Spain in 755 to win himself a new dominion at the head of those tribes. This prince was *ʿAbd al-Raḥmān I*, a man of such audacity and steadfastness of purpose that he was called "The Falcon of the Quraysh" (and reputedly first so named by the ʿAbbāsid Caliph himself): a scion of the Umayyads who restored his family's rule in the west and founded the Umayyad dynasty of Spain, which over a period of nearly 300 years guided the Islāmic realm in that land to a peak of political and economic greatness and to a high pitch of intellectual and artistic creativity.

MUSLIMS AND CHRISTIANS

The interchange of ideas which took place in Spain between the ruling Muslim Arabs and Berbers and the subject Christian Spaniards or Portuguese and Jews had a character of its own. In this particular conquered land, Islām did not come in the course of the Middle Ages to prevail as the religion of the majority; here (and in Sicily) alone, the great mass of the subject people remained loyal to the Christian faith and were able to keep intact their native culture and language. In all the other lands which were under Muslim rule during the same centuries, the Prophet's religion came, as is well known, to be embraced by the great majority of the population; and in the lands already inhabited by Semitic or partly Semitic peoples, such as Egypt, the Arabic language also won the day. Such pertinacity in the Christian faith is not seen elsewhere till several centuries later, among the Greeks and Balkan Slavs under Turkish rule. (The Armenians, Georgians and Russians lived under their own princes and are not comparable). Explanations of this phenomenon can only be conjectural. While the Spaniards may be presumed to have possessed an instinct of religious conservatism, the theological schisms which rent the Near East may perhaps have made its populations more responsive to the simple and easily intelligible basic teachings of Islām. In Egypt and Persia at least, the proportion of conquerors to subjects was certainly no higher than in Spain; yet 90 percent of the inhabitants of the Nile valley and practically all those of Persia became Muslims, though in the latter country Islām had to admit certain peculiar modifications and reinterpretations. Another factor, and certainly one of importance, was that oriental Christianity did not have a focus or (except in Nubia and Abyssinia, with which links were weak) a body of fellow-communicants to look to outside Muslim-controlled territory, whereas the Spaniards and later the Balkan peoples could look to such rallying points and lived alongside countries of similar faith and denominations.

INTELLECTUAL AND ECONOMIC LIFE

Relations with the religiously disparate subject population thus played a vital part in Spanish Muslim history, and much more conspicuously so than in the east (though there too this was at first by no means a negligible factor). Nevertheless, the Umayyad régime, established in 756 with headquarters at *Córdoba*, was strong enough during the first two hundred and more years of its existence to overcome the resultant tensions. In the cultural field it very soon earned distinction, mainly for *belles lettres*. On Spanish soil, Arabic poetry acquired a particular personal note unheard at the time in other Islāmic lands. One of the earliest to voice it was none other than ʿAbd al-Rahmān I, when he sang praises to the first palm-tree brought by him to Spain as a living souvenir of his Syrian homeland. ʿAbd al-Raḥmān's importation was, incidentally, the forbear of the very important date-growing industry of medieval Spain; and the tree became a symbol of the Islāmic Arab civilization, whose territorial range, indeed, largely coincides with the habitat of the palm, as a glance at the map will show [1]. In Spain, as in Sicily, the Arabs were responsible for important agricultural progress. They introduced rice growing, orange-planting and several other new orchard and garden crops. They also excelled in the handicrafts and did much to promote mining. In the opinion of Adolf Friedrich, Count von Schack, who was the first Western scholar to make a systematic study of Spanish Arabic

[1] Cf. the map in Brockhaus's *Konversationslexikon* (1930/35 ed.) accompanying the article on dates (*Dattel*).

literature and the translator of many fine German versions from it, the individualist poetry of Arab Spain reflects something of the lyric art of the Romance languages and of the human spirit of the West. In its abundant production, influences of Western thinking are certainly apparent, particularly in the court poetry. This latter, by some channel which can no longer be traced in detail, probably influenced the poetry of the troubadours, as recent investigations have redemonstrated [1]. In this as in other ways the two great civilizations of the Mediterranean, each in several fundamental respects a child of classical antiquity, made contact with one another. In architecture, no less than in poetry, the art of the Spanish Moors combined Eastern elements with indigenous and Visigothic components from the West — for instance in the characteristic horse-shoe arches and the peculiar square minarets still to be seen in the Giralda tower of Seville, and in the renowned mosque of nineteen aisles at Córdoba which took more than two hundred years (785-997) to build and now serves as a cathedral church.

THEOLOGY

Equally peculiar was the position of theology within Spanish Islām. The doctrinal problems which had convulsed but sharpened the wits of the eastern Muslims went almost unheeded in Spain, as also in Egypt. (In Western Europe during the early middle ages, large-scale "heresies" were likewise unknown, from the Arians down to the Albigensians). After the failure of a local school of Islāmic Law, the Spaniards adhered to the relatively rigorous interpretation of the Mālikite school. It seems as if the *genius loci*, or the national spirit, had analogous effects on both Islām and Christianity; and the mutual enmity of the two religions must certainly have reinforced the conformism which became so marked on both sides.

From this rigid religious standpoint, inferences were drawn which to us seem deplorable but to the contemporary mind were self-evident: for instance when the library of the Spanish Umayyad Caliph *Ḥakam II*, reputedly one of extraordinary wealth, was destroyed volume by volume, not even theologically unimpeachable works being spared; or when after the final extinction of Moorish rule in the peninsula great numbers of Arabic books were burnt.

---

[1] See note on p. 88.

CULTURAL RELATIONS WITH THE OCCIDENT

While the theological literature produced in the Iberian peninsula was limited for several centuries to strictly orthodox works of scant intellectual and historical interest to the modern student, this shortcoming was offset by a remarkable growth of scientific and philosophical literature, born of revulsion against a theology which was becoming over-scholastic and of preference for spheres where the heritage of the ancients was accessible and the workings of the individual mind were allowed free expression. It was above all in Spain, and especially at the university of Granada and the city of Saragossa (Christian after 1230), that recensions and Latin translations were made of Arabic works on the natural sciences and of Greek scientific works taken over by the Arabs (p. 56 f.), thus providing the Christian Occident with its first perceptions of Arabic thought and an enhanced insight into the erudition of antiquity. Details of this process must be sought in histories of science. The philosophy of Muslim Spain, whose great development came when Mālikite theology had begun to decline, will be discussed in connection with the religious upheavals of the later period (p. 111).

ʿABD AL-RAḤMĀN I

All these developments depended on the political setting. After installing the Umayyad power in Spain in 755, *ʿAbd al-Raḥmān I* had to sustain a number of internal struggles with contumacious governors and other officials before he could effectively establish his authority and assert his independence from the ʿAbbāsids at Baghdād. His task was made easier by the Berber insurrection in North Africa, which raged from 740 to 761 and greatly impeded overland communications with the east. On the other hand, he did not succeed in stamping out the Christian states of León and Navarre in the mountain country of northern Spain. These constituted bases for the unremitting Christian countermovement against the Muslims, and doubtless also a hope for the Christians living under Muslim rule. Probably for this reason the latter were generally considered unreliable and seldom employed in governmental posts. In consequence the rate of lapse from Christianity remained comparatively low. Conversions to Islām occurred nevertheless, on a scale which cannot be determined with any precision; and as a result much Celto-Iberian blood was added to the veins of the Arabs and Berbers, and a considerable cultural stimulus was thrown in.

THE LATER UMAYYADS

ʿAbd al-Raḥmān made himself master of the country as far as Barcelona and Saragossa. An intrusion in 777-8 by Charlemagne, who had been called in by the disaffected local governors (whether he was also in league with the ʿAbbāsids is uncertain), came to an abortive end when a great part of his army was destroyed in the defile of Roncesvalles, made famous by the *Chanson de Roland*. By the time of ʿAbd al-Raḥmān's death in 788, his régime was firmly grounded, and his successors *Hishām I* (788-796) and *Ḥakam I* (796-822) were in a position to give the territory external and internal security and to patronize cultural exertions. In the middle of the 9th century, this calm was threatened by a movement of Christian zealots in quest of martyrdom, which disturbed the harmonious contractual symbiosis of the two religious groups and sent a fair number of Christians to freely chosen deaths. Further serious difficulties for the Umayyad state arose from the side of its Muslim citizens. Separatist intrigues at Toledo led in 852 to the formation in that city of an aristocratic republic which lasted for 80 years; and various malcontent elements sprang into revolt — Berbers with grievances of a national stamp and others with social and religious complaints. The most important was a rebellion led by *Ibn Ḥafṣūn* and his sons, who consolidated themselves in the mountains near Málaga and kept the realm in turmoil from 894 to 928. Clashes between Arabs and Berbers were frequent and, as in Mesopotamia and Egypt, the imported slave troops formed groups of pretorian guards and became completely insubordinate. All this seriously weakened the power of the Umayyad state. The pretorians in this case were mostly Slavs taken captive and sold to Spain from eastern Germany, with a minority of Berber prisoners of war and Mediterranean coast-dwellers seized on plundering expeditions; the principal market for the slaves from central Europe was then at Verdun, and the purveyors were mainly Jewish merchants. These mercenary forces were generally known by the Arabic name for the Slavs who formed their chief component, *Ṣaqlab*, plural *Ṣaqālib*, whence are derived the French and German words *esclave* and *Sklave* with the same intrusive *k*, dropped in the English *slave*.

ʿABD AL-RAḤMĀN III AND THE FALL OF THE DYNASTY

In the course of these troubles, the Christian states of the north, though they too had plenty of internal discords, found opportunities to advance their frontiers to the south. Barcelona had already fallen into

Christian hands in 801. From 843 onwards, the Normans made repeated attacks, and a grave threat appeared from the south where the Fāṭimids in an attempt to extend their control over the western part of North Africa had eliminated the hitherto evenly balanced local dynasties. This on several occasions forced the Umayyads to intervene, until the deflection of the Fāṭimids to Egypt eliminated any danger from them in the second half of the 10th century and thereafter. Peace in the main prevailed abroad and at home during the reign of *'Abd al-Raḥmān III*, mightiest of the Spanish Umayyads (912-961). When tensions arose between León and Castile over a disputed royal succession, he played the part of mediator between Christian states. As a retort to the Fāṭimid claims to the Caliphate, and as a clear sign that his realm had achieved a degree of civilization and military strength abreast of Baghdād, he assumed in 929 the title of *Caliph*; his predecessors had been content to use the term *Amīr*. Compared with the contemporary 'Abbāsid state, helpless before its Turkish soldiery and the Būyid menace and culturally already on the wane, Spain was in fact much the brighter star; the cultural movements outlined above had now reached or were fast approaching their zenith. 'Abd al-Raḥmān's son and successor *Ḥakam II* (961-976) successfully maintained the country's high political standing, except that in 973 he had to abandon Fraxinetum (La Garde Freinet/Var) in Provence, a fortress held by the Muslims since 891 whence they pillaged and intimidated wide stretches of southern France and the Alps. Ḥakam II was also the chief collector of the celebrated library, whose destruction in the next reign has been alluded to above. Under his son *Hishām II*, who came to the throne as a minor and had been brought up to take little interest in anything but theology, the authority of the state declined, especially as the regency jointly exercised by his Basque mother *Aurora* (known to the Arabs by the translated name *Ṣubḥ*) and her minister and favourite *al-Manṣūr*[1] was not acknowledged without cavil by the grandees. Al-Manṣūr was nevertheless an efficient administrator and an outstanding military leader, who fought fifty-two campaigns against the Christians, humbled León and retook Barcelona by storm in 985. Being anxious to make his power hereditary and so institute a ministerial dynasty like those which were such a feature in the east (p. 51), he took steps before his death in 1002 to bequeath to his son the office of *ḥājib* (as wazīrs were called in Spain following the ancient title in use under the Syrian Umayyads). The displeasure of the grandees now knew no bounds. When al-Manṣūr's son met his end in 1008, the

[1] Spanish *Almanzor*.

sovereign prestige of the incompetent and obscurantist Caliph Hishām II was also dragged down. He was twice deposed, in 1009 and 1013, and followed by a rapid succession of Umayyad pretenders, no one of whom could make any mark, until in 1031 the Umayyad dynasty was ejected altogether.

PETTY STATES

Muslim Spain now broke up into a multiplicity of small states under their own princelings (*Mulūk al-Ṭawā'if*). At Córdoba an aristocratic republic took control, as earlier at Toledo; and Berbers and Slavs carved out domains for themselves with swiftly changing frontiers. Among all these petty states, that of the *'Abbādids* of Seville (1026-1085) achieved most importance. At a time when the Christian Spaniards were recovering strength and some of their states were amalgamating, the Muslims were crippling one another more and more. For the first time the Christians were now in a military position to take the initiative, and after a long siege they captured Toledo for good in 1085 — an event which has already been noted as constituting in Oriental estimation the first move of the Crusades, that is, of the Occidental offensive against Islām.

Intellectual life continued to flourish in Spain throughout the 11th century, and as in the east the setting up of so many different princely courts enabled savants and poets to seek protection and reward first at one, then at another. The novel tendencies which appeared in Spanish thought during the 12th century resulted from a transformation in the political aspect of the country.

THE ALMORAVIDES IN NORTH AFRICA

For an understanding of this change, a glimpse must be cast at affairs in North Africa as they had developed since the conquest of Egypt by the Fāṭimids in the middle of the 10th century. Following that event, the western part of North Africa had slipped out of their control and various native dynasties had established themselves in the area — — *Zīrids* in Tūnis, *Ḥammādids* in Algeria, etc. These had their mutual tussles, but an approximate balance was maintained between them until the middle of the 11th century, when the immigration of the more or less uncivilized Arab tribes of the *Banū Hilāl* and *Banū Sulaym* wrought havoc in Tunisia and much of the land beyond. Around the same time, a reform movement inspired by Islām began to spread, without at first attracting much attention, among a clan of the great *Ṣanhājah* group of Berber tribes. Its aim was a return to the doctrines of primitive Islām together with social reform and reduction of the pecuniary obligations imposed by contemporary governments. Its founders had no great success at first and withdrew to a fortified hermitage on an island in the River Senegal (which name is cognate with Ṣanhājah). The Arabic term for such hermitages being *ribāṭ*, they became known as "*al-Murābiṭūn*", something like "the Hermits". This party first acquired political importance around 1056 under the leadership of *Yūsuf ibn Tāshfīn*, who with the aid of his wife *Zaynab* developed an outstanding capacity for organization and also displayed no mean talents as a military leader. As a new headquarters, he founded the city of Marrakech (Marrākush) in 1062, and by 1082 he had subdued the whole of the present-day Morocco and Algeria. Other Murābiṭ troops moved south to spread Islām among the negroes of West Africa.

THE ALMORAVIDES IN SPAIN

These events occurred at the time when the Islāmic states in Spain were having to bear the full weight of the defensive struggle against the Christian countries. After the fall of Toledo in 1085, their position was so precarious that they turned for help to the new North African empire of the Murābiṭs. Yūsuf responded to their appeal and in alliance with the Spanish Muslims defeated the Castilians at the battle of *Sacralias* (*Zallāqah*) in 1086, in consequence of which the Christians lost extensive territories in the east of the peninsula, including Valencia and the Saragossa district. As soon, however, as the Spanish Muslims felt some relief from the strain, dissensions again broke out among their princes and new opportunities to strike were thus offered to the Christians. In the resultant fighting the renowned *Cid Campeador* (d. 1099) played a prominent part as an auxiliary on both sides — by no means only on that of the Christians. Yūsuf took advantage of the situation to intervene once more, and having received a favourable ruling from the Muslim legal authorities he proceeded this time to eliminate the petty princes from Spain and govern the country in his own name. The word used to designate his religious following, *al-Murābiṭūn*, was modified in Spanish to *Almoravides* and applied also to his dynasty. It did not last long. After his death in 1106, control of affairs passed during the reign of his son *'Alī* into the hands of an ultra-orthodox Islāmic party, which even condemned the works of the theologian al-Ghazzālī (p. 83), then just becoming known in Spain, and called for a complete religious reaction. The Christians of Spain, a section of whom had by now adopted Arabic as their daily speech and hence were termed "arabicized" (*Mustaʿrib*, Spanish *Mozarabe*), had also to face many sufferings, some of them being deported to Morocco. A number of Jews chose likewise to emigrate, including the Judeo-Arab theologian and philosopher *Maimonides* (1135-1204; p. 111), who was born at Córdoba and later became court physician to Ṣalāḥ al-Dīn in Egypt, where he died.

THE ALMOHADES

The resurgence of religious reaction under the Almoravides encountered opposition from a new reforming party among the Berbers. *Muḥammad ibn Tūmart* (d. 1128), son of a Berber mosque-janitor, had studied at Baghdād and acquainted himself there with the Ashʿarite theological principles (p. 73); as against the literalist Qur'ānic exegesis of the Mālikite school still prevalent in the west, he stood for a more intellectual interpretation as taught by al-Ash'arī's disciples. His followers, from their profession of the unity of God (*Tawḥīd*), took the name *al-Muwaḥḥidūn*. The centre from which they diffused their doctrine was in the Moroccan Atlas; and in the early decades of the 12th century their influence and power spread far afield until, in the three or four years following the death of the Almoravide ruler ʿAlī in 1143, they were able to seize that dynasty's entire North African domain. Meanwhile, Muslim Spain once more fell apart into a number of small states. The Christians had captured Saragossa in 1118; and in a new move, undertaken in conjunction with the Second Crusade, they gained possession in 1147 of Lisbon, a regional capital around which the future Portugal took shape. An occasion was thus presented to the Muwaḥḥids under their leader *ʿAbd al-Mu'min*, an associate of the founder of the movement with considerable military and theological talents, to step across into Spain. In Spanish their name became *Almohades*. Between 1146 and 1154 the principal Muslim cities of that country — Córdoba, Almería, Granada — fell into their hands, and in 1163 Tūnis was joined to the African part of their empire. ʿAbd al-Mu'min's son and later his grandson carried on his forward policy in Spain, and the latter, *Yaʿqūb al-Manṣūr*, dealt a blow to the Christians at Alarcos in 1195; but this success was more than offset by the great Christian victory at *Las Navas de Tolosa (Ḥiṣn al-ʿUqāb)* in 1212. From then on the power of the Almohades crumbled away, especially after the rise of a rival Berber dynasty, the *Marīnids*, in Morocco; and in 1275

MAP 4

Islam in Spain, from 711 to 1492

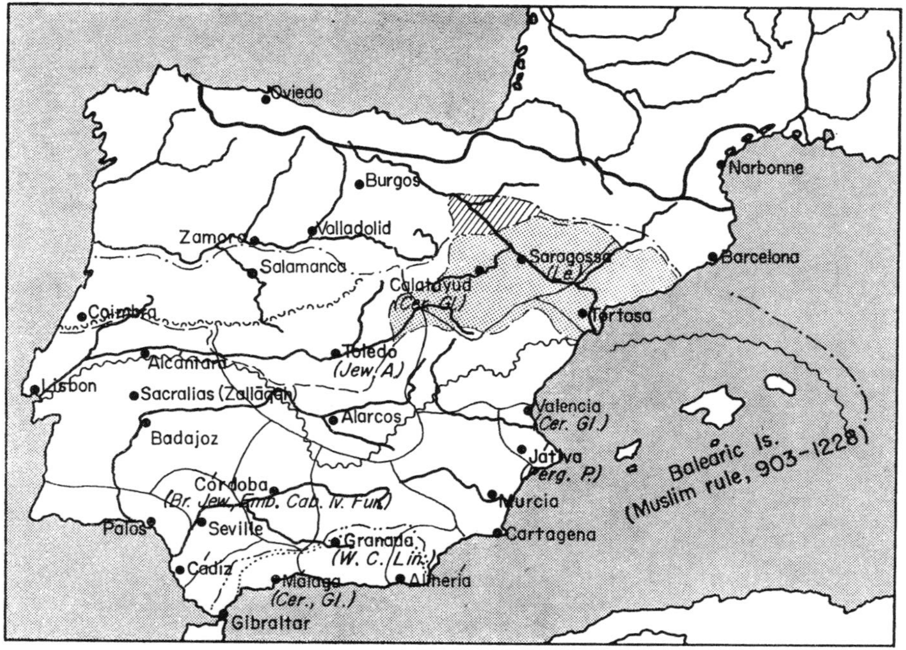

KEY

- Limit of Islāmic occupation after 711-713
- Limit of Islāmic occupation at the fall of the Umayyads, 1021
- Frontiers of the Muslim petty states (Mulūk al-Ṭawā'if), 1031-1085
- Domain of the Banū Hūd on the middle Ebro, 1014-1041
- Limit of Islāmic occupation c. 1072
- Almoravide territory after 1085
- Lands held by vassal princes under the Almoravides
- Almohade territory 1130-1269
- The state of Granada in 1257
- The state of Granada in the 15th cent. (till 1492)

A	= Arms
Br.	= Brocade
Cab.	= Cabinet making
Cer.	= Ceramies
C	= Cotton goods
Emb.	= Embossed work
Fur	= Fur dressing
Gl.	= Glass
Iv.	= Ivory work
Jew.	= Jewelry
Le.	= Leather goods
Linn.	= Linen goods
P	= Paper
Par.	= Parchment
W.	= Woollen goods

its last vestiges were destroyed. They had evacuated Spain as far back as 1225. Tunisia had broken loose in 1259 under another independent Berber dynasty, the *Ḥafṣids*, who assumed the title of *Caliph* and for a brief spell were recognized as such in Makkah and Egypt; they ruled the country till 1574.

THE RISE OF ARABIC AND JEWISH PHILOSOPHY

The Almohades hold an important place in history, for more than one reason. The concentration in their vigorous hands of all political power in North Africa and Muslim Spain made possible the final absorption of the Berbers into Islām and delayed the advance of the Christian Spanish states for several decades. At the same time they made it possible for the Spanish Muslim mind to grow in greater freedom. It has already been seen how the development of philosophy in Spain had hitherto been held back under the fetters of Mālikite orthodoxy. When the Almohades did away with the exclusive jurisdiction of that school, things changed. In the field of philosophy, Muslim Spain was to show achievements which elicited the interest of the occidental Christians and profoundly affected their ideas. Here in Spain, *Ibn Rushd* (1126-1198), known to Western Europe as *Averroës* and celebrated also as a physician, now worked out in reaction against al-Ghazzālī a philosophical system which had great repercussions in the West, notably on the Emperor Frederick II. Here too, the mystic speculations of *Ibn 'Arabī* (1165-1240) found currency, and *Ibn Ṭufayl* (c. 1108-1185) composed on lines first set by Ibn Sīnā a much esteemed utopian romance, *Ḥayy ibn Yaqẓān* (*"The Living, Son of the Awakening"*), in which he pleaded the competence of the human mind to attain independently to higher knowledge.

To this intellectual growth, an important contribution was made in the philosophical field by the Jewish inhabitants of Spain. In close connection with the parallel development among the Muslims, they woke to an intellectual life of their own. Already, in the philosophical and theological dissertations of *Salomo ben Gabirol (Avicebron,* c. 1020-c. 1070), and then of *Maimonides* who, as seen, was exiled from Spain with his father (p. 110), they had produced work of lasting intellectual value. Later there appeared the Hebrew imitations of Ḥarīrī's *Maqāmāt* by *Yuda ben Salomo Kharīsī* (d. before 1235). In general, Muslims and Jews in Spain lived side by side without friction, and at times Jews held high official positions and even that of *ḥājib* (wazīr). Such anti-Jewish manifestations as occured were induced by motives similar to those behind the anti-Christian outbursts in Egypt and elsewhere described earlier. It was in Spain that Jews first made contact with the intellectual life of Europe and that the first sprouts appeared of a Jewish school of learning, which later shifted to France and Italy and afterwards long had its centre in Germany. The Christians, on the other hand, never played in Spain such a part in Arabic intellectual life or in the Muslim administration as they had done in Egypt and western Asia. The explanation of this is to be found in the general political situation, which was such that they were bound to appear as partisans of the hostile states in the north of the country.

VOYAGERS AND HISTORIANS

In the field of travel narratives and geographical descriptions, the western lands of Islām came equally to the fore during these centuries and produced two outstanding minds: *Ibn Jubayr* of Valencia (1145-1228), who wrote a most vivid account of the Muslim countries of the Mediterranean and also of Sicily, and *Ibn Baṭṭūṭah* of Tangier (1304-1377), who in twenty five years of wandering reached the Volga, India and thence the coast of China. No less high-ranking in another field are the historians *Ibn al-Khaṭīb* (1317-1374), annalist of Granada, and *Ibn Khaldūn* of Tūnis. The latter, in the Prolegomena (*Muqaddimah*) of his historical treatise, for the first time in the Islāmic world propounded a philosophy of history and made a sociological survey of the development of the Muslim peoples; and in the section of his work on the history of the Berbers, he was the first to present a monographic study of a single national group. Each of these historians resided in Spain but had to move to Africa, and Ibn Khaldūn betook himself as far as Egypt, where he held a high judicial post until his death (1332-1406).

THE END OF MOORISH RULE

The closing period of Moorish rule in the Iberian peninsula is best known to us Occidentals for a last blossoming of the plastic arts. We owe to it that consummate masterpiece of the architecture and craftsmanship of western Islām, the *Alhambra*, i.e. the "*Red* (*Castle*)" at *Granada*, which has remained in almost perfect preservation and has been described in detail by many writers. This castle was the residence of a family of rulers who emerged from the wreck of the Spanish dominion of the Almohades, and for two and a half centuries held for Islām a strip of country in the south east, around Granada, Almeria and Málaga. Once having founded their state, the *Naṣrids* (as this dynasty was called) maintained their position by dint of a highly adroit foreign policy and enjoyed sufficient security to find time and means for cultural concerns. Their chief external difficulties in the 14th century were with the Marīnids of Morocco and the Ḥafṣids of Tūnis. During this time, however, struggles between opposing claimants to the throne and intrigues among rival families of wazīrs began to sap the structure of the Naṣrid state; and they continued into the 15th century, which cannot be treated in any detail because contemporary written sources are almost entirely lacking, having subsequently been destroyed by the Spaniards from motives of religious zeal. Of the internal cultural and economic development of this residue of Islāmic territory, no knowledge thus remains. The growing power of the Spanish Christian kingdoms and the union of Castile and Aragon in 1479 enabled them to strike a decisive blow against the Muslims. Favoured by internecine quarrels withing the Naṣrid state, Isabella the Catholic and her husband Ferdinand II of Aragon (V of Castile) broke through to Granada in 1491 and took the city on January 2, 1492. Moorish rule on the soil of western Europe thus came to an end at the beginning of the year in which Christopher Columbus discovered America and near the close of the century during which the fall of Constantinople fastened Turkish rule onto eastern Europe for several centuries to come.

The fate of the Muslims who remained behind in Spain, became pseudo-Christians and were named by the Spaniards "*Moriscos*"; their revolts against Spanish rule during the 16th century, especially in 1571, and their deportation in 1609: all these are subjects which must be pursued in studies of Spanish history. It need only be added that in 1492 the bulk of the Jews were expelled and that most of them migrated to the east and settled in various cities of the Levant and the Balkans, especially in Salonika, where they are known as *Spaniolos* and still use a form of Spanish as their everyday speech.

DYNASTIC TABLES

In these tables, only the commencing date of a reign is shown if its close coincided with the accession of the next ruler; when nothing is added, this can accordingly be taken to have occurred. In all other cases, the closing date of the reign is also indicated.

I. THE UMAYYADS

21. I. 661 Muʻāwiyah I, son of Abū Sufyān.
... IV. 680 Yazīd I, son of the above.
... XI—20. XII. 683 Muʻāwiyah II, son of the above.
22. VI. 684 Marwān I, son of Ḥakam, second cousin of Muʻāwiyah I.
7. V. 685 ʻAbd al-Malik, son of the above.
8. X. 705 Walīd I, son of the above.
23. II. 715 Sulaymān, brother of the above.
22. IX. 717 ʻUmar II, nephew of ʻAbd al-Malik.
31. I. 720 Yazīd II, brother of Sulaymān.
28. I. 724 Hishām, brother of the above.
6. II. 743 Walīd II, son of Yazīd II.
17. IV. 744 Yazīd III, son of Walīd I.
20. IX. 744 Ibrāhīm, brother of the above.
23. XI. 745—5. VIII. 750 Marwān II, nephew of ʻAbd al-Malik.

In Spain

... VII. 755 ʻAbd al-Raḥmān I, nephew of Hishām.
15. IX. 788 Hishām I, son of the above
17. IX. 796 Ḥakam I, son of the above.
23. V. 822 ʻAbd al-Raḥmān II, son of the above.
22. IX. 852 Muḥammad I, son of the above.
4. VIII. 886 Mundhir, son of the above.
29. VI. 888 ʻAbd Allāh, brother of the above.
19. X. 912 ʻAbd al-Raḥmān III, grandson of the above.
15. X. 961 Ḥakam II, son of the above.
1. X. 976 Hishām II, son of the above.
22. II. 1009 Muḥammad II, great-grandson of ʻAbd al-Raḥmān III.
5. XI. 1009 Sulaymān, great-grandson of ʻAbd al-Raḥmān III.

21. VI. 1010 Hishām II (second time).
... 1013 Sulaymān (second time).
28. VI. 1016 'Alī ibn Ḥamūd, called al-Nāṣir, an 'Alid.
22. III. 1018 'Abd al-Raḥmān IV, great-grandson of 'Abd al-Raḥmān III.
... 1019 al-Qāsim, brother of 'Alī.
26. XII. 1023 'Abd al-Raḥmān V, brother of Muḥammad II.
9. II. 1024 Muḥammad III, great-grandson of 'Abd al-Raḥmān III.
17. VI. 1025 Yaḥyà, son of 'Alī.
1. III. 1026—30. XI. 1031 Hishām III, son of 'Abd al-Raḥmān IV (d. 1037).

2. THE 'ABBĀSIDS

6. XI. 749 Abū l-Abbās 'Abd Allāh al-Ṣaffāḥ.
9. VI. 754 al-Manṣūr, brother of the above (b. 712).
7. X. 775 al-Mahdī, son of the above.
4. VIII. 785 al-Hādī, son of the above.
15. IX. 786 Hārūn al-Rashīd, brother of the above (b. 766).
24. III. 809 al-Amīn, son of the above (b. 787).
25. IX. 813 al-Ma'mūn, brother of the above (b. ... IX. 786).
7. VIII. 833 al-Mu'taṣim, brother of the above (b. 795-97).
5. I. 842 al-Wāthiq, son of the above (b. 812).
10. VIII. 847 al-Mutawakkil, brother of the above (b. II/III. 822).
11. XII. 861 al-Muntaṣir, son of the above (b. 837).
25. VI. 862 al-Musta'īn, grandson of al-Musta'ṣim (b. 832?, d. ... X. 866).
5. I. 866 al-Mu'tazz, son of al-Mutawakkil (b. 845?, d. mid-VII. 869).
11. VII. 869 al-Muhtadī, son of al-Wāthiq.
21. VI. 870 al-Mu'tamid, son of al-Mutawwakkil (b. 843/45).
15. X. 892 al-Mu'taḍid, nephew of the above and son of the Regent al-Muwaffaq (b. 856 or 863).
5. IV. 902 al-Muqtafī, son of the above (b. 887).
13. VIII. 908 al-Muqtadir, brother of the above (b. 895).
31. X. 932 al-Qāhir, brother of the above (d. 950).
24. IV. 934 al-Rāḍī, son of al-Muqtadir (b. ... XII. 909).
23. XII. 940 al-Muttaqī, brother of the above (d. ... VII. 968).
12. X. 944 al-Mustakfī, son of al-Muqtafī (d. IX/X. 949).
29. I. 946 al-Mutī', son of al-Muqtadir (d. IX/X. 974).

5. VIII. 974 al-Ṭā'i', son of the above.
1. X. 991 al-Qādir, grandson of al-Muqtadir.
29. XI. 1031 al-Qā'im, son of the above.
2. IV. 1075 al-Muqtadī, grandson of the above.
4. or 8. II. 1094 al-Mustaẓhir, son of the above (b. 1078?).
6. VIII. 1118 al-Mustarshid, son of the above (b. 1093-94).
29. VIII. 1135 al-Rashīd, son of the above (b. 1107, d. 6-7 VI. 1138).
17. IX. 1136 al-Muqtafī, uncle of the above (b. 9. IV. 1096).
12. III. 1160 al-Mustanjid, son of the above (b. 13. VIII. 1116).
20. XII. 1170 al-Mustaḍī' (b. 23. III. 1142).
25/30 III. 1180 al-Nāṣir, son of the above (b. 1158).
6. X. 1225 al-Ẓāhir, son of the above.
11. VII. 1226 al-Mustanṣir son of the above.
15. XI. or 5. XII. 1242-10. II. 1258 al-Musta'ṣim, son of the above (b. 1212-13, d. 20. II. 1258).

(So-called) Caliphs in Egypt

13. VI. 1261 al-Mustanṣir II, son of al-Ẓāhir (?)
22. XI. 1262 al-Ḥākim I, great-great-grandson of al-Rashīd (?)
22. I. 1302 al-Mustakfī II, son of the above.
4. V. 1340 al-Wāthiq II, grandson of al-Ḥākim I.
18. VI. 1340 al-Ḥākim II, son of al-Mustaqfī II.
VII/VIII. 1352 al-Mu'taḍid II, brother of the above.
III. 1362 al-Mutawakkil II, son of the above.
VII. 1377 al-Mu'taṣim II, son of al-Wāthiq II.
VIII. 1377 al-Mutawakkil II (second time).
IX. 1383 al-Wāthiq III, son of al-Wāthiq II.
13. XI. 1386 al-Mu'taṣim II (second time).
7. V. 1389 al-Mutawakkil II (third time).
7. XII. 1405—I. 1406 al-Musta'īn II, son of al-Mutawakkil II. (d. 1420/30).
9. III. 1414 al-Mu'taḍid III, brother of the above.
23. VII. 1441 al-Mustakfī III, brother of the above.
23. II. 1451 al-Qā'im II, brother of the above (d. 1458).
VI/VII. 1455 al-Mustanjid II, brother of the above.
24. IV. 1479 al-Mutawakkil III, son of al-Musta'īn II.
24. X. 1497 al-Mustamsik, son of the above.
1508-09 al-Mutawakkil IV, son of the above.
1516 al-Mustamsik (reinstated as regent for his son; d. 1521).
1516/23 I. 1517 al-Mutawakkil IV (second time; d. 1538).

3. THE IMĀMS

(Descendants of ʿAlī ibn Abī Ṭālib)

17. VI. 656-24 I. 661 Caliph: ʿAlī ibn Abī Ṭālib, cousin of the Prophet, husband of his daughter Fāṭimah (d. 632).

2nd Imām: al-Ḥasan, son of the two above, d. 669.

3rd Imām: al-Ḥusayn, brother of the above, killed 10. X. 680 at Karbalāʾ.

4th Imām: (ʿAlī) Zayn al-ʿĀbidīn, son of the above, d. 712/13.

5th Imām: Muḥammad al-Bāqir, son of the above, d. 731/33. (His brother Zayd, executed in 739 at Kūfah, was the first special Imām of the Zaydites — see p. 66 f.).

6th Imām: Jaʿfar al-Ṣādiq, son of Muḥammad Bāqir, d. (poisoned?) 765.

7th Imām: Musà al-Kāẓim, son of the above, d. 799. [His brother Ismāʿīl, d. 760, was the Imām of the Ismāʿīlites (see p. 67) and purportedly the ancestor six generations back of ʿUbayd Allāh al-Mahdī, the first Fāṭimid (see next table].

8th Imām: ʿAlī al-Riḍà (see p. 65), son of the above, d. (poisoned?) 818.

9th Imām: Muḥammad al-Taqī, son of the above, d. 835.

10th Imām: ʿAlī al-Naqī, son of the above, d. 868.

11th Imām: Hasan al-ʿAskarī, son of the above, d. 873/74 or 878/79.

12th Imām: Muḥammad al-Mahdī, son of the above, the Ṣaḥib al-Zamān (see p. 66), b. 869, reputedly disappeared in 873/74 at Sāmarrā.

4. THE FĀṬIMIDS

15. I. 910 ʿUbayd Allāh, called al-Mahdī (see Table 3, 7th Imām) (b. 873); in North Africa.

3-4. III. 934 al-Qāʾim, son — or adoptive son? — of the above (b. ... IV. 893). Purported descent from Fāṭimah is questionable.

18. V. 946 al-Manṣūr, son of the above (b. 914/15).

18. III. 953 al-Muʿizz, son of the above (b. 27. IX. 931), occupied Cairo 7. VII. 969.

10. XII. 975 al-ʿAzīz, son of the above (b. 10. V. 955).

14. X. 996 al-Ḥākim, son of the above (b. 13. VIII. 985, d. ....?).

13. IX. 1021 al-Ẓāhir, son of the above (b. 12. III. 1005).

13. VI. 1036 al-Mustanṣir, son of the above (b. 2. VII. 1029).

29. XII. 1094 al-Mustaʿlī, son of the above (b. 15. VIII. 1074).

8. XII. 1101 al-ʿĀmir, son of the above (b. 30. XII. 1096).

7. X. 1130 al-Muntaẓar, pseudo-Caliph.
4. XII. 1131 al-Ḥāfiẓ, cousin of al-ʿĀmir (b. ... IX. 1074).
11. X. 1149 al-Ẓāfir, son of the above (b. 23. II. 1133).
16. IV. 1154 al-Fāʾiz, son of the above (b. 31. V. 1149, d. 23. VII. 1160).
20. VII. 1160/6. IX. 1171 al-ʿĀḍid, cousin of the above (b. 9. V. 1151, d. 13. IX. 1171).

5. THE SALJŪQS

A. The Great Sajlūqs

c. 1038 Ṭoghril (Tuğrul) Beg, son of Mīkāʾil and grandson of Selcük.
4. IX. 1063 Alp Arslān, son of Chaghrī (Çağrï) Beg and nephew of the above (b. c. 1030-31).
24. XII. 1072 Malik Shāh I, son of the above (b. 1054).
18/19. XI. 1092 Maḥmūd, son of the above (b. 1087).
... XI. 1094 Barkiyārūq, brother of the above (b. 1078-80).
22. XII. 1104 Malik Shāh II, son of the above (b. 1100).
8. II. 1105 Muḥammad, uncle of the above (b. 1082).
18. IV. 1118—IV/V.1157 Sanjar, brother of the above (b. 1086?). Further petty princes till 1194.

B. The Saljūqs of Rūm (in Asia Minor)

1077-78 Süleyman I, son of Kutlumïş and great-grandson of Selcük.
1086-87 Interregnum.
1092 Kïlïc Arslan I, son of Süleyman.
1106-7 Melikşah I, son of the above.
1116-17 Rükneddin Mesʾud I, brother of the above.
1156 İzzeddin Kïlïc Arslan II, son of the above.
1192 Gïyaseddin Keyhusrev I, with 11 brothers as part-rulers.
1196 Rükneddin Süleyman II, elder brother.
6. VII. 1204 İzzeddin Kïlïc Arslan III, son of the above.
... XI. 1204 Keyhusrev I (reinstated).
... VII. 1210 İzzeddin Keykâvus I, son of the above.
1219-20 Alâeddin Keykubad I, brother of the above.
1236-37 Gïyaseddin Keyhusrev II, brother of the above.
1246/47-1257 İzzeddin Keykâvus II, son of the above (d. 1279/80).
1248/49-1265 Rükneddin Kïlïc Arslan IV, brother of the above.
1249/50-1257 Alâeddin Keykubad II, brother of the above.
1265 Gïyaseddin Keyhusrev III, son of Kïlïc Arslan IV.

1282—83 Gїyaseddin Mes'ud II, son of Keykâvus II.
1284 Alâeddin Keykubad III, nephew of the above.
1284—85 Mes'ud II (second time).
1293 Keykubad III (second time).
1294 Mes'ud II (third time).
1300-01 Keykubad III (third time).
1302-03 Mes'ud II (fourth time).
1304-05 Keykubad III (fourth time).
1307/08—1317 (at the latest) Gїyaseddin Mes'ud III, son of the above.

6. THE AYYŪBIDS

(in Egypt)

6. IX. 1171 Ṣalāḥ al-Dīn (Saladin) son of Ayyūb, (b. 1137).
3. III. 1193 al-Malik al-ʿAzīz I, son of the above (b. 7. I. 1172).
29. XI. 1198 al-Malik al-Manṣūr, son of the above.
1199 al-Malik al-ʿĀdil I, brother of Salāḥ al-Dīn.
31. VIII. 1218 al-Malik al-Kāmil I, son of the above (b. 19. VIII. 1180).
8. III. 1238 al-Malik al-ʿĀdil II, son of the above (b. ... II. 1221, d. 9. II. 1248).
31. V. 1240 al-Malik al-Ṣāliḥ, brother of the above (b. 26. I. 1207).
21. XI. 1249 al-Malik al-Muʿaẓẓam, son of the above.
3. V. 1250—1252 (nominally) al-Malik al-Ashraf, cousin of the above (b. 1244-45, d. 1254?).
3. V. 1250—14. IV. 1257 (as regent) Shajarat al-Durr, widow of al-Malik al-Saliḥ, wife by her second marriage on 31. VII. 1250 of:
31. VII. 1250—10. IV. 1257 Aybak, the first Mamlūk Amīr.
10. IV. 1257—... XI. 1259 al-Manṣūr Nūr al-Dīn, son of the above two.
... XI. 1259 rule of the Baḥrite Mamlūks.

NOTE. Tables of all Muslim Dynasties which ever attained any importance, and numerous family genealogies, are given by EDUARD VON ZAMBAUR, *Manuel de généalogie et de chronologie pour l'histoire de l'Islam*, Hanover 1927, 2nd ed. 1955, but unfortunately only with *hijrī* dates. A general outline of the Umayyads, ʿĀlids and ʿAbbāsids, with indications of non-Arab origin on the mother's side, will be found on p. 560 ff. of RUDI PARET, *Der Islam und die Araber bis gegen Ende des Mittelalters* I (see Bibliography p. 125). STANLEY LANE-POOLE, *The Mohammadan dynasties*, London 1893 (photographically reprinted, Paris 1925), though still useful, does not incorporate the results of subsequent research.

BIBLIOGRAPHY

The relevant literature is so vast that only a tentative list of the more important modern works can be given here. The list has been rearranged and slightly enlarged for the English edition. Particulars of the available source material are not given, but can be found in many of the books which are listed and in the *Encyclopaedia of Islam* and *İslâm Ansiklopedisi*.

REFERENCE WORKS

Encyclopaedia of Islam, ed. by MARTINUS THEODORUS HOUTSMA et al., Leiden-Leipzig 1913-1936 (4 vols. and supp.). New ed., by JOHANNES HENDRIK KRAMERS et al., 1945 ff, (1959, to Bast). In English, French and (first ed.) German. Turkish ed.: *Islam Ansiklopedisi*, Istanbul 1939 ff. (to Muhammed).

Shorter Encyclopaedia of Islam, ed. by Sir H. A. R. GIBB and J. H. KRAMERS, Leiden 1953. In English, French and German.

PAREJA, FÉLIX M., with the collaboration of A. BAUSANI and L. HERTLING, *Islamologia*, Rome 1951. Enlarged Spanish tr., 2 vols., Madrid 1952-54. (Admirable summaries of the entire field, with bibliographies).

MENSCHING, GUSTAV, *Handbuch der Religionswissenschaft*, Berlin, 1948. Vol. X, article *Islam* (as religion), with bibliography. Also other articles.

SPULER, BERTOLD, *Der Vordere Orient in islamischer Zeit*, Berne, 1952. (Lists works published 1937-1951).

SAUVAGET, JEAN, *Introduction à l'histoire de l'Orient musulman. Eléments de bibliographie*, Paris 1948.

PFANNMÜLLER, GUSTAV, *Handbuch der Islam-Literatur*, Berlin and Leipzig 1923.

ETTINGHAUSEN, RICHARD, *A selected and annotated bibliography of books and periodicals in Western languages dealing with the Near and Middle East*, 2nd ed. with supp., Washington 1954.

ZAMBAUR, EDUARD VON, *Manuel de généalogie et de chronologie pour l'histoire de l'Islam*, Hanover 1927, 2. ed. 1955.

POOLE, STANLEY LANE-, *The Mohammadan dynasties*, Paris 1925.

BROCKELMANN, CARL, *Geschichte der islamischen Völker und Staaten*, 2nd ed., Munich 1943; tr. by JOEL CARMICHAEL and MOSHE PERLMANN, *History of the Islamic Peoples*, New York, 1947.

CAETANI, LEONE, Prince of Teano, Duke of Sermoneta, *Chronographia Islamica*, 5 vols., Paris 1912-

HAZARD, HARRY W., and COOKE, H. LESTER, *Atlas of Islamic History*, Princeton 1951 (elementary).

WESTERMANN'S *Atlas zur Weltgeschichte*, 3 vols. in 1, Brunswick 1955.

Historical Atlas of the Muslim peoples, Amsterdam (Djambatan) 1957.

PRE-ISLAMIC ARABIA AND THE NEAR EAST

GUIDI, MICHELANGELO, *Storia e cultura degli Arabi fino alla morte di Maometto*, Florence 1951.

NALLINO, CARLO ALFONSO, *Raccolta di scritti*; vol. III, part I, *Storia dell'Arabia pre-islamica*, Rome 1941.

O'LEARY, DE LACY EVANS, *Arabia before Muhammad*, London 1927.

JAWĀD ʿALĪ, *Taʾrīkh al-ʿArab qabl al-Islām*, 3 vols., Baghdād 1951-53.

NIELSEN, DITLEF, *Handbuch der altarabischen Altertumskunde*; I, *Die altarabische Kultur*, Copenhagen 1927.

HARTMANN, MARTIN, *Der islamische Orient, Berichte und Forschungen*; vol. 2, *Die arabische Frage...*, Leipzig, 1909.

CAETANI, LEONE, *Studi di storia orientale*, 3 vols., Milan 1911-14.

RYCKMANS, GONZAGUE, *Les religions arabes préislamiques*, Louvain 1951.

LAMMENS, HENRI, *L'Arabie occidentale avant l'hégire*, Beirut 1928.

FARÈS, BICHR, *L'honneur chez les Arabes avant l'Islam*, Paris 1932.

DUSSAUD, RENÉ, *Les Arabes en Syrie avant l'Islam*, Paris 1907.

CHARLES, HENRI, *Le christianisme des Arabes nomades sur le limes et dans le désert syro-mésopotamien aux alentours de l'hégire*, Paris 1936.

NYBERG, HENRIK SAMUEL, *Die Religionen des alten Iran*, tr. by HANS HEINRICH SCHAEDER, Leipzig 1938.
NÖLDEKE, THEODOR, *Geschichte der Perser und Araber zur Zeit der Sasaniden (nach Tabarī mit Erläuterungen und Ergänzungen)*, Leiden 1879.
CHRISTENSEN, ARTHUR, *L'Iran sous les Sassanides*, 2nd ed., Copenhagen 1944.
GHIRSHMAN, ROMAN, *L'Iran des origines à l'Islam*, Paris 1951; tr. by the *author*, *Iran from the earliest times to the Islamic conquest*, London 1954.
BRÉHIER, LOUIS, *Le monde byzantin*, 3 vols., Paris 1947-50.
OSTROGORSKY, GEORG, *Geschichte des byzantinischen Staates*, 2 vols., Munich 1952.
VASILIEV, ALEXANDER ALEXANDROVICH, *History of the Byzantine empire* 324-1453, Madison 1952.
ABEL, FELIX MARIE, *Histoire de la Palestine depuis la conquête d'Alexandre jusqu'à l'invasion arabe*, 2 vols., Paris 1952.
BELL, HAROLD IDRIS, *Egypt from Alexander the Great to the Arab conquest*, London 1948.
JULIEN, CHARLES-ANDRÉ, *Histoire de l'Afrique du Nord*, vol. I, Paris 1951.

ISLAM: ORIGINS, BELIEFS AND INSTITUTIONS

WENSINCK, ARENT JAN, *The Muslim creed, its genesis and historical development*, Cambridge 1932.
GIBB, Sir HAMILTON ALEXANDER ROSSKEEN, *Mohammedanism, an historical survey*, 2nd ed., London 1953.
GUILLAUME, ALFRED, *Islam*, London 1954.
TRITTON, ARTHUR STANLEY, *Islam, beliefs and practices*, London 1951.
GAUDEFROY-DEMOMBYNES, MAURICE *Les institutions musulmanes*, Paris 1946; tr. by JOHN P. MACGREGOR, *Muslim institutions*, London 1950.

WATT, W. MONTGOMERY, *Muhammad at Mecca*, Oxford 1953.
——, *Muhammad at Medina*, Oxford 1956.
ANDRAE, TOR, *Mohammed, sein Leben und sein Glaube*, Göttingen 1932; tr. by THEOPHIL MENZEL, *Mohammed, the man and his faith*, London 1936; tr. by JEAN GAUDEFROY-DEMOMBYNES, *Mahomet, sa vie et sa doctrine*, Paris 1945.
BUHL, FRANTS, *Das Leben Mohammeds*, German tr. by HANS HEINRICH SCHAEDER, Leipzig 1930. 2., 1955.
BLACHÈRE, RÉGIS, *Le problème de Mahomet*, Paris 1952.
DERMENGHEM, EMILE, *La vie de Mahomet*, Paris 1929; tr. by ARABELLA YORKE, *The life of Mahomet*, London 1930; tr. by REŞAT NURI, *Muhammedin hayati*, Istanbul 1930.
WENSINCK, ARENT JAN, *Mohammed en de Joden te Medina*, Leiden 1908.
GUILLAUME, ALFRED, *The life of Muḥammad; a translation of Isḥāq's Sīrat Rasūl Allāh with introduction and notes*, London 1955.
ABBOTT, NABIA, *Aishah the Beloved of Mohammed*, Chicago 1942.

SNOUCK HURGRONJE, CHRISTIAAN, *Mekka*, 2 vols., Leiden 1888.
WELLHAUSEN, JULIUS, *Reste arabischen Heidentums*, 2nd ed., Berlin 1897.
——, *Prolegomena zur ältesten Geschichte des Islams*, Berlin 1899.

NÖLDEKE, THEODOR, *Geschichte des Qorāns*, 2nd ed. bearbeitet von FRIEDRICH SCHWALLY, 3 vols., Leipzig 1909-38 (vol. III by G. BERGSTRASSER and O. PRETZL).
BELL, RICHARD, *Introduction to the Qur'an*, Edinburgh 1953.
HOROVITZ, JOSEF, *Koranische Untersuchungen*, Berlin and Leipzig 1926.
GOLDZIHER, IGNAZ, *Die Richtungen der islamischen Koranauslegung*, Leiden 1920, 2nd. ed., 1952.
BLACHÈRE, RÉGIS, *Introduction au Coran*, Paris 1950.
JEFFERY, ARTHUR, *The foreign vocabulary of the Qur'an*, Baroda 1928.
——, *Materials for the history of the text of the Qur'an*, Leiden 1937.
——, *The Qur'an as scripture*, New York 1952.
PARET, RUDI, *Mohammed und der Koran*, Stuttgart 1951.

MACDONALD, DUNCAN BLACK, *The religious attitude and life in Islam*, Chicago 1909.
ANDRAE, TOR, *Die Person Muhammeds in Lehre und Glauben seiner Gemeinde*, Stockholm 1918.

ANDRAE, TOR, *Les origines de l'Islam et le christianisme*, French tr. by JULES ROCHE, Paris 1955.
BELL, RICHARD, *The origin of Islam in its Christian environment*, London 1926.
TORREY, CHARLES CUTLER, *The Jewish foundation of Islam*, Oxford 1924.

GOLDZIHER, IGNAZ, *Muhammedanische Studien*, 2 vols., Halle a.S., 1890; vol. II tr. in part by LEON BERCHER, *Etudes sur la Tradition islamique*, Paris 1952.
GUILLAUME, ALFRED, *The Traditions of Islam*, Oxford 1924.

GOLDZIHER, IGNAZ, *Vorlesungen über den Islam*, 2 Heidelberg 1925; tr. by FELIX ARIN, *Le dogme et la loi de l'Islam*, Paris 1920.
GARDET, LOUIS, and ANAWATI, GEORGES C., *Introduction à la théologie musulmane*, Paris 1948.
TRITTON, ARTHUR STANLEY, *Muslim Theology*, London 1947.
SWEETMAN, J. WINDROW, *Islam and Christian theology*, Lutterworth 1945- (1957, to vol. II, part I).
WATT, W MONTGOMERY, *Free will and predestination in early Islam*, London 1948.
DONALDSON, DWIGHT MARTIN, *Studies in Muslim ethics*, London 1953.

SCHACHT, JOSEPH, *The origins of Muhammadan jurisprudence*, Oxford 1950 (cf. J. W. FÜCK in "*Bibliotheca Orientalis*" X/5 (Leiden 1953, p. 196/8).
MACDONALD, DUNCAN BLACK, *The development of Muslim theology, jurisprudence and constitutional theory*, New York 1913.
NALLINO, CARLO ALFONSO, *Raccolta di scritti*; vol. IV, *Diritto musulmano - Diritti orientali cristiani*, Rome 1942.
SNOUCK HURGRONJE, CHRISTIAAN, *Verspreide geschriften*; vol. II, *Geschriften betreffende het Mohammedaansche recht*, Leipzig 1923.
MILLIOT, LOUIS, *Introduction à l'étude du droit musulman*, Paris 1953.
SANTILLANA, D., *Istituzioni di diritto musulmano...*, 2 vols., Rome 1926-33.
TYAN, EMILE, *Histoire de l'organisation judiciaire en pays d'Islam*, 2 vols., Paris 1938.
——, *Institutions du droit musulman*; *I. Le califat*, Paris 1954; II. *Califat et sultanat*, 1955.
ARNOLD, Sir THOMAS WALKER, *The Caliphate*, Oxford 1924
BECKER, CARL HEINRICH, *Bartholds Studien Über Chalif und Sultan*, in "*Islam*" VI (1916), pp. 350-412.
BARTHOLD, VASILIĬ VLADIMIROVICH, *Sultan i Chalif*, in "*Mir Islama*" I (1912), pp. 203-226, 345-400.
SHERWANI, HAROON KHAN, *Studies in Muslim political thought and administration*, Lahore 1945.
AGHNIDES, NICOLAS PRODROMOU, *Mohammedan theories of finance*, New York 1916.
SIDDIQI, S. A, *Public finance in Islam*, Lahore 1948.
KHADDURI, MAJID, *War and peace in the law of Islam*, Baltimore 1955.
——, and LIEBESNY, HERBERT JOSEPH, *Law in the Middle East*; vol. I, *Origin and development of Islamic law*, Washington 1955.

KHĀRIJISM AND SHĪ'ISM

SALEM, ELIE ADIB, *Political theory and institutions of the Khawārij*, Baltimore 1956.
BLOCHET, EDGAR, *Le messianisme dans l'hétérodoxie musulmane*, Paris 1903.
WELLHAUSEN, JULIUS, *Die religiös-politischen Oppositionsparteien im alten Islam*, Berlin 1901.
VLOTEN, GERLOF VAN, *Recherches sur la domination arabe, le chiitisme et les croyances messianiques sous le khalifat des Omayades*, in *Verhandelingen Kon. Akad. Wetenschappen Amsterdam, Afdeel. Letterkunde*, vol. I, 3, 1894.
ARENDONCK, CORNELIS VAN, *De opkomst van het zaidietische imamaat in Yemen*, Leiden 1919.
STROTHMANN, RUDOLF, *Das Staatsrecht der Zaiditen*, Strasbourg 1912.
——, *Der Kultus der Zaiditen*, Strasbourg 1912.
DE GOEJE, MICHAEL JAN, *Mémoire sur les Carmathes de Bahrain et les Fatimides*, 2nd ed., Leiden 1880.

HODGSON, MARSHALL G. S., *How did the early Shi'a become sectarian?*, in *Journal American Oriental Soc.*, vol. 75, 1, Jan.-March 1955.
——, *The order of the Assassins*, The Hague 1955.
LEWIS, BERNARD, *The origins of Ismā'īlism*, Cambridge 1940.
IVANOW, VLADIMIR ALEKSIEYEVICH, *The alleged founder of Ismailism*, Bombay 1946.
——, *Brief survey of the evolution of Ismailism*, Leiden 1952.
DONALDSON, DWIGHT MARTIN, *The Shi'ite religion*, London 1933. (Twelver Shī'ism).
MADELUNG, WILFERD, *Fāṭimiden und Baḥrainqarmāten*, in "*Islam*" XXXIII/3 (1959).
KĀSHIF AL-GHIṬĀ', MUḤAMMED ḤUSAYN, *Aṣl al-Shī'ah wa uṣūlhā*, Najaf 1359-1950. (Twelver Shī'ism).

ṢŪFISM

ARBERRY, ARTHUR JOHN, *An introduction to the history of Sūfism*, London 1947.
NICHOLSON, REYNOLD ALLEYNE, *The mystics of Islam*, London 1914.
——, *Studies in Islamic mysticism*, Cambridge 1921.
SMITH, MARGARET, *Readings from the mystics of Islam*, London 1950. (With historical account and biographical notes).
DEPONT, OCTAVE, and COPPOLANI, XAVIER, *Les confréries religieuses musulmanes*, Paris 1897.

ISLAM AND OTHER RELIGIONS

ARNOLD, Sir THOMAS WALKER, *The preaching of Islam*, London 1913.
TRITTON, ARTHUR STANLEY, *The Caliphs and their non-Muslim subjects*, London 1930.
BROWNE, LAWRENCE EDWARD, *The eclipse of Christianity in Asia*, Cambridge 1933.
FRITSCH, ERDMANN, *Islam und Christentum im Mittelalter*, Breslau 1932.
FISCHEL, WALTER JOSEPH, *Jews in the economic and political life of medieval Islam*, London 1937.

MUSLIM CIVILIZATION

KREMER, ALFRED, Freiherr VON, *Geschichte der herrschenden Ideen des Islams*, Leipzig 1868.
——, *Culturgeschichtliche Streifzüge auf dem Gebiete des Islams*, Leipzig 1873.
——, *Culturgeschichte des Orients unter den Chalifen*, 2 vols., Vienna 1875-77.
KHUDABUKHSH, SALAHUDDIN, *Contributions to the history of Islamic civilization*, 2nd ed., 2 vols., Calcutta 1929-30. (Includes original papers and translations from VON KREMER).
MEZ, ADAM, *Die Renaissance des Islams*, Heidelberg 1927; tr. by SALAHUDDIN KHUDA BUKHSH and DAVID SAMUEL MARGOLIOUTH, *The Renaissance of Islam*, London 1937.
SHUSTERY, A. M. A., *Outlines of Islamic culture*, 2 vols., Bangalore 1938.
BECKER, CARL HEINRICH, *Islamstudien*, 2 vols., Leipzig 1924-32.
KRAMERS, JOHANNES HENDRIK, *Analecta orientalia*, Leiden 1954.

LEVY, REUBEN, *The social structure of Islam*, Cambridge, 1957.
GARDET, LOUIS, *La cité musulmane, vie sociale et politique*. Paris 1954.
TAESCHNER, FRANZ, *Islamisches Ordensrittertum zur Zeit der Kreuzzüge*, in *Die Welt als Geschichte* X (1938), pp. 387-402. (*Futūwah*; guilds).
LAMBTON, ANN KATHARINE SWYNFORD, *Landlord and tenant in Persia*, Oxford 1953.
MAZAHÉRI, ALY, *La vie quotidienne des musulmans au moyen âge, Xe. au XIIIe. siècle*, Paris 1951 (with many mistakes).

ARNOLD, Sir THOMAS WALKER, and GUILLAUME, ALFRED, ed., *The legacy of Islam*, Oxford 1931.
ARBERRY, ARTHUR JOHN, ed., *The legacy of Persia*, Oxford 1953.
GRUNEBAUM, GUSTAVE EDWARD VON, *Medieval Islam, a study in cultural orientation*, 2nd ed., Chicago 1947.
——, *Islam, essays on the nature and growth of a cultural tradition*, London 1955.
——, ed., *Unity and variety in Muslim civilization*, Chicago 1955.
O'LEARY, DE LACY EVANS, *Arabic thought and its place in history*, revised ed., London 1939.
——, *How Greek science passed to the Arabs*, London 1939.
PARET, RUDI, *Der Islam und das griechische Bildungsgut*, Tübingen 1950.
CARRA DE VAUX, BERNARD, Baron, *Les penseurs de l'Islam*, 5 vols., Paris 1921-26.

SHALABI, AHMAD, *History of Muslim education*, Beirut 1954.
PELLAT, CHARLES, *Le milieu basrien et la formation de Ǧahiz*, Paris 1953.
ṬALAS, AS'AD, *L'enseignement chez les Arabes; la madrasa Nizamiyah et son histoire*, Paris 1939.
TRITTON, ARTHUR STANLEY, *Materials on Muslim education in the middle ages*, London 1957.

BROCKELMANN, CARL, *Geschichte der arabischen Litteratur*, 2 vols., and supplement, 3 vols., Leiden 1938-1949.
NICHOLSON, REYNOLD ALLEYNE, *A literary history of the Arabs*, Cambridge 1930.
GIBB, Sir HAMILTON A. R., *Arabic literature; an introduction*, London 1926.
ABD-EL-JALIL, JEAN MARIE, *Brève histoire de la littérature arabe*, Paris 1943.
PELLAT, CHARLES, *Langue et littérature arabes*, Paris 1952.
GABRIELI, FRANCESCO, *Storia della letteratura araba*, Milan 1952.
BLACHÈRE, RÉGIS, *Histoire de la littérature arabe des origines à la fin du XVe. siècle de J. C.*, 5 vols., Vol. 1, Paris 1952.
NALLINO, CARLO ALFONSO, *Raccolta di scritti*; vol. 6, part 1, *La letteratura araba dagli inizi all'epoca della dinastia umayyade*, Rome 1948. Tr. by CHARLES PELLAT, *La littérature arabe des origines à l'é l'époque de la dynastie arabe*, Paris 1950.
GONZÁLEZ PALENCIA, ANGEL, *Historia de la literatura arabigo-española*, Barcelona 1945.
FÜCK, JOHANN, *Arabiya; Untersuchungen zur arabischen Sprach- und Stilgeschichte*, Berlin 1950.
——, *Documenta islamica inedita*, Berlin 1952.

STOREY, CHARLES AMBROSE, *Persian literature. A bio-bibliographical survey.* 4 fasc. London 1927-53.
BROWNE, EDWARD GRANVILLE, *A literary history of Persia.* 4 vols. Cambridge 1928. (Also most valuable for political history).
LEVY, REUBEN, *Persian literature; an introduction*, London 1923.

MARGOLIOUTH, DAVID SAMUEL, *Lectures on Arabic historians*, Calcutta 1930.
ROSENTHAL, FRANZ, *A history of Muslim historiography*, Leiden 1952.
SAUVAGET, JEAN, *Historiens arabes; pages choisies*, Paris 1946.
DE BOER, TJITZE J., *Geschichte der Philosophie im Islam*, Stuttgart 1901; tr. by E. R. JONES, *History of Philosophy in Islam*, London 1933.
HORTEN, MAX, *Die Philosophie des Islam*, Munich 1924.
GAUTHIER, LEON, *Introduction à l'étude de la philosophie musulmane*, Paris 1923.

SARTON, GEORGE ALFRED LÉON, *Introduction to the history of science*, 3 vols., Baltimore 1927-49.
MIELI, ALDO, et al., *La science arabe et son role dans l'évolution scientifique mondiale*, Leiden 1938.
BROWNE, EDWARD GRANVILLE, *Arabian medicine*, Cambridge 1921.
RENAUD, H. P. J., *La médecine arabe*, Paris 1933.
ELGOOD, CYRIL, *A medical history of Persia and the eastern Caliphate*, London 1951.
NALLINO, CARLO ALFONSO, *Raccolta di scritti; vol. V. Astrologia, astronomia, geografia*, Rome 1944.

MARÇAIS, GEORGES, *L'art de l'Islam*, Paris 1946.
GLÜCK, HEINRICH, and DIEZ, ERNST, *Die Kunst des Islam*, Berlin 1925.
MIGEON, GASTON, and SALADIN, HENRI, *Manuel d'art musulman.* 2 vols. I, *Arts plastiques et industriels*, by G. MIGEON; II, *L'architecture*, by H. Saladin. Paris 1907.
RICHMOND, ERNEST T., *Moslem architecture*, 623 *to* 1516, London 1926.
CRESWELL, KEPPEL ARCHIBALD CAMERON, *Early Muslim architecture: Umayyads, early 'Abbāsids and Ṭūlūnids.* 2 vols., Oxford 1932-40.
——, *A provisional bibliography of the Muhammadan architecture of India*, Bombay 1922.
——, *A provisional bibliography of the Moslem architecture of Syria and Palestine*, London 1924.
ARNOLD, Sir THOMAS WALKER, *Painting in Islam*, Oxford 1928.
POPE, ARTHUR UPHAM, ed., *A survey of Persian art from prehistoric times to the present.*, 6 vols., London and New York, 1938-39.
——, *An introduction to Persian art since the seventh century A.D.*, New York 1931.

BODE WILHELM VON, and KÜHNEL, ERNST, *Vorderasiatische Knüpfteppiche aus älterer Zeit*, 3rd ed., Leipzig 1922; tr. by RUDOLF MEYER RIEFSTAHL, *Antique rugs from the Near East*, New York 1922.
ERLANGER, RUDOLPHE, Baron D', *La musique arabe*, 5 vols., Paris 1930-49.
FARMER, HENRY GEORGE, *A history of Arabian music to the XIIIth century*, London 1929.

SCHWARZ, PAUL, *Iran im Mittelalter nach arab. Geographen*, 9 fasc., 1896-1936.
LE STRANGE, GUY, *The lands of the eastern Caliphate*, Cambridge 1930.
MILLER, KONRAD, *Mappae arabicae*, 3 vols., Stuttgart 1926-31.
JACOB, GEORG, *Studien in arabischen Geographen*, Berlin 1892.
——, *Der nordisch-baltische Handel der Araber im Mittelalter*, Leipzig 1887.
BLACHÈRE, RÉGIS, *Extraits des principaux géographes arabes du moyen âge*, Paris 1932.
NAFIS AHMAD, *Muslim contribution to geography*, Lahore 1947.
HEYD, WILHELM, *Geschichte des Levanthandels im Mittelalter*, 2 vols., Leipzig 1879; tr. by the author, *Histoire du commerce du Levant au moyen âge*, 2 vols., Leipzig 1885-86, 2nd enlarged ed. Leipzig 1923.
LEWIS, ARCHIBALD ROSS, *Naval power and trade in the Mediterranean, A.D. 500-1100*, Princeton 1951.
FAHMY, ALY MOHAMMED, *Muslim seapower in the eastern Mediterranean from the 7th to the 10th century A.D.*, London 1950.
HOURANI, GEORGE FADLO, *Arab seafaring in the Indian Ocean in ancient and early medieval times*, Princeton 1951.
FERRAND, GABRIEL, *Relations de voyages et de textes géographiques arabes, persans et turcs relatifs à l'extrème orient du VIIIe. au XVIIIe. siècle*, 2 vols., Paris 1913.
HADI HASAN, *A history of Persian navigation*, London 1928.
HUZAYYIN, SULIMAN AHMAD, *Arablia and the Far East*, Cairo 1942.

THE EMPIRE OF THE CALIPHS

CAETANI, LEONE, *Annali dell'Islam*, vols. I-X, Milan 1905-26.
WELLHAUSEN, JULIUS, *Das arabische Reich und sein Sturz*, Berlin 1902; tr. by MARGARET GRAHAM WEIR, *The Arab kingdom and its fall*, Calcutta 1927.
VECCIA-VAGLIERI, LAURA, *Il conflitto 'Alī-Mu'āwaiya e la secessione khārigita*, in *Annali dell' Istituto Universitario Orientale di Napoli*, N.S. IV (Naples 1952), p. 1-94; Documenti, Vol. V 1954.
LØKKEGAARD, FREDE, *Islamic taxation in the classic period, with special reference to circumstances in Iraq*, Copenhagen 1950.
DENNETT, DANIEL CLEMENT, *Conversion and the poll tax in early Islam*, Cambridge (Mass.) 1950.
LAMMENS, HENRI, *Etude sur le siècle des Ommayades*, Beirut 1930.
PÉRIER, JEAN, *La vie d'al-Hadjdjâdj ibn Yousof d'après les sources arabes*, Paris 1904.

SHERWANI, NAWAB . . . MUHAMMAD HABIBUR RAHMAN KHAN, *Hadrat Abu Bakr*, tr. by Syed MOINUL HAQ, Lahore 1947.
SHIBLI NU'MANI, *Al-Farooq; Umar the Great*, vol. I, tr. by . . . ZAFAR 'ALI KHAN, 3rd ed., Lahore 1947.
HUSAINI, SYED ABDUL QADIR, *Muslim administration*, Madras 1949.

TAESCHNER, FRANZ, *Geschichte der arabischen Welt*, Heidelberg, Berlin and Magdeburg 1944.
DIEHL, CHARLES, and MARÇAIS, GEORGES, *Le monde oriental de 395 à 1087*, 2nd ed., Paris 1944.
ANDREAS, WILLY, ed., *Neue Propyläen-Weltgeschichte*, vol. II, Berlin 1940; chapters by RUDI PARET, *Der Islam und die Araber bis gegen Ende des Mittelalters*, pp. 541-576, and FRANZ TAESCHNER, *Iran im Mittelalter*, pp. 577-624.
TAUER, FELIX, *Dějiny a Kultura islámu* (History and Culture of Islam), I and II, in *Dějiny lidstva*, III and IV, Prague 1936-43.
LEWIS, BERNARD, *The Arabs in history*, London and New York 1951.
HOGARTH, D. G., *Arabia*, Oxford 1922.
THOMAS, BERTRAM, *The Arabs*, London 1937.

WEIL, GUSTAV, *Geschichte der Chalifen*, 5 vols., Heidelberg and Stuttgart 1846-62.
HUART, CLÉMENT, *Histoire des Arabes*, 2 vols., Paris 1912-13.
MUIR, Sir WILLIAM, *The Caliphate, its rise, decline and fall*, 4th ed., Ediburgh 1914. (Thin in places).

VLOTEN, GERLOF VAN, *De opkomst der Abbasiden in Chorasan*, Leiden 1890.
LEVY, REUBEN, *A Baghdad chronicle*, Cambridge 1929.
LE STRANGE, GUY, *Baghdad during the Abbasid caliphate*, London 1924.
NÖLDEKE, THEODOR, *Orientalische Skizzen*, 2 vols., Berlin 1892; tr. by JOHN SUTHERLAND BLACK, *Sketches from eastern history*, London and Edinburgh 1892.
ABBOTT, NABIA, *Two queens of Baghad*, Chicago 1937.
AUDISIO, GABRIEL, *La vie de Haroun-al-Raschid*, Paris 1930; tr. *Harun ar Rashid, Caliph of Bagdad*, New York 1931.
PHILBY, HARRY ST. JOHN BRIDGER, *Harun al-Rashid*, New York and London 1934.
BOUVAT, LUCIEN, *Les Barmécides d'après les historiens arabes et persans*, Paris 1912.
GABRIELI, FRANCESCO, *Al-Ma'mūn e gli 'Alidi*, Leipzig 1929.
HERZFELD, ERNST, *Geschichte der Stadt Samarra*, Hamburg 1948.
SŪSĀ (SOUSA), AḤMAD, *Rayy Sāmarrā' fī 'ahd al-khilāfah al-'abbāsīyah* (The irrigation system of Sāmarrā' during the 'Abbāsid Caliphate), Baghdād 1948. (Valuable also for the civilization of the period).
BOWEN, HAROLD, *The life and times of 'Alī ibn 'Īsā*, Cambridge 1928.
GUIDI, MICHELANGELO, *La lotta tra l'Islam e il Manicheismo*, Rome 1927.
VASILIEV, ALEXANDRE ALEXANDROVICH, *Byzance et les Arabes*, 2 vols., Paris 1935-50.
LAURENT, J., *L'Arménie entre Byzance et l'Islam depuis la conquête arabe jusqu'en* 886, Paris 1919.
GROUSSET, RENÉ, *Histoire de l'Arménie des origines à* 1071, Paris 1947.
MINORSKY, VLADIMIR FEDOROVICH, *Studies in Caucasian history*, London 1953.

PERSIA

SYKES, Sir PERCY MOLESWORTH, *A history of Persia*, 3rd ed., 2 vols., London 1930.
——, *A history of Afghanistan*, 2 vols., London 1940.
HINZ, WALTHER, *Iran. Politik und Kultur von Kyros bis Reza Schah*, Leipzig 1938.
GROUSSET, RENÉ; CHRISTENSEN, ARTHUR; MASSÉ, HENRI, et al., *La civilisation iranienne*, Paris 1952.
WIET, GASTON, *Soieries persones*, Cairo 1948. (With historical sketch).
SPULER, BERTOLD, *Iran in früh-islamischer Zeit: Politik, Kultur, Verwaltung und öffentliches Leben zwischen der arabischen und der seldschukischen Eroberung*, 633 *bis* 1055, Wiesbaden 1952.
SIDDIQI, AMIR HASAN, *Caliphate and Kingship in medieval Persia*, Lahore 1942.
NĀẒIM, MAḤMŪD, *The life and times of Sulṭān Maḥmūd of Ghazna*, Cambridge 1931.
SANAULLAH, FĀḌIL, *The decline of the Saljūqid empire*, Calcutta 1938.
NAFĪSĪ, SA'ĪD, *Tārīkh-i khāndān-i Ṭāhirī*, Tehran 1335/1956.

TURKS

BARTHOLD, VASILIY VLADIMIROVICH, *Turkestan down to the Mongol invasion*. 2nd ed. Tr. from the original Russian and revised by the author with the assistance of H. A. R. GIBB, London 1928.
——, *Zwölf Vorlesungen über die Geschichte der Türken Mittelasiens*. Deutsche Bearbeitung von THEODOR MENZEL. Berlin, 1935. Tr. by Mme. M. DONSKIS, *Histoire des Turcs d'Asie Centrale*, Paris 1945.
MACGOVERN, WILLIAM MONTGOMERY, *The early empires of Central Asia*, Chapel Hill 1939.
JAHN, KARL, *Enkele beschouwingen over de geschiedenis en beschaving der Oud-Turkse volkeren*, Leiden 1954.
CZAPLICKA, MARIE ANTOINETTE, *The Turks of Central Asia in history and at the present day*, Oxford 1918. (Ethnology and bibliography).
BERNSTAMM, ALEKSANDR, *Social'no-ékonomicheskii stroy Orkhono-eniseyskikh Tiurok VI-VIII vekov* (The socio-economic structure of the Orkhon and Yenisei Turks in the 6-8th cents.), Moscow and Leningrad 1946.

KISELËV, S. V., *Drevniaya istoriya Yuzhnoy Sibiri* (Ancient history of South Siberia), 2nd (much altered) ed., Moscow 1951.
GIBB, Sir HAMILTON A. R., *The Arab conquests in Central Asia*, London 1923.
PRITSAK, OMELIAN, *Karachanidische Studien*, I-X, typewritten thesis, Göttingen 1948. (Turkish tr. in preparation). Parts printed in *Oriens* III (1950), pp. 209-228, and Zeitschrift der Deutschen Morgenländischen Gesellschaft 101 (1951), pp. 270-300.
SPULER, BERTOLD, *Geschichte Mittelasiens*, in *Weltgeschichte in Einzeldarstellungen*, pub. by Verlag Bruckmann, vol. "*Asien*", Munich 1950, pp. 309-360.
GORDLEVSKIĬ, VLADIMIR A, *Gosudarstvo Sel'dzhukidov Maloy Azii* (The Sāljūq state in Asia Minor), Moscow and Leningrad 1941.
KÖYMEN, MEHMED ALTAY, *Büyük Selcük İmparatorluğu* (The Empire of the Great Seljūqs), 2 vols.; Ankara 1953-4.
YINANÇ, MÜKRIMIN HALIL, *Selcuklular devri I: Anadolu'nun fethi* (The Saljūq period; I, The conquest of Anatolia), Istanbul 1944.
LAURENT, J., *Byzance et les Turcs Sejdjoucides dans l'Asie occidentale jusqu'en* 1081, Nancy 1913.

SYRIA-PALESTINE

LE STRANGE, GUY, *Palestine under the Moslems* (650 *to* 1500), London 1890.
HITTI, PHILIP KHURI, *History of Syria, including the Lebanon and Palestine*, London 1951.
——, *The origins of the Druze people and religion*, New York 1928.
LAMMENS, HENRI, *La Syrie. Précis historique*, 2 vols., Beirut 1921.
MEDNIKOV, N., A., *Palestina ot zavoevaniya eya Arabami do krestovykh pokhodov po arabskim istochnikam* (Palestine from its conquest by the Arabs till the Crusades according to Arab sources), 4 vols., St. Petersburg 1897-1907.
WATSON, Sir CHARLES MOORE, *The story of Jerusalem*, London 1918.
CANARD, MARIUS, *Histoire de la dynastie des H'amdanides de Jazira et de Syrie*. Vol. I, Paris 1953.
CAHEN, CLAUDE, *La Syrie du nord à l'époque des croisades*. Paris, 1940.
SAUVAGET, JEAN, *Alep. Essai sur le développement d'une grande ville syrienne, des origines au milieu du XIXe siècle*, 2 vols., Paris 1941.
RUNCIMAN, STEVEN, *A history of the Crusades*, 3 vols., Cambridge 1951-54.
SETTON, KENNETH MEYER ed., *A history of the Crusades*. 5 vols. planned. Vol. 1, by MARSHALL W. BALDWIN, *The first hundred years*, Philadelphia 1955.
STEVENSON, WILLIAM BARRON, *The Crusaders in the East*, Cambridge 1907.
BARKER, Sir ERNEST, *The Crusades*, London 1923. (Useful short summary).
GROUSSET, RENÉ, *Histoire des croisades et du royaume franc de Jérusalem*, 3 vols., Paris 1934-36.
KRAEMER, JÖRG, *Der Sturz des Königreichs Jerusalem* (1187), Wiesbaden 1952.
POOLE, STANLEY LANE-, *Saladin and the fall of the Kingdom of Jerusalem*, 2nd ed., London 1926.
RICHARD, JEAN, *Le royaume Latin de Jérusalem*, Paris 1953.

EGYPT

BECKER, CARL HEINRICH, *Beiträge zur Geschichte Ägyptens unter dem Islam*, Strassburg 1911-12.
WIET, GASTON, *L'Egypte arabe, de la conquête arabe à la conquête ottomane*, 2nd ed., Paris 1946. (*Histoire de la nation égyptienne*, ed. by GABRIEL HANOTAUX, vol. IV).
POOLE, STANLEY LANE-, *A history of Egypt in the middle ages* (600-1500), London 1901, 4th ed., 1925.
BUTLER, ALFRED JOSHUA, *The Arab conquest of Egypt and the last thirty years of the Roman dominion*, Oxford 1902.
HASSAN, ZAKY MOHAMED, *Les Tulunides. Étude sur l'Égypte musulman à la fin du IXe. siècle*, Paris 1933.
WÜSTENFELD, FERDINAND, *Geschichte der Fatimidenchalifen*, Göttingen 1881.
O'LEARY, DE LACY EVANS, *A short history of the Fatimid Khalifate*, London 1923.
SCHIMMEL, ANNEMARIE, *Kalif und Kadi in spätmittelalterlichem Ägypten*, in *Die Welt des Islams*, XXIV (1942), pp. 1-128.
CLERGET, MARCEL, *Le Caire: étude de géographie urbaine et d'histoire économique*, 2 vols., Cairo 1934.

NORTH AFRICA

JULIEN, CHARLES-ANDRÉ, *Histoire de l'Afrique du Nord*, vol. 2, Paris 1952.

FAURE-BIGUET, GABRIEL ISIDOR, *Histoire de l'Afrique Septentrionale sous la domination musulmane*, Paris 1905.
HAMEL, J., *Histoire du Maghreb*, Paris 1923.
DELAFOSSE, MAURICE, *Histoire de l'Afrique Occidentale Française*, Paris 1926.
GAUTIER, ÉMILE FÉLIX, *L'islamisation de l'Afrique du Nord; les siècles obscurs du Maghreb*, Paris 1927. Reprinted 1942 with title *Le passé de l'Afrique du Nord.*
CAUDEL, MAURICE, *Les premières invasions arabes dans l'Afrique du Nord*, Paris 1900.
FOURNEL, L, *Les Berbers*, 2 vols., Paris 1877-81.
VONDERHEYDEN, M., *La Berbérie orientale sous la dynastie des Banou l-Arlab*, Paris 1927. (Aghlabids).
MARÇAIS, GEORGES, *La Berbérie musulmane et l'Orient au moyen âge*,Paris 1946.
GSELL, STÉPHANE; MARÇAIS, GEORGES, and YVER, GASTON, *Histoire de l'Algérie*, 5th ed., Paris 1930.
CAMBON, HENRI, *Histoire de la régence de Tunisie*, Paris 1948.
——, *Histoire du Maroc*, Paris 1952.
BRUNSCHVIG, ROBERT, *La Berbérie orientale sous les Hafsides*, 2 vols., Paris 1930.
TERRASSE, HENRI, *Histoire du Maroc des origines à l'établissement du protectorat français*, vol. I, Casablanca 1949.
BEL, ALFRED, *La religion musulmane en Berbérie*; I, *Établissement et développement de l'Islam en Berbérie du VIIe. au XXe. siècle*, Paris 1938.

SICILY

AMARI, MICHELE, *Storia dei Musulmani di Sicilia*, 2nd ed. revised by CARLO ALFONSO NALLINO, 4 vols., Catania 1933-39.
MOSCATO, G. B., *Cronaca dei Musulmani in Calabria*, San Lucido 1902.

SPAIN

LÉVI-PROVENÇAL, ÉVARISTE, *Histoire de l'Espagne Musulmane.* I, *La conquête et l'émirat hispano-umaiyade*, 710-912, Paris and Leiden 1950. II, *Le califat umaiyade de Cordoue*, 912-1031, Paris and Leiden 1950. III, *Le siècle du califat de Cordoue*, Paris 1953. Tr. by EMILIO GARCÍA GÓMEZ, *España Musulmana hasta la caida del Califato de Córdoba*, 711-1031 *de J.C.*, Madrid 1950.
——, *L'Espagne musulmane au Xe. siècle. Institutions et vie sociale.* Paris 1932.
DOZY, REINHART, *Histoire des Musulmans d'Espagne jusqu'à la conquête de l'Andalousie par les Almoravides* (711-1110), new ed. revised by É. LÉVI-PROVENÇAL, Leiden 1932.
——, *Recherches sur l'histoire et la littérature de l'Espagne pendant le moyen âge*, 3rd ed., 2 vols., Leiden and Paris 1881.
POOLE, STANLEY LANE-, *The Moors in Spain*, 2 nd ed., London 1920.
GONZÁLEZ PALENCIA, ALFONSO, *Historia de la España Musulmana*, 3rd ed., Barcelona 1932.
SÁNCHEZ ALBORNOZ, CLAUDIO, *La España Musulmana*, Buenos Aires 1946.
SCHACK, ADOLF FRIEDRICH, Graf VON, *Poesie und Kunst der Araber in Spanien und Sizilien*, 2nd ed., 2 vols., Stuttgart 1877.
NYKL, ALOIS RICHARD, *Hispano-Arabic poetry and its relations with the old Provençal troubadours*, Baltimore 1946.
MILLET, RENÉ, *Les Almohades. Histoire d'une dynastie berbère*, Paris 1923.

INDICES

Many of the Arabic etc. names and terms which appear are subject-headings of articles in the *Encyclopaedia of Islam*. (N.B. Č = Ch, Dj = J and Ḳ = Q in *E.I.*).

INDEX A: Persons etc.

Names of persons, families, tribes, religious communities

Abāḍites *see* Ibāḍites
'Abbādids (dynasty) 108
'Abbās (uncle of Muḥammad) 15, 48
'Abbāsids (Caliphal dynasty) 48-65, 68-69, 71-72, 73-74, 76, 82, 88, 98-100, 105, 106, 107
'Abd Allāh ibn Ṭāhir (Ṭāhirid ruler) 60
'Abd Allāh ibn Zubayr (anti-Caliph) 40-41
'Abd al-Malik (Umayyad Caliph) 41 f., 47
'Abd al-Mu'min (Almohade ruler) 110
'Abd al-Raḥmān I (Umayyad ruler in Spain) 49, 102, 103, 105, 106
'Abd al-Raḥmān III (Umayyad Caliph in Spain) 106 f.
Abraham *(Ibrāhīm)* (prophet) 9
Abūl-'Abbās al-Saffāḥ *see* al-Saffāḥ
Abū Bakr (Caliph) 6, 8, 16, 18-20
Abū Ja'far al-Manṣūr *see* al-Manṣūr
Abū Muslim (Īrānian leader) 48-49, 51, 54
Abūl-Qāsim Manṣūr *see* Firdawsī
Abū Ṭālib (uncle of Muḥammad) 7
Achaemenids (ancient Persian dynasty) 1, 21, 23, 51
al-'Āḍid (Fāṭimid Caliph) 92
'Aḍud al-Dawlah (Būyid ruler) 75
Afshīn (Turkish title of a Caliphal general) 55, 60
Aghlabids (dynasty) 70 f.
Aḥmad Būyeh or Buwayh: *see* Mu'izz al-Dawlah
Aḥmad ibn Ḥanbal (theologian) 65 note
Aḥmad (Sāmānid ruler) 77
Aḥmad ibn Ṭūlūn (ruler in Egypt) 69
'Ā'ishah (wife of Muḥammad) 16, 18, 31, 32
Akrites (Byzantine frontier guards) 75
'Alawites *see* Nuṣayrīs
Albigensian Christians 104
Alexander the Great *(Iskandar)* 21
'Alī ibn Abī Ṭālib (Caliph) 6, 7, 31-34, 36, 39, 65, 85, 98
'Alī (Almoravide ruler) 109, 110
'Alī al-Riḍā *(Imām)* 65
'Alids (descendants of 'Alī) 39, 46, 48, 49, 63, 65, 66, 67, 68
Almanzor *see* al-Manṣūr
Almohades *(al-Muwaḥḥidūn*; dynasty) 110, 111, 112
Almoravides *(al-Murābiṭūn*; dynasty) 108, 109, 110
Alp Arslān (Saljūq ruler) 82, 83
al-Amīn ('Abbāsid Caliph) 58
Amr ibn al-'Āṣṣ (general) 19, 22, 24, 30, 32 f., 36, 38
'Amr ibn Layth (Ṣaffārid ruler) 61
Anṣār *see* "Helpers"
Arian Christians 43, 107
Aristotle *(Arisṭūṭālīs)* 56
Artuqids (dynasty) 91
al-Ash'arī (theologian) 73, 83, 110
Assassins (Nizārī Ismā'īlites) 86 f., 93, 98, 99
Atabegs ("guardians", later rulers) 87 f., 91 98
Atsïz (Khwārizm-Shāh) 97
Aurora *see* Ṣubḥ
Averroes *see* Ibn Rushd
Avicenna *see* Ibn Sīnā
Avicebron *see* Salomo ben Gabirol
'Aws (tribe in Madīnah) 8
Ayyūb (father of Ṣalaḥ al-Dīn) 92
Ayyūbids (dynasty) 91-94, 96
al-Azhar *(madrasah)* 72, 83, 92

Bābak (Khurramite leader) 55
Bal'amī (historian and *wazīr*) 78
Banū Hilāl (Arab tribe) 108
Banū Naḍīr, Qaynuqā' and Qurayẓah (Jewish tribes) 11 note
Banū Sulaym (Arab tribe) 108
Baptist sects 27, 68
Barmakids *(wazīrs)* 51, 58 f.
al-Basāsīrī (general) 82
Bektashi *(darvīsh* order) 98
Buddhists 82
Būyids or Buwayhids (dynasty) 74-75, 76, 77, 77, 81, 82

Çağrı Beg Dā'ūd *see* Chaghrī
Carmathians *(Qarāmiṭah*, sing. *Qarmaṭī)* (Ismā'īlite sect) 50, 68, 73, 86
Catholic Christians 43, 101-113. *See also* "Latin" Christians.
Chaghrī Beg Dā'ūd (Saljūq ruler) 81
Charlemagne (Frankish emperor) 58, 106
Christians *(Naṣārà)* 4, 6 f., 9 f., 19, 23 f., 25 f., 28, 37, 38, 41, 43, 47, 56, 67, 84, 85, 88-94, 95 f., 97, 100, 101-113.
Christopher Columbus 113

INDEX B

Names of places, nations, languages

INDEX C

Technical terms

INDEX D

Authors cited